THE SPINSTER
AND HER ENEMIES

FEMINISM AND SEXUALITY 1880–1930

■**Sheila Jeffreys** is a lesbian and a revolutionary feminist who has been active in the Women's Liberation Movement for twelve years, mainly in Women Against Violence Against Women. She has contributed to publications which include *The Sexual Dynamics of History* (London Feminist History Group, 1983), and *The Sexuality Papers* (Coveney, Jackson, Jeffreys and Mahoney, 1984). She continues her work on the history of sexuality, teaching it too in Women's Studies in adult and extra-mural education.

THE SPINSTER

AND HER ENEMIES

FEMINISM AND SEXUALITY 1880–1930

SHEILA JEFFREYS

LONDON AND NEW YORK

PANDORA

for Carolle S. Berry with love

First published in 1985 by Pandora Press
(Routledge & Kegan Paul Ltd)
Reprinted in 1987

11 New Fetter Lane, London EC4P 4EE
Published in the USA by
Routledge and Kegan Paul Inc.
in association with Methuen Inc.
29 West 35th St., New York NY10001

Set in 10 on 11pt Sabon
by Inforum Ltd, Portsmouth
and printed in Great Britain
by The Guernsey Press Co. Ltd,
Guernsey, Channel Islands

Library of Congress Cataloguing in Publication Data

Jeffreys, Sheila.
The spinster and enemies.

Bibliography: p.
Includes index.
1. Feminism—England—History.   2. Sexual ethics—
England—History.   3. Single women—England—Sexual
behaviour—History.   I. Title.
HQ1599.E5J44   1985   305.4'2'0942   85–9279
British Library CIP Data also available

ISBN 0–86358–050–5

CONTENTS

ACKNOWLEDGMENTS

In the Patriarchy Study Group from 1978 to 1981 I was able to refine my ideas on sexuality through weekends of intense and exciting discussion with other revolutionary feminists including Al Garthwaite, Jackie Plaister, Lal Coveney, Leslie Kay, Margaret Jackson, Marianne Hester, Pat Mahoney, Sandra McNeill, Valerie Sinclair. I am grateful to them all. The lesbians I have worked with in Women against Violence against Women have sustained me both personally and politically, particularly Linda Bellos and Jill Radford. I would like to thank the women in the South West London Women's Studies Group through which I was launched into women's studies teaching, and the women in my classes who have been consistently supportive and encouraging.

I would like to thank those who gave me practical help in my research. I am grateful to Jalna Hanmer and Hilary Rose of the Department of Applied Social Studies at the University of Bradford for encouraging me to take up research and providing the facilities to begin this project. David Doughan of the Fawcett Library has shown unfailing interest and given me invaluable assistance. Special thanks to Maggie Christie who compiled the index and to my editor, Philippa Brewster.

Most of all I am indebted to Carolle S. Berry for the love and support which she has given me throughout the writing of this book. She has spent a great number of hours listening to me, contributing her thoughts and clarifications and organising piles of papers and lists of what I was to do next.

If this acknowledgments page sounds like a tribute to womens's love and friendship that is because it is that love and friendship that has enabled me to keep my ideas running against the grain for so long.

INTRODUCTION

This book looks at a watershed period in the history of sexuality. The traditional historical interpretation of the years 1880–1930 is that the sexual puritanism of Victorian England gave way to the first sexual revolution of the twentieth century. From a feminist perspective the picture is different. This period witnessed a massive campaign by women to transform male sexual behaviour and protect women from the effects of the exercise of a form of male sexuality damaging to their interests. There is little or no reference to this campaign in the histories of the women's movement in Britain. Other aspects of the feminist struggle such as the suffrage campaign, the movement to improve women's education and work opportunities and to gain changes in the marriage law, have all received attention. When historians have mentioned the work of the same feminist campaigners in the area of sexuality they have represented them as prudes and puritans, criticising them for not embracing the goal of sexual freedom or women's sexual pleasure and finding in their writings a source of useful humorous material. While their activities and demands have been seen as challenging and progressive in other areas, the activities of the very same women in the area of sexuality have been seen as backward and retrogressive.

The first five chapters look at the ideas and activities of feminist campaigners around sexuality. The first chapter deals with the involvement of feminists in those organisations usually seen as purely conservative and anti-sex, for example, the National Vigilance Association, the Moral Reform Union. It examines the way feminist concerns shaped social purity in the 1880s and 1890s. It ends with a comparison of these earlier organisations with the clearly non-feminist Alliance of Honour, whose membership was exclusively male, in the period before the First World War. The

1

chapter entitled 'Continence and Psychic Love' examines the theories and strategies of those feminists who were involved in relationships with men. It looks in particular at the philosophy of sex developed by Elizabeth Wolstenholme Elmy and Francis Swiney. The next two chapters are devoted to the women's campaign against the sexual abuse of girls. This campaign has been chosen as an example of practical feminist activity where feminist theory was put into effect, because it was so extensive and wide-ranging and has been substantially ignored by historians. The other major sexual issue on which feminists campaigned, prostitution, has received some attention.[1] The chapter on spinsterhood encompasses the ideas and motivations of those feminists who were choosing to reject sexual relationships with men.

There are certain basic assumptions underlying the work of historians on the history of sexuality which must be overturned if the significance of the women's campaigns is to be understood. The most pervasive is the assumption that the last 100 years represent a story of progress from the darkness of Victorian prudery towards the light of sexual freedom.[2] Implicit in this view is the idea that there is an essence of sexuality which, though repressed at times in the past, is gradually fighting its way free of the restrictions placed upon it. On examination this 'essence' turns out to be heterosexual and the primary unquestioned heterosexual practice to be that of sexual intercourse. Despite the wealth of work by sociologists and feminists on the social construction of sexuality, the idea remains that a natural essence of sexuality exists.[3] Another assumption is that there is a unity of interests between men and women in the area of sexuality, despite the fact that sexuality represents above all a primary area of interaction between two groups of people, men and women, who have very different access to social, economic and political power. Thus historians who concern themselves with writing the history of the 'regulation of sexuality', that is the way in which people's sexual behaviour has been restricted by repressive ideology and the state, without paying serious attention to the way in which the power relationship between the sexes is played out on the field of sexuality, can be seen to be subsuming the interests of women within those of men.[4] A most fundamental assumption is that sexuality is private and personal. It may be understood that social and political pressures influence what happens in the bedroom, but sexual behaviour is not recognised as having a dynamic effect in its own right on the structuring of the power relationships in the world which surrounds the bedroom. When sexuality is understood to be the most personal area of private life, it is not surprising that the women's campaigns to set limits to the exercise of male sexuality should be regarded with incomprehension or totally misunderstood. Ideas and campaigns which are developing within the current wave of feminism give us a very different basis for looking at the work of our foresisters.

Contemporary feminists have detailed the effects upon women of both the fear and the reality of rape, showing that the exercise of male sexuality in the form of rape, functions as a form of social control on women's lives.[5] Rape as social control has the effect of restricting where women may go, what women may do, and serves to 'keep us in our place' which is subordinate to men, thereby helping to maintain male domination over women. Work is now being done by feminists on the damaging effects upon women caused by the exercise of other aspects of male sexuality. The sexual abuse of children, prostitution, pornography and sexual harassment at work are all now being documented and examined.[6] Feminists are showing that these sexual practices by men are crimes against women though they have consistently been represented as victimless forms of male behaviour. Considering that contemporary feminists are having to wage a difficult struggle to get forms of male behaviour which are essentially crimes against women taken seriously, it is not at all surprising that women's campaigns around precisely the same issues in the last wave of feminism are all but invisible to contemporary historians. Much of the feminist theoretical work on male sexual behaviour and its effects on women has been designed to show the ways in which sexual harassment in childhood and in adulthood, at work, on the street and in the home, restricts the lives and opportunities of women and generally undermines our confidence and self-respect. As the impact of men's sexual violence on all the different areas of women's lives is documented, it becomes clear that male sexual control is of enormous importance in maintaining women's subordination. It is clear that we must look at the area of sexuality, not as merely a sphere of personal fulfilment, but as a battleground; an arena of struggle and power relationships between the sexes.

Current feminist debate on sexuality has gone futher than an examination of the effects of male sexuality on women outside the home to a critique of the institution of heterosexuality and its role in the control and exploitation of women. Questions are now being raised about the effects on women of the experience of sexual activity within all heterosexual relationships in terms of the maintenance of male dominance and female submission.[7] Feminists are exploring ways of making it possible for more women to have real choices around sexuality, so that more than a brave and embattled minority may have the right of loving other women. Such questioning allows us to see the feminists engaged in struggles around sexuality in previous generations not simply as the victims of a reactionary ideology, but as women manoeuvring, both to gain more power and control within their own lives, and to remove the restrictions placed upon them by the exercise of male sexuality inside and outside the home.

On the basis of this reassessment of what pre-First World War feminist theorists and campaigners around sexuality were doing, it is necessary also to reassess the significance of the so-called 'sexual revolution' of the 1920s. The propagandists of sex reform in the 1920s and 1930s attacked the earlier feminists for being prudes and puritans. Contemporary historians, for whom the new ideology of the 1920s has become the conventional wisdom, have replicated this attack. When looking at the 1920s they have been unable to be objective or critical. The last five chapters of this book examine the values and assumptions, and provide a new interpretation of this 'sexual revolution'.

Chapter 6 looks at the way in which ideas about the acceptable form of women's friendships was changed through sexological prescriptions in the late nineteenth century, as the stereotype of the 'real' lesbian was created. The chapter on the sex reform movement before the First World War critically examines the work of Havelock Ellis and other sexologists of the period. It shows how the feminist theory was undermined by the creation of a new prescription of correct female and male sexual behaviour with all the authority of science. Male sexuality was characterised as active and aggressive and female sexuality as passive and submissive. A substitute form of feminism was promoted which consisted of the glorification of motherhood combined with a vigorous attack on spinsters. The chapter on the 'new feminism' shows how the new form of feminism, promoted by the sexologists, was adopted in the 1920s, as the older form of feminism, which included a critique of male sexual behaviour and the promotion of spinsterhood, declined. As part of the enforcement of heterosexuality and the attack on women's resistance to sexual intercourse, women's frigidity was invented. It was a potent weapon to worry women into enthusiastic participation in the sexological prescription. This development is described in Chapter 9. The concluding section shows how, by the end of the 1920s, a sexual ideology was in wide currency which was in total contradiction to the feminist theory of the pre-war period. It examines the concept of the prude which was used to undermine the feminist critique.

The effect of the 'sexual revolution' was to cripple the feminist campaign to assert woman's right to control her own body, and to exist, as Wolstenholme Elmy put it, 'Free from all uninvited touch of man'. This aim has never been given its deserved significance by historians as part of the range of political objectives of the nineteenth-century women's movement. This may be because the right to bodily integrity has not been included in the political platform of any male political struggle, and only those objectives which men have seen to be important for themselves have been given serious attention. Men are not subject to physical invasion by a powerful ruling class and can take possession of their own physical space for granted. Woman's right to escape from being the involuntary object of men's sexual desires has not earned itself a place in the pantheon of human rights. Woman's 'frigidity' became an issue in the 1920s as attempts were made to construct a female sexuality which would complement that of men. The struggle of women to assert their right to say no gradually faded into insignificance whilst male sex theorists debated astride the conquered territories of women's bodies.

CHAPTER 1

Feminism and Social Purity

In the 1880s in Britain, a movement, described by its proponents as being for the advancement of 'social purity', was gathering momentum. The social purity movement reached through hundreds of societies into the lives of a considerable proportion of the male and female population. Historians, whose vision has been blinkered by the ideology of the 'sexual revolution', have tended to see social purity as simply an evangelical, anti-sex, repressive movement. Robert Bristow, in his book *Vice and Vigilance*, includes 1880s social purity within what he sees as four peaks of 'anti-vice' agitation.[1] He places these in the 1690s, the late eighteenth and early nineteenth centuries, the 1880s and the early twentieth century. His explanation for the birth of each is the same: 'Each was fed by the religious revivals that converted young men and channelled waves of sublimated anti-sexual energy against the erotic.'[2] Another approach has been to speak of the anxieties caused by social disruption being displaced onto a concern about sexuality, and to represent the social purity movement as a form of moral panic.[3] These writers acknowledge the involvement of feminists in nineteenth-century social purity but regard the feminist input as a red-herring caused by the difficulty those feminists had in overcoming their old-fashioned puritanical ideas about sex. In fact feminist ideas and personnel played a vitally important part in the 1880s social purity movement and can be seen as having shaped its direction and concerns.

The primary aims of social purity were the elimination of prostitution and of the sexual abuse of girls. Women and girls are the objects of prostitution and sexual abuse, and men are the exploiters. It cannot therefore be expected that one form of explanation could describe why both men and women were involved in campaigning against a form of sexual behaviour to which men and women bore such a very different relationship. The explanations of the male historians may well help us to understand the involvement of men in social purity. The men were concerned, for whatever reason, in controlling the behaviour of their own sex. Women were concerned with preventing the exploitation of theirs. In analysing the motives of the women and men involved in what has been seen by some as the contemporary equivalent of social purity, organisations like the British National Viewers and Listeners' Association or the Responsible Society, the same problem of interpretation exists. However these contemporary phenomena have no feminist input and have an anti-feminist stance on most important issues. The 1880s social purity movement was very different, since feminist ideas and personnel played such an important part in it.

Two distinctly different currents flowed into the social purity movement of the 1880s. One was religious revivalism and the other was the agitation against the Contagious Diseases Acts. These Acts of the 1860s allowed compulsory examination of women suspected of working as prostitutes in garrrison towns and ports. The campaign for their repeal gave women the experience of thinking and speaking about previously tabooed topics. The feminists who opposed the Acts pointed out that the examinations were an infringement of women's civil rights.

Feminists in the Ladies National Association, inspired by Josephine Butler, inveighed against the double standard of sexual morality which enforced such abuse of women in order to protect the health of men who, as they pointed out, had infected the prostitutes in the first place. The progenitors of the social purity movement of the 1880s included men and women who had been involved in the repeal campaign. The Social Purity Alliance was set up in 1873 by men involved in the campaign to unite those of their sex who wished to transform their conduct and that of other men, so that self-control could be promoted and prostitution rendered unnecessary. From the 1880s onwards and particularly from 1886 when the Contagious Diseases Acts were finally repealed, women who had been involved in the abolition campaign and others who espoused the same principles, joined the proliferating social purity organisations in large numbers and brought with them a strong and determined feminist viewpoint. The social purity movement provided a vehicle which the feminists could use to make their influence felt. Feminists within social purity saw prostitution as the sacrifice of women for men. They fought the assumption that prostitution was necessary because of the particular biological nature of male sexuality, and stated that the male sexual urge was a social and not a biological phenomenon. They were particularly outraged at the way in which the exercise of male sexuality created a division of women into the 'pure' and the 'fallen' and prevented the unity of the 'sisterhood of women'. They insisted that men were responsible for prostitution and that the way to end such abuse of women was to curb the demand for prostitutes by enjoining chastity upon men, rather than by punishing those who provided the supply. They employed the same arguments in their fight against other aspects of male sexual behaviour which they regarded as damaging to women, such as sexual abuse of children, incest, rape and sexual harassment in the street. This chapter will look at some of those social purity organisations in which women's influence was dominant, whether these women saw themselves as self-conscious feminists or not, in order to assess their motives and ideas.

Josephine Butler

Josephine Butler was involved in many other feminist campaigns besides that against the Contagious Diseases Acts, notably the movement for higher education for women. Her feminism was informed by her interest in the defence of individual liberty as pursued by the National Vigilance Association for the Defence of Personal Rights. This was a liberal, radical organisation, concerned with defending the individual against state interference with rights and liberties. On the issue of sexuality Butler's feminism was strong and clear. She did not merely fight state interference, in the form of the Contagious Diseases Acts, with women's civil rights, she also conducted a propaganda campaign against men's abuse of women in the institution of prostitution. In a pamphlet entitled *Social Purity* and published on behalf of the Social Purity Alliance,[4] Josephine Butler outlined the gist of the feminist message behind the social purity movement. The pamphlet reproduces an address given by Butler at Cambridge in May 1879 to undergraduates. The question she was asked by the young men was, 'What can we do practically to promote Social Purity and to combat the evil around us?'[5] Josephine Butler proclaimed that the root of the evils of prostitution and impurity was: 'the unequal standard in morality; the false idea that there is one code of morality for men and another for women . . . which

8

has within the last century been publicly proclaimed as an axiom by almost all the governments of the civilised and Christian world.'[6] She explained that the double standard led to the condemnation of women and the excusing of men and quoted proverbial expressions which illustrated this – expressions which could only be used of men, such as 'He is only sowing his wild oats' and 'A reformed profligate makes a good husband'. The women who attacked the double standard were assaulting traditional male privileges in a way that was intended to be embarrassing and difficult for men. The result of the double standard, according to Butler, was 'that a large section of female society has to be told off – set aside, so to speak, to minister to the irregularities of the excusable man'.[7] She attributed the blame for this situation to men and particularly those of the upper classes such as were in her audience:

> Licentiousness is blasting the souls and bodies of thousands of men and women, chiefly through the guilt of the men of the upper and educated classes. The homes of the poor are blighted – the women among the poor are crushed – by this licentiousness, which ever goes hand-in-hand with the most galling tyranny of the strong over the weak.[8]

Then, as now, men of all classes were involved in the use of women in prostitution. The radical part of Butler's attack was to target the middle and upper-class men who were in the habit of sounding off about the immorality of the 'lower orders' whilst hiding behind a mask of respectability. After outlining the problem, Butler explained that she did not think that her audience was suited to rescue work, their role was in the forming of a 'just public opinion'.

J. Ellice Hopkins

The name of J. Ellice Hopkins, unlike that of Josephine Butler, is not generally mentioned in connection with the history of feminism. She had more influence than any other woman or man on the development of 1880s social purity. She is one of those who became involved in social purity through religious revivalism and had no previous involvement in feminist causes. Yet if we look closely at what she had to say it is clear that in relation to sexuality her position was almost identical to that of the most radical feminist campaigners. Hopkins was born and brought up in Cambridge and began her evangelical work there with a

9

mission for working men. She moved to Brighton in 1866 and became involved in the preventive work of a rescue home in that town. Preventive work was concerned with keeping young women out of prostitution and could include help with finding jobs or the setting up of homes for girls considered to be in danger of falling into prostitution, to ease their passage into other ways of making a living. Rescue workers set up refuges for women working in prostitution with the aim of rehabilitating them. From her time in Brighton onwards, Hopkins dedicated herself to the task of preventive work, both directly with those women who might become prostitutes and with the potential clients, by working to transform the sexual behaviour of men. Her work and influence lie behind the creation of the Ladies Association for Friendless Girls, the White Cross Army and the Church of England Purity Society. She also contributed to the formation of many other purity organisations in the 1880s through her speaking tours and writings. She formed a close friendship with James Hinton, a medical specialist and philosopher, who made a deathbed appeal to her in 1875 to carry out the work he had been unable to do in preventive work among the female poor. It seems that Hopkins by no means fully implemented Hinton's aims. Hinton had believed that prostitution could be eliminated by the rehabilitation of sexuality, so that non-prostitute women would be more compliant in servicing men's needs.[9] Havelock Ellis, who, as we shall see in Chapter 6 was one of the main progenitors of the sex reform movement which set out to eroticise women in the service of men's sexuality, claimed to have been inspired by reading Hinton's work. Hopkins saw her mission very differently. She set out to restrict men's sexual behaviour. This is a good example of the way in which the desire to eliminate prostitution could inspire men and women in very different ways. The main motivation of the women involved in 1880s social purity was to transform men's sexual behaviour through challenging the idea that men had an urgent sexual need which required to be serviced by women. The sex reform movement, on the other hand, totally accepted the imperative nature of men's sexual urges, and sought to conscript all women into the active servicing of male sexuality.

In 1879 Hopkins submitted to a committee of convocation *A Plea for the Wider Action of the Church of England in the Prevention of the Degradation of Women*, later published as a pamphlet. The 'Plea' is a very courageous attack on the hypocrisy of the church and its indifference to the elimination of prostitution, and an impassioned demand for action. The committee of convocation had been set up specifically to deal with the problem of prostitution and Hopkins expressed in the preface to the pamphlet, the hope that it would result in the formation of a powerful church organisation to 'attack it root and branch, and proclaim the absolute authority, for men and women alike, of those great moral laws on which the welfare and health of nations have most depended'.[10] The tenor of Hopkins's approach is suggested by her use of the phrase 'degradation of women' in place of 'prostitution'. Her interest lay, not in punishing women who 'fell', but in protecting women from the damage caused to them by the double standard and men's sexual practice. The effect of male sexual behaviour she described thus: 'at the heart of our great Christian civilisation there has grown up an immense outcast class of helpless women, and still more helpless children.'[11] The plight of girl children was exacerbated by the English law which recognised:

> That a woman comes of age, at the age of 13, for the purposes of vice, – in other words, that if a little bird-witted child of 13 consents to be ruined for life, the law throws on that moral baby the responsibility, and the man who has betrayed a child escapes scot free.[12]

Josephine Butler had been unable to shock the Church of England out of its apathy towards prostitution. Ellice Hopkins was to succeed in doing so. The transformation of opinion was necessary since, in Hopkins's words, 'the majority of men, many of them good Christian men, hold the necessity of the existence of this outcast class in a civilised country, where marriage is delayed; the necessity of this wholesale sacrifice of women in body and soul'.[13] Hopkins accused the church of making no attempt to change the attitude towards prostitution of the average Englishman who thought:

> What's the use, . . . of our bearing the burden of self-control which civilised life throws upon us, whilst *we have plenty of women*? . . . What recks it that weak women are crushed and degraded, as long as we strong men find life the easier and pleasanter.[14]

Hopkins outlined the action which she wanted the church to take. At that time the only church organisation which existed to deal with the problem was the Church Penitentiary Association. Hopkins was angry that the church saw fit to offer 'only penitentiaries' in which the women involved in prostitution would be given the chance to repent. She wanted the church to deal with the real cause of prostitution.

She had no doubt as to the identity of the real cause; it was men. She wrote that penitentiaries 'only cure the evil after it is done, when they only touch women, and leave the vital factor, *the man*, untouched, and only save women in infinitesimal numbers'.[15] She declared that while penitentiaries were given by the church as the 'sole specific', then the church actually ministered to the evil cause of prostitution, by accepting the double standard, and tacitly acknowledged its existence.

Hopkins demanded the creation of men's chastity leagues to deal with the 'real cause'. It is this which most clearly distinguishes her work from that of women involved in work around prostitution before her. She carried the battle to protect women from sexual exploitation beyond the defensive activities of preventive and rescue work with women. She directed her energies to the transformation of male sexual behaviour because she believed that that was where the cause of the problem lay. She thought that men needed help in self-control and that would be best given by men banding together to help each other.

> What I crave is some agency that would infuse into young men
> a good, strong passionate sense of the pitifulness of degrading
> women, inflicting a curse which they do not share with so
> much as their little finger – going back to their own jolly lives,
> their pleasant homes, their friends, their career, their power of
> marrying; and leaving the unhappy girl to become an outcast,
> cutting *her* off from ever being an honourable wife and
> mother, exposing her to a hideous disease, dooming her to live
> a degraded life and die a Godless, Christless, hopeless death.[16]

Hopkins, though she was herself a strong and independent, lifelong spinster, expressed herself in terms of the Victorian ideals of wifehood and motherhood. The significance of her contribution lay not so much in her ideas on woman's role as in her plans for men's role. She was a woman directing men's behaviour in the interests of defending women. She was not the originator of the idea of men's purity leagues, as the Social Purity Alliance was already in existence, but she was responsible for converting the Church of England to the idea and for popularising it so that purity leagues mushroomed throughout the 1880s in Britain.

A White Cross League pamphlet tells us what came from her

efforts. Hopkins made a speech at a church congress held in Derby in 1882 which made such a deep impression that a committee was formed to see what action could be taken. From this committee in 1883, came the formation of the Church of England Purity Society, which was the central organ of the church for 'promoting purity amongst men, and preventing the degradation of women and children'.[17] In February of the same year, the White Cross Army was set up. Hopkins spoke at a meeting in Edinburgh presided over by the Bishop of Durham. The bishop asked all men who accepted the five obligations mentioned in her speech to come forward. Two hundred men were enrolled and received pledge cards containing the obligations which were as follows:

1 To treat all women with respect, and to endeavour to defend them from wrong.
2 To endeavour to put down all indecent language and jests.
3 To maintain the law of purity as equally binding on men and women.
4 To endeavour to spread these principles among my companions, and to try and help my younger brothers.
5 To use every possible means to fulfil the command, 'Keep THYSELF pure'.[18]

The Purity Society was intended to have an oversight of preventive and rescue work whilst the White Cross Army circulated literature and enlisted the support of men. In 1891 the organisations combined to form the White Cross League which spread to India, Canada, South Africa, the United States, France, Germany, Holland, Switzerland and many more nations. The majority of White Cross League pamphlets in the 1880s and 1890s were written by Hopkins.

What was Hopkins's relationship to feminism? Her general attitude to the relationship between the sexes owes more to the principles of chivalry than to those of feminism as she reveals in comments such as 'the man is the head of the woman, and is therefore the servant of the woman'. Hopkins is an example of those many women who have used one variety of religion or another as a means of improving the situation of women and causing men to change their abusive behaviour. The language she uses is strongly Christian and her statements often seem ambivalent and contradictory. An unsigned White Cross League pamphlet of 1891, which is likely to have been written by Hopkins or at least strongly influenced by her, calls for a chivalrous respect for womanhood:

Not simply because women are the weaker sex; in all but the strictly physical sense this is becoming more and more untrue; but (1) because of the great dignity of the position of wife and mother to which every woman may be called, and (2) because in marriage or otherwise woman has a soul of her own and a spiritual destiny of her own to work out. She is not to be the servant of man's convenience or pleasure, either in marriage or apart from it . . . woman is not to be patronised; she is different, not inferior.[19]

She asserts the Christian virtues of wifehood and motherhood and that women have different roles, yet at the same time her sentiments about woman's relationship to man are strongly feminist. Hopkins's writing recognised that there was a confrontation between the interests of men and women. In the sexual system she described, women were the objects of men's exploitation and men the aggressors. This was a very different message from that which emerges from our contemporary equivalents to social purity. The writings of Mary Whitehouse, for instance, attack the sexual behaviour of 'people' rather than men, and Whitehouse makes no personal identification with women and what is happening to them. Hopkins's condemnation of men for the abuse of women and her anger at them, are unequivocal in the following statement from her social purity pamphlet *The Ride of Death*. Hopkins described prostitutes who had 'lost their way' and were close to 'disease, degradation curses, drink, despair'. She asked:

For who has driven them into that position? Men; men who ought to have protected them, instead of degrading them; men who have taken advantage of a woman's weakness to gratify their own selfish pleasure, not seeing that a woman's weakness was given to call out a man's strength. Ay, I know that it is often the woman who tempts; these poor creatures must tempt or starve. But that does not touch the broad issue, that it is men who endow the degradation of women; it is men who, making the demand, create the supply. Stop the money of men and the whole thing would be starved out in three months' time.[20]

Hopkins saw men's demands as the underlying cause of prostitution. She recognised that poverty and the limited opportunities allowed to women for making a decent living, were the reasons many women entered prostitution and she saw that poverty as the result of discrimination against women. She asked, 'Is it fair for you men, who can compel a fair wage for your work, to sit in judgement on her, and say it is her fault?'[21]

One indicator of the feminist current in the social purity movement is the way that the fate of individual women or groups of women who suffered male abuse was seen to be the concern of all women since all women were united by a common womanhood. Hopkins took this stance and wrote, 'as slavery fell before the realisation of a common humanity, this deeper evil of the degradation of woman will fall before the realisation of a common womanhood.'[22] It was common for women involved in the social purity movement to see themselves as being of one accord with what they described as the 'women's movement', particularly with respect to work in the area of sexuality. Hopkins clearly saw herself as part of the women's movement, as she makes clear in this rousing clarion call to other women to join her to fight the sexual abuse of girl children:

I appeal to you . . . not to stand by supinely any longer, and see your own womanhood sunk into degradation, into unnatural uses – crimes against nature, that have no analogues in the animal creation; but, whatever it costs you, to join the vast, silent women's movement which is setting in all over England in defence of your own womanhood . . . I appeal to you . . . to save the children.[23]

Hopkins would not have meant anything specifically feminist by the women's movement. For her it represented a massive uprising by women against men's sexual abuse.

Another woman in social purity who does not seem to have set out from a feminist perspective, but was certainly promoting a feminist message about prostitution and the double standard, was Laura Ormiston Chant. She was active in the Gospel Purity Association which was set up as a specifcially nonconformist organisation. The White Cross Army had originally been intended as a nondenominational society, but was swiftly associated with the Church of England. The GPA, set up in 1884, had a men's and a women's branch. Ormiston Chant, who later became editor of the *Vigilance Record*, journal of the National Vigilance Association whose work will be considered in the next chapter, was a frequent speaker for the GPA. In 1884 she is reputed to have given 400 talks, mainly to men's purity leagues. She wrote a pamphlet published by the White Cross League which shows her to have been as powerful a propagandist as Butler or Hopkins. Ormiston Chant writes that she received a letter from a friend which stated that it was more dreadful for a woman to 'fall into sin' than for a man. Chant's reply was a firm denial of this idea. She explained that women had been taught to accept that double standard and that:

> Unchastity is necessary for men – that it is the masculine prerogative – that a certain class of women must be sacrificed to this necessity, and that no good woman does, or ought, to know, anything about it; and that such a thing as chastity in the bridegroom, who requires it as an absolute necessity in his bride, is really asking too much of the so-called stronger sex.[24]

After attacking the Contagious Diseases Acts as being designed to make unchastity safe for men, by medical inspection of prostitutes, she employed a dramatic example of role reversal to bring the iniquity of the double standard home to her readers:

> Think of good women and men, knowing that I was a rake (feminine), inviting me to their houses, winking at my loathesomeness, but making feeble attempts to shut my victim up in a refuge, and branding him as 'fallen'! And think, oh think, of my blatantly talking of my brutality as necessity – of my requiring my husband to believe it – a coward, a liar, and a perjuror, who vowed a marriage vow, and deliberately broke it.[25]

Jane Ellice Hopkins was very strongly involved in the campaign to prevent men's abuse of girl children. She campaigned for the Criminal Law Amendment Act of 1885 which raised the age of consent for sexual intercourse to 16, with the aim of reducing the use of young girls in prostitution. She gave evidence before the 1881 House of Lords Commission on the protection of girls, stimulated petitioning up and down the country – particularly through the Ladies Associations for Friendless Girls, which were her inspiration – on the age of consent, and spent the two years prior to the passing of the Act in an exhausting national speaking tour on the subject. It was her concern with preventing the abuse of children which led her into an aspect of her work which was strongly criticised by feminists. She was worried that children who lived in brothels would take up the same career as their mothers. She supported the passing of the Industrial Schools Act of 1880 which allowed local authorities to remove children suspected of being in moral danger to board and receive training in Industrial Schools. The Act does not seem to have worked very well as Hopkins was complaining in 1882 that it was a 'dead letter' in London. Her association with this Act made her infamous amongst those campaigners who were opposed to restrictive legislation, i.e. legislation meant to reduce prostitution by interfering with the civil rights of women. The Act is described in the journal of the Vigilance Association for the Defence of Personal Rights as 'the wholesale kidnapping, that is, of little girls who may not have perfect domestic surroundings, and their consignment to large prison schools.[26] The journal's comment on Ellice Hopkins is that, 'It is sad, also, to see a woman thus endorsing the common faith that "the centre of evil" is in little girls.'[27] It seems that in her enthusiasm to create a foolproof scheme for the elimination of prostitution, Hopkins was prepared to endorse some actions which infringed upon the civil liberties of women. None the less she opposed the Contagious Diseases Acts throughout her writings whilst saying that she did not feel it necessary to become actively involved in the abolition campaign since so many good and able women and men were involved.

The scope of Hopkins's vision for the elimination of prostitution was such that she planned to cover the country in a safety net consisting of three kinds of organisations in each town. These were men's purity leagues to develop men's self-control, vigilance associations to deal with the prosecution of male offenders against women, and brothel visiting, and Ladies Associations to do preventive work among girls. Under her inspiration and with her support, Ladies Associations for the Care and Protection of Friendless Girls were set up in towns throughout Britain. The associations were to set up homes for girls who were homeless, had come to town looking for work or were between jobs and who might otherwise drift into prostitution. The girls were to be trained in domestic work, fitted with clothing through clothing clubs, given employment through a Free Registry Office which would not, as apparently many registry offices were at the time, be a front for entrapment into prostitution. The lady members would visit the girls in their situations and endeavour to provide a watchful guidance until they were sure the girls were settled down and happy in regular employment. By 1879 such associations were established in Birmingham, Bristol, Nottingham, London, Edinburgh, Torquay, Cheltenham, Southampton, Winchester, Bradford, Dundee and Perth and during the 1880s they were formed in many other towns after a visit and a rousing speech and general advice from Hopkins.

It is only church historians who have paid much attention to Hopkins's work. Where she has been mentioned by those concerned with the history of sexuality, she has been represented as a straightforward prude, and little attention has been paid to interpretation of her work. One aspect that has met with derision and misunderstanding from historians is the encouragement to Ladies Association members to give talks to working-class mothers involving simple sex instruction and advice which she believed would lower the risk of incest, such as not bathing children of both sexes together or letting them sleep together. Her concern about incest was not 'prudish'. She believed that it had very damaging effects on the female children who experienced it. There was a recognition amongst social purity workers of the link between incestuous abuse and prostitution through the possibility that a girl whose body was sexually used by male relatives as a child would find it only too easy to take up a career in which she was sexually exploited in later life. Hopkins was personally hostile to what she termed the 'dregs of asceticism' which led to bodies being seen as 'more or less the seat of evil, [and the idea] that there is something low and shameful about some of their highest functions which leads the British parent to make a conscience of ignoring the whole subject.'[28] She did not believe in sexual ignorance and encouraged the middle-class women in the Ladies Associations to train up their own sons to an awareness of the necessity for chastity and respect for women, and this required the discussion of subjects which they would rather have avoided.

Judith Walkowitz, an American historian, when writing of the impact of a Ladies' Association on Plymouth, summed up Hopkins thus: 'Ellice Hopkins, with her inadvertent appeal to middle class male prurience, represented one of the strands of social purity that arrived on the scene in Plymouth.'[29] There was in fact nothing inadvertent about her work. Her appeal to men of all classes, and the White Cross Army started amongst working men, depended upon the creation of guilt which would provide internal controls on their sexual behaviour.

The Moral Reform Union

An organisation which published and sold quantities of pamphlets by Hopkins was the Moral Reform Union, active from 1881 to 1897. The Union seems to have been the most overtly and

18

determinedly feminist wing of the social purity movement. According to the reports, it sprang from the inspiration of the Social Purity Alliance which had been founded by members of the campaign to repeal the Contagious Diseases Acts. Its founding statement declared that it was inspired by those organisations which 'accept the doctrine of the equal moral standard for both sexes', have 'faith in the possibility of chastity for men as well as women' and 'denounce the blasphemous lie that prostitution is a necessity'.[30] The origins of the Union lay in a meeting of twelve women including Dr Elizabeth Blackwell and the energetic organising secretary of the Moral Reform Union, Thomazine Leigh Browne. They described their motivation thus: 'Several ladies, appalled by the ever-increasing tide of corruption, which had culminated in immoral legislation, desired to confer with others who were planning remedial measures.'[31] The immoral legislation was that of the Contagious Diseases Acts. Blackwell and Browne invited concerned women to meet and work out how to attain their desired aim because they felt that 'union was strength'. The Union, which was originally intended to be a women's organisation, included some men at the second meeting who had expressed interest but there is no doubt that the women were the moving force. Of the 69 members whose names are given in the first report, only 15 were men and the names of those men seldom appear in the reports. The objects of the Union were:

1 To study, and confer upon, all subjects which especially affect the moral welfare of the young.
2 To collect, sell, distribute, or publish literature for moral education.
3 To consider how best to carry out practical measures for the reform of public opinion, law, and custom on questions of sexual morality.[32]

The provision of moral education literature was always a major part of the work and the Union was proud to be able to provide literature for the wants of the 'several classes whom it is necessary to interest in this great moral work'.[33] The literature contained many titles by Hopkins, Butler, Elizabeth Blackwell, by Wolstenholme Elmy, a feminist whose work we will look at in Chapter 2, and many more, hundreds of titles in all.

The Union carried out much of its work, such as petitioning and lecturing on the Contagious Diseases Acts and the age of consent, through drawing-room meetings of women. Such meetings were a very common form of women's political organising in the nineteenth century. One aspect of its work, which it saw as very important, was to provide communication between and therefore strengthen, other societies which existed to protect women and children from sexual exploitation. From the beginning these societies included the Social Purity Alliance, the Society for the Abolition of State Regulation of Vice, the Society for the Suppression of the Traffic in Girls, societies for the protection of young servants, the YMCA, and the Vigilance Association for the Defence of Personal Rights, amongst many others.

The overall project was to transform the sexual behaviour of men, or, as Mrs Bruce of Boston urged at the Union's first meeting, 'to demand purity and righteousness in men'. The Union was vigorous in taking the battle into the enemy camp by exposing and aiding in the prosecution of individual men as well as denouncing the behaviour of men as a group. The Union received many applications for assistance and advice in cases of corruption and seduction. Where appropriate these were handed on to other organisations, including after 1885, the National Vigilance Association. The Union talked of gaining legislation to allow for prosecution of seducers of women of all ages, not just very young women. The members also wanted 'protection [to be] afforded to women and girls against persecution by immoral men' and protested strongly when Great Yarmouth town council passed new bye-laws directed only at women who solicited and not at men.[34] In response to attempts made to apply a character test to women voters in municipal elections, which outraged women members, the Union began to call for the disqualification of male holders of public positions who had been accused in courts of justice of 'gross and disgusting criminal immorality' towards women. After the woman who ran an exclusive brothel to which MPs and members of the aristocracy repaired in great numbers, was imprisoned and the clients had received no penalty, the Union circulated an article entitled, 'The naming of some of the high-placed accomplices of Mrs Jeffries'.[35] The Union was concerned about incest and appealed for a 'stronger law to deal with crimes against morality in cases of near relationship'. At this time there was no legislation against incest. Union members also discussed with alarm the implications of the fact that Canada had enacted into statute law 'the revolting dictum that a husband may force his wife without being punishable', and thus legalised rape in marriage.[36] All these concerns – equal legislation on prostitution, incest, and rape in marriage – were to be major feminist concerns up to the First World War.

The Moral Refrom Union's interaction with other social purity groups shows up clearly the clash of interests within the social purity movement between feminists and non-feminists. The conflict was always between those who were prepared to support restrictive legislation against women in order to eliminate prostitution or impurity, and either ignore the double standard or merely make pious statements about the equal responsibility of men and those of feminist orientation who insisted that women should never be the subject of unjust legislation. The Union denounced

> unjust legislation in regard to the sexes, particularly that legislation which, founded upon the monstrous assumption that an enormous class of purchased women is a necessaray part of society, condones the act of the purchase, and attempts to reduce the trade.[37]

The first clash with another organisation was with the Central Vigilance Committee for the Repression of Immorality. The Union's report for 1883–4 explains that a weekly Union meeting was suspended so that all members could go to one of the first meetings of this new group, presumably to find out what sort of organisation they were and whether they were suitable for the Moral Reform Union to be associated with. The Union members concluded that the Vigilance Committee's speakers could not possibly arrive at a practical solution of the problem they were examining, which was prostitution, without the co-operation of women and lamented the fact that no women representatives of the committee had been at the meeting. The Union wrote to the Central Vigilance Committee about the necessity for the co-operation of women. The Committee replied that 'the including of women with them in their deliberations would not promote the objects they had in view.'[38] The reason for this seemed evident to the Moral Reform Union. It was the fact that the 'petition they are projecting goes upon the old lines of persecuting women for the protection of men' and women would be likely to disagree.

Much the same sort of exchange was conducted with the Church of England Purity Society which was another organisation which the union wrote to deploring the lack of women's point of view in the forming of its policy. The Union report stated, 'while in hearty sympathy with much of the work of the Church of

21

England Purity Society, we think the exclusion of women from its councils a fatal mistake.'[39] The CEPS replied that they did not think prostitution or sexual misbehaviour to be suitable subjects for discussion by women. The Union was most indignant. Another example of the Union's spirited defence of feminist principles is the way in which they severed connection with the National British Women's Temperance Association. Lady Henry Somerset, president of the association, executed a dramatic volte-face and decided to condone the 'regulation of vice' for the British army in India. This would mean the registration of prostitutes and compulsory examination for disease, which condoned the double standard and removed women's civil rights. Lady Somerset was also president of the British branch of the International Council of Women and her treachery in betraying the women's cause on prostitution caused consternation amongst feminist ranks.

The spectrum of organisations concerned with the protection of women and children was broad, ranging from the Vigilance Association for the Defence of Personal Rights, which concentrated on civil rights, through men's and women's organisations which campaigned around the elimination of the double standard from a civil rights perspective – such as the Social Purity Alliance, the Moral Reform Union and the National Vigilance Association – to organisations which included proponents of both regulation and anti-regulation opinions such as the Ladies Associations, and groups like the Central Vigilance Committee and the Church of England Purity Society which were unequivocally promoting legislation against women. The Moral Reform Union was firmly established in the part of the social purity movement which upheld feminism and the civil rights of women.

The internationalism of feminist social purity workers shows that the crusade to eliminate the double standard was constantly cross-fertilised by ideas from women in other countries. In particular whatever we find happening in Britain is likely to be reflected in events in the United States and vice versa. Delegates from the Moral Reform Union were invited to international conferences such as the 1891 International Congress of Women in Chicago. The internationalism is demonstrated by the fact that the woman who was due to represent the Union was unable to attend and Frau Fischer-Lette of Berlin went on behalf of the Union instead and stayed on for the World's Congress on Social Purity. The report on the Women's Congress stressed the need for maintaining international contacts.

An example of a speech made by an American feminist in 1888 at the International Council of Women held in Washington shows the strength of the feminist ideas with which British social purity women were in contact. The conference was attended by speakers from all over Europe including several from Britain. One British speaker was Mrs Ormiston Chant who concentrated on the practical aspect of preventive work with girls and the necessity to campaign against restrictive legislation. Some of the American speakers were far more outspoken on sexuality. Mrs Lucinda B. Chandler, speaking on 'Marriage Reform', expressed a strong dislike of the way that marriage legitimated the sexual slavery of women in terms very similar to her British counterparts Elizabeth Wolstenholme Elmy and Francis Swiney, whose work we will be considering later. She said that women wanted choice in exercising the reproductive function and in possessing ther children:

> It is the riot of carnalism, which the license of marriage claims to sanctify, that perpetuates the lustful, selfish propensities in force and fury, intensifies the downward revolution of the life, toward the animal, and creates the perversity that is so much more degraded than the animal . . . Man's legal institution of marriage was based upon the idea that woman's office in social economy is chiefly that of childbearing . . . Women as well as men must eliminate from marriage the features of prostitution, for when prostitution ceases inside of marriage it will disappear outside . . . How shall a woman be educated to know she has the right to control her own person? By listening to the voice of her own soul, and setting aside every inbred idea that has come down from male theology and statute.[40]

There seems to have been a closer direct link between social purity and temperance in the US than in Britain. In 1891 Dr Kate Bushnell, who was visiting with her co-delegate from the American Women's Christian Temperance Union, gave a talk at a Moral Reform Union meeting on combatting the three great evils, intemperance, impurity and the opium habit and traffic. Bushnell's address made plain what she felt to be the connection between temperance and social purity and suggested that the connection had been forgotten elsewhere:

> The word temperance, she thought, had been narrowed down till it only meant total abstinence. In America, the women of the Christian Temperance Union had accepted it in its higher

> meaning, the combatting of depraved appetite in every form,
> and for the abolition, all the world over, of all laws that
> protect depraved appetite. Intemperance worked more deadly
> evil upon women than upon men, because women became the
> victims of depraved appetites in men. When degraded, they
> were doubly degraded – first, being enslaved by their own
> appetites, and secondly by the appetites of men.[41]

In America, when international conferences were held, temperance often occupied almost as much space on the agenda as social purity and campaigns to protect women and children.

Through the network of national and international social purity organisations, women were able to exert considerable influence over men's consciences if not their behaviour, and to validate the feelings of other women about male sexuality. They saw themselves as part of the 'women's movement' and identified with all the women who were the objects of male sexual abuse. They attributed responsibilty to men, unequivocally, for the abuse they were fighting. By engaging in social purity work women were able to express their anger and indignation against men in a legitimate setting. Under the banner of social purity and with the moral clout of the Christian religion behind them, women were free to fight the forms of male sexual behaviour they found oppressive and to name *men* as the perpetrators of sexual injustice against women. There were elements within social purity which opposed them and wished to eliminate vice by restrictive legislation against women, but in the early days of social purity, these were no stronger than the feminist tendency.

The social purity feminists concentrated on fighting sexual abuses outside marriage, but through their campaigns against such abuses they were able to promote continence and sexual self-control for men and inspire guilt in men about their sexual desires. Thus women who wished to avoid sexual intercourse would be advantaged in their individual relationships with men. The project of the transformation of male sexual behaviour was undertaken by those women in social purity of a feminist persuasion, in a way which distinguishes them from other women working to the same ends. They took their message directly to men through talks and propaganda for men's chastity leagues. Where later feminists put their trust in the vote or spiritual systems, the social purity women set themselves straightforwardly to the task of getting men to control themselves.

After 1900 a new wave of social purity organisations sprang up in which feminism seems to have played little or no part. Social purity seemed now to be diverging completely from the ideals of feminists. An example of this new kind of organisation is the Alliance of Honour, set up in 1904. It was a men's organisation which included among its founders Baden Powell, of boy scout fame, and Bramwell Booth of the Salvation Army. The 14 points of the Alliance of Honour sum up its philiosophy. They include sentiments very similar to those of the White Cross Army such as 'an equally high moral standard for women and men'. But there were significant differences. The 14 points did not restrict themselves to sexual conduct or the defence of women. They included a large dose of general political philosophy of a highly conservative nature. This was directed towards the protection of 'religion, home and empire'.[42] The 14 points set out a programme for the promotion of loyal and obedient citizenship and patriotism. It was a nationalist programme. Members of the Alliance were enjoined to 'True Patriotism; Clean Citizenship; Public Moral Health and Public Physical Health'.

A major concern of the Alliance was pornography, particularly in the forms in which they saw it to be proliferating at this time, in theatre advertisements, for example, indecent postcards and indecent papers, i.e. news items reporting on sexual crime and the reporting of divorce cases. The way in which their concern over pornography was expressed made it clear that their objections stemmed from a root which had little to do with feminism. In an article entitled 'Pernicious Literature', Canon Rawnsley of Carlisle wrote:

> An enormous output of demoralising fiction and periodicals is poisoning the nation's character at its fountain-head. Side by side with this factor in the nation's degradation is found the deluge of the disgusting and vulgar post card and the indecent photograph.[43]

It is evident that their concern was for the protection of the nation at a time when there was a general alarm at the decline of Britain's imperial strength. They express no interest in the degradation of women in pornography, and very little in the effect of such depictions of women on men's behaviour towards women. The Alliance of Honour attracted 100,000 young men in the period immediately before the First World War. It continued its purity campaign throughout the 1920s and 1930s. The Alliance wanted young men to develop self-control and avoid masturbation in order to construct a strong empire and state, whereas the feminists saw self-control by men as necessary to prevent the sexual abuse of women.

There was a proliferation of empire-orientated social purity organistions in this period. Some earlier organisations continued their work but with a different emphasis and the loss of any feminst perspective. The tradition continued well into the 1930s. It is this tradition which is the root of social purity as we know it today in the form of the Festival of Light and the National Viewers and Listeners' Association. Such organisations make no specific reference to women even when it would seem difficult to avoid. The Longford Report, for example, which emerged from the work of the Festival of Light, does not mention that pornography depicts women as objects for men, and devotes only a few paragraphs to the significance of pornography to men's wider view of women.

In the period after 1900 the concerns of those feminists who had earlier worked within social purity seem to have been integrated into the propaganda of the suffrage campaign, which was renewed with unparallelled vigour after 1906. It is possible that feminists were able to pursue their aims of an equal moral standard and the control of male sexuality for the protection of women, through their pursuit of the vote, which was seen as a symbolic achievement through which women's other wrongs might be righted. The Ladies National Association which was set up to fight the Contagious Diseases Acts, continued after their repeal to campaign around the same kind of issues in the International Abolitionist Federation. This sought to eliminate the regulation of prostitution by the state and to destroy the white slave traffic worldwide. In 1913 the Ladies National Association joined up with the men's association to form a new organisation, the Association for Moral and Social Hygiene, directed by Alison Neilans, a former militant suffragist. The work of the AMSH in the campaign against the sexual abuse of children is examined in Chapters 3 and 4. In the following chapter we will look at the ideas feminists were developing from the 1890s to the First World War about sexuality. These are the ideas which motivated those feminists who became involved in the campaign against sexual abuse.

CHAPTER 2

Continence and Psychic Love

The women whose ideas and strategies are examined in this chapter saw themselves as feminists and had abandoned the constraints of Christianity and Christian-dominated social purity. These feminists have been derided as prudes and puritans by historians. They are women whose contributions to other areas of feminist struggle have been seen as radical and progressive, whilst their ideas on sexuality have been seen as rather outdated and embarrassing. In fact these women theorists were involved in the development of a complex philosophy of sex, designed to show both how women's subjection had originated and how women were maintained in subjection to men from day to day. As Dale Spender points out in *Women of Ideas*, women's theory has been routinely dismissed and written out of history whereas men's ideas have been called philosophy or politics.[1] In no instance is this clearer than in the case of the feminist philosophy of sex that we will be looking at here. The contempt with which these theories have been treated doubtless owes a great deal to the significance of their challenge to the dominant male ideology of sex.

The language with which these feminists described sexuality, in terms such as 'sexual excess' and 'continence', has proved a stumbling block for contemporary feminist historians. The language available to them when they were trying to express their anxieties and their hopes was not created by the women themselves. Similarly today, feminists wrestle to gain some grasp on their feelings about sex within an ideology of compulsory sexual activity, using terms such as 'sexual needs', 'orgasm' and 'frustration' which would have been quite as alien to the feminists of the 1890s and are not necessarily more useful to us today in articulating our experience and hopes about sexuality.

Elizabeth Wolstenholme Elmy

Elizabeth Wolstenholme Elmy made a major contribution to feminist ideas on sexuality through her books and articles. In a very active feminist career which spanned 60 years she worked alongside those women who were taking the most radical stand on sexuality such as Josephine Butler and Christabel Pankhurst. Her main campaigning activities were in the areas of higher education for women, women's suffrage, reform of the laws on marriage and the custody of children and the abolition of the Contagious Diseases Acts. She began her efforts for the improvement of women's position by forming an association of schoolmistresses and a society for furthering the higher education of women in 1861. In 1865 she was a founding member and honorary secretary of the Manchester Women's Suffrage Society. In 1867 she revived the agitation in suppport of the Married Women's Property Act, became secretary of the Married Women's Property Committee and held that office until 1882 when the last Married Women's Property Act was passed. The 1882 Infants' Act, giving widowed mothers custody of their children, was largely due to her efforts. While most other workers in the movement for women's education stood aloof from the Contagious Diseases Acts agitation, Wolstenholme Elmy threw herself into abolition work from the beginning and was a very prominent member of the committee of the Ladies National Association throughout its existence.

In 1889 she was a founding member of the Women's Franchise League along with Richard and Emmeline Pankhurst and Josephine Butler, among others. Her connection with the Pankhursts, severed briefly in 1891 when she founded her own Women's Emancipation Union, was later resumed when she joined the Women's Social Political Union in which she remained until 1914 despite the splits, as a devoted supporter of Christabel and her mother. A statement from the aims of the Women's Emancipation Union in 1895 gives an idea of the shape of Wolstenholme Elmy's feminism at that time:

> [the WEU] recognises that the slavery of sex is the root of all slavery, and that injustice to womanhood, especially injustice within the family, is the perennial source of all other injustice, it seeks the legal, political, social, and individual emancipation

of women, as the vital indispensable condition of all other true and lasting reforms; and affirms these claims as paramount to all personal, sectional, or party considerations whatsoever.[2]

She was uncompromising in putting women first and seeing the fight for women's emancipation as the fundamental political struggle.

Wolstenholme Elmy generally wrote under the pseudonyms of Ellis Ethelmer or Ignota (the unknown woman). Of her major works, two were books of sex education for children, one, *Woman Free*, was a heavily annotated long poem mainly concerned with women's biology and the effects of sexual abuse, and another, *Phases of Love*, is concerned with the ideal form of the sex relation between men and women. Many of her articles pursue the same themes. Her activities in the Ladies National Association and in marriage reform gave her practical outlets for her views. Sylvia Pankhurst attributed the writing of *Woman Free* to Wolstenholme Elmy's husband, Ben Elmy.[3] It is very unlikely that a work which so clearly expressed woman's experience of sexual abuse was by a man. It is much more likely that this is a case, like so many documented in Dale Spender's book, in which a woman's work has been appropriated by a man.

She showed her unconventionality in the area of sexuality by living with her future husband, Ben Elmy, before they married. This was a quite exceptional flouting of Victorian middle-class convention. When it was clear that she was pregnant, she was forced by fellow suffragists to marry lest she harm the suffrage cause with scandal. When she married in 1875 she adopted the surname Wolstenholme Elmy as a gesture against the patriarchal nature of marriage. Her clear and simple descriptions of the human reproductive process for children at a time when ignorance was considered to be correct for adult women let alone for children, are further evidence of her flouting of the conventions. Her book for older children, published in 1892, was entitled *The Human Flower*. It began with a description of reproduction in flowers and went on to describe human reproduction in a manner designed, as she said, to prevent any stigma of 'impurity' from attaching to any part of the body. In pursuit of this aim the human genitals are described as 'flower-like' organs. The book for younger children was entitled, appropriately, *Baby Buds*.

A central theme of Wolstenholme Elmy's writings is the right of women to control their own bodies. This control was to extend to deciding when and how sexual activity should take place and whether or not to bear children. In *The Human Flower* she described the plight of the married woman in relation to sex and reproduction in detail, with the aim of implanting the idea of mutuality and woman's right to decide at an early age:

> Seeing the still existent unjust conditions, legal or social, in marriage and noting the misery so frequently the lot of the wife – too usually led or left to accept marriage ignorant of the actual incidents of matrimony, and with no word of forewarning as to marital physical intimacies which, unless of reciprocal impulse, may prove repugnant and intolerable to her; involving moreover the sufferings and dangers of repeated and undesired childbearing – the conviction is every day growing that under no plea or promise can it be permissible to submit the individuality, either mental or physical, of the wife, to the will and coercion of the husband; the functions of wifehood and motherhood must remain solely and entirely within the wife's own option. Coercion, like excess, is in itself a contravention and annihilation of the psychic nature of the sexual relation; since no true affection or love would either prompt or permit to inflict a grief or an injustice on a reluctant partner, and to submit her thus to the possibility of undesired maternity is a procedure equally unjustifiable and inhuman to the mother and the 'unwelcome child'.[4]

Such a sympathetic understanding of the effects of unwanted sexual intercourse upon women will not be found in contemporary sex education literature for children. It is a very clear statement of woman's right to physical integrity and self-determination.

Wolstenholme Elmy hoped to relieve some of the misery of wives caused by ignorance as to what their husbands expected of their bodies. She was particularly concerned about the concept of 'conjugal rights' which gave the husbands the backing of the law in requiring sexual use of their wives' bodies whether they were willing or not. The law allowed wives no redress against husbands who forced them into sexual intercourse. The situation is no different today as the contemporary feminist 'Rape in Marriage' campaign is seeking to point out. An article in the *Westminster Review* entitled 'Judicial Sex Bias' by Ignota shows how Wolstenholme Elmy, along with other women, had been fighting a long battle to alter the law. Ignota quotes extracts from a paper read by herself under the name Wolstenholme Elmy to the Dialectical Society in March 1880 about the attempt which was then being made, via the Criminal Code Bill of that year, to embody in statute law the fact that a man could not rape his wife. The Bill defined rape as 'the act of a man, not under the age of 14 years, having carnal knowledge of a woman, *who is not his wife*, without her consent'. Her paper commented that rape,

> being a violation of a primary natural right, is and ought to be, wholly independent of any legal or otherwise artificially created relationship between the parties, and that it would be a gross immorality to enact as the section I have just quoted proposes implicitly to do, that any act by a husband, however base and cruel it may be, is justified by the matrimonial consent of the wife once given and never to be retracted.[5]

She stated that embodying such a provision in law would reduce the wife to 'bodily slavery'. Though the Bill did not become law, Ignota pointed out that decisions by judges had enshrined the principle in common law none the less. The 'bodily slavery' of the wife is still a principle behind English law, but some legal battles were won to improve the right of a woman to control her own body in marriage. The 1884 Matrimonial Causes Act ended the power of the husband to imprison a wife who refused conjugal rights. The Clitheroe case of 1891 established that a woman who refused to live with her husband could not be seized by him or on his behalf or imprisoned by any court.

The ideal form of relationship between the sexes which Wolstenholme Elmy promoted did not include sexual intercourse except for the purposes of reproduction. In her sex education manual *The Human Flower* she acknowledged that some couples might choose to engage in sexual intercourse more often and recommended a safe period to avoid conception. The 'safe' period was, in accordance with the medical opinion of the time, that which we now recognise as least safe! The idea that a fulfilling love relationship which excluded sexual intercourse could exist between men and women is unfamiliar if not incomprehensible to the minds of those brought up during or after the 'sexual revolutions' of the twentieth century which have defined 'sex' specifically as sexual intercourse. It is probably this unfamiliarity which has caused contemporary historians to characterise the feminists who thought as Wolstenholme Ely did as 'anti-sex' or as prudes. In *Phases of Love* she explained the political basis of what she called 'psychic love'. The book is described as 'A history of the human passion and of its advance from the physical to the psychic character and attribute'. The first two pages describe the sensations of a man and a woman lying on a riverbank. The modern reader might suppose from the description that the couple were experiencing ecstasy after an episode of genital sexual activity. Wolstenholme Elmy then explains that what had actually taken place was 'psychic love'. She explained that psychic love was only possible in those bred to a 'realisation of justice, equality, and sympathy between the sexes'. The rest of the book is the history of the transformation of physical into psychic love. She writes of previous historical systems that 'into each of these masculine schemes was interwoven, with a singular unanimity, the bodily subjection (and hence the degradation) of women'.[6] Throughout history men had misused women by 'positive physical oppression and excess' which had resulted in a restriction of woman's 'native individuality of mental power and action'. Her anger at the way that a woman was reduced by men's obsession with physical love to a merely sexual function is echoed again and again through the development of feminist thought from the mid-nineteenth century through to the 1920s. Wolstenholme Elmy's solution was to promote the ideal of sexual self-control and its counterpart of 'psychic love'. Her aim was to free women from the 'degradation of her temple to solely animal uses', so that she might take a full part in all the areas of life previously arrogated to man. The only roughly equivalent concept to exist in the contemporary wave of feminism is that of women being seen as 'sex objects'. The concept in the late nineteenth century was much broader. The use of woman as simply a sexual function was seen as underlying the whole system of the oppression of women.

In order to justify the importance of physical self-determination for women, Wolstenholme Elmy used eugenic arguments and stressed woman's role as mother. In *Woman Free* she quoted approvingly from Professor Alfred Wallace, a supporter of the suffrage movement, who stated that when women were in a position to choose their mates freely without any compulsion from poverty or social pressure, then more would choose to stay unmarried and those that married would select the fittest men and produce superior children. The concepts of motherhood and eugenics were used by feminists of all persuasions in the period to give extra weight to their arguments. The idea that a superior human being could be bred by whatever means, was a fashionable idea with socialists, feminists and right across the political spectrum. Feminists like Wolstenholme Elmy never lauded motherhood at the expense of woman's right to satisfying work outside the home. It may be that because bodily integrity was a basic human right for which men had never had to strive and would probably not understand, an armoury of arguments was felt to be necessary. In *Phases of Love* Wolstenholme Elmy wrote that the potency of motherhood in women was becoming ever more deeply esteemed and she saw 'this esteem and reverence by both sexes ensure to woman inviolably and continuously the self-sovereignty of her own person'. In a powerful verse of the poem in *Women Free* she linked the ideas of woman's right to control her own body, eugenics and motherhood,

> For but a slave himself [man] must ever be,
> Till she to shape her own career be free; –
> Free from all uninvited touch of man,
> Free mistress of her person's sacred plan;
> Free human soul; the brook that she shall bear,
> The first – the truly free, to breathe our air;
> From woman slave can come but menial race,
> The mother free confers her freedom and her grace.[7]

The phrase 'all uninvited touch of man' shows the breadth of her understanding of the importance of bodily integrity for women.

Wolstenholme Elmy did not confine herself to the problem of sexual abuse in marriage. As a member of the national committee of the Ladies National Association for the Abolition of the Contagious Diseases Acts she drew direct connections between the existence of prostitution and the sexual slavery of all women in or out of marriage. She wrote that Acts like the Contagious Diseases Acts, 'tend to intensify in the minds of men the horrible notion that woman is merely an appanage to man for the purpose of the gratification of his basest sensuality'.[8] Such sentiments contradict the common nineteenth- and twentieth-century defence of prostitution, which is that it protects the virtue of happily married women by providing a safety valve for men's rape tendencies. Feminists involved in the campaign around prostitution said that such abuse of women depended for its existence on a system in which all men were able to exploit and abuse all women sexually, in or out of marriage. Wolstenholme Elmy summed up the effects of prostitution on the women who were used as 'Profanation of the dignity and individuality of women'. These are very much the same words she used to describe the effects of unwelcome sex within marriage. She does not distinguish between the experience of bodily slavery for women whether it is in marriage or prostitution. She attacked the regulation of prostitution on account of its class bias as well as its sex bias. Here she accuses the supporters of the Contagious Diseases Acts:

> The building up of a false social system on the basis of *class* (for be it remembered, it is practically only poor women whom this wicked system assails) and sex injustice is the endeavour, here openly avowed, of the men who deny to women the right to help govern themselves.[9]

It is interesting that today political theorists of the left whom one might expect to recognise the class, if not the sex injustice of prostitution generally acknowledge neither. The only problem they recognise in respect of prostitution is that of unjust legislation. Their desire to see prostitution as just a job like any other causes them to be quite blind to the arguments of either the first or the present wave of feminism. The views of the contemporary socialist historians are discussed in the Afterword.

Wolstenholme Elmy is most remembered and quoted not for her outspoken attacks on coercion in marriage, nor her brave accounts of human reproduction for children, but for saying that menstruation was pathological and caused by men's sexual abuse of women.

> Revolting was the shock to the writer, coming, some years ago, with unprejudiced and ingenuous mind, to the study of the so-called 'Diseases of Woman', on finding that nearly the whole of these special 'diseases', including menstruation, were due, directly or collaterally, to one form or other of *masculine* excess or abuse.[10]

The fact that she entertained this idea about menstruation does not indicate an eccentric and individual horror at the effects of male sexuality upon women. She quotes medical evidence such as Dr Caroline B. Winslow of Boston, in support of her statement. This medical opinion had influenced both the American and English women's movements to some extent. Like many other feminists, Francis Swiney in particular, she was horrified to discover from contemporary medical sources how many female ailments could be attributed to sexual intercourse. She was wrong about menstruation but right about the pains and complications of unwanted childbirth, which clearly originated from this source, along with many other infections and complications of the female reproductive system.

Francis Swiney

Francis Swiney began writing in the 1890s and published a great quantity of books, pamphlets and articles up to the First World War. Wolstenholme Elmy described Swiney in her letters as a very reliable woman in Cheltenham who could be trusted to look after woman suffrage affairs in that town. Ignota reviewed her *Awakening of Woman* in 1899 in the *Westminster Review* with great enthusiasm. Her ideas seem to have had most influence on the militant wing of the women's movement. Her works were advertised in the *Suffragette*, journal of the Women's Social and Political Union. Treatment of her by historians has tended to be cursory and dismissive, interpreting her as either a crank or a prude. Like Wolstenholme Elmy she saw the sexual subjection of women as fundamental to the oppression of women by men. She offered a similar solution in the elimination of genital sexual activity between men and women as far as possible, and the promotion of sexual self-control for men. Wolstenholme Elmy's solution was 'psychic love'. Swiney's was her own unique brand of theosophy promoted through the League of Isis which she organised herself.

There is no doubt as to the strength of Swiney's feminism. She wrote of women's oppression with passionate rage:

> For, consider what man-rule, man-made religion, man's moral code has implied to woman. She has seen her female child, Nature's highest development in organic evolution, ruthlessly murdered as superfluousness. She has seen her son the 'defective variation' biologically the outcome of malnutrition and adverse conditions, and therby imperfect, placed over her as master, Lord, and tyrant.[11]

The murder of the female child to which she referred is the practice of infanticide of girls in subsistence economies where girls, particularly when dowries were required for them, were seen as an economic burden. At the root of women's wrongs, according to Swiney, lay women's sexual subjection to men. She explained, 'She [the female animal] stands the martyr of the organised and systematic sexual wrongdoing on the part of the man who should be her mate, and whom she alone has evolved to the human plane.'[12] She saw women's sexual subjection as fundamental to the establishment of 'man-rule'. She believed that this subjection began when men destroyed the matriarchate in order to make women into sexual slaves who would satisfy men's sexual desires. The importance she attached to the sexual aspect of women's oppression is expressed in such statements as 'Now the sex-subjugation of woman has always been more or less the father of men's thoughts.'[13] She accused men of having reduced woman to a purely sexual function:

> Men have sought in women only a body. They have possessed that body. They have made it the refuse heap of sexual pathology, when they should have reverenced it as the Temple of God, the Holy Fane of Life, the Fountain of Health to the human race.[14]

The greatest burden of this subjection was that women were forced to submit to sexual intercourse at all times, whenever the male desired, and even at those times which Swiney considered should be the most sacred, during pregnancy and immediately after childbirth. She considered such use of the woman's body to be abusive and employed quantities of biological, medical and anthropological evidence to prove her point. She catalogued the effects upon women and the 'race' caused by a 'selfish, lustful and diseased manhood'. She stated that men's sexual impositions during pregnancy led to infants being born covered in the 'vernix caseosa', a 'cheesy mess' formed from 'inanimate decomposed zoosperms', since sperm in excess was a 'virulent poison'. This covering was said to lead to eczema, skin diseases, eye disease and many more ailments in children. The sperm was said to contain alcohol, nicotine or syphilis which had dreadful effects on infant mortality and child health. In the woman, she stated, 'masculine excess' could lead to painful childbirth and puerperal fever, and the resumption of intercourse too soon after childbirth prevented the reproductive organs from recuperating and dried up the mother's milk. She claimed that such sexual abuse led to the human species being 'diseased by sexual vice, overpopulated with degenerates, imbeciles, and malformed individuals'. The accuracy of Swiney's statements was only as good as her sources, and she relied on the medical opinion of her day. Current medical opinion is beginning to lend credence to one of her assertions. She spoke of excess sperm leading to cancer. A link is now being suggested between sexual intercourse using non-barrier methods of contraception and cervical cancer. It is important to see her list of ailments and more bizarre conclusions in the light of the excitement which women like Swiney must have experienced on discovering, from gynaecological work in the nineteenth century, that women were not naturally weak and subject to mysterious illnesses. There was great indignation that many of women's woes, including venereal disease and its many complications, resulted from an activity, sexual intercourse, which they saw as unnecessary.

Swiney's solution to the problem of excess sexual intercourse was the 'Law of continence' or 'Natural Law'. She stated that sexual intercourse should only take place for the purposes of reproduction and on no accout during the periods of lactation and gestation. According to her plan, which included very lengthy periods of lactation, a woman could be expected to bear children at intervals of four to five years. To support her argument she referred to a period of history which she called the matriarchate, when the 'mothers' rule' was obeyed, such extended intervals in childbearing were the rule and the diseases which 'fill our asylums and hospitals with thousands of victims of sexual excess' were rare. Swiney drew her evidence of primitive peoples from the work of contemporary anthropologists who were describing societies in which women had no more than three or four children and would not allow men sexual access to them for periods of from two to three years. Evidence of such practices has been produced by anthropologists throughout the twentieth century.[15] These revelations have not, since Swiney's time, created any discussion or interest in the subject of women's relation to sexual intercourse. This is probably because the coital imperative which rules at present has rendered them incomprehensible. Swiney did realise the implications and used the evidence as a weapon against the idea that sexual intercourse was vital to the health and happiness of women.

Swiney's 'Natural Law' was embodied in the six rules of observance of the theosophical society she founded and administered, the League of Isis, which included both women and men. The following rules 2 and 5 give an idea of the aims of her society:

2   To hold in reverence and sanctity the creative organs and

functions, only exercising them for their natural, ordained and legitimate use.

5   To keep, as far as possible by individual effort, the Temple of the Body pure and undefiled; raising sex relations from the physical to the spiritual plane, and dedicating the creative life in the body to the highest uses, Man regarding Woman as the creatrix of the Race, Woman regarding Man as the appointed coadjutor in the supreme task of racebuilding, both labouring in Love to produce a perfect work.[16]

Continence seems to have been the main if not the only route to spiritual experience in Swiney's system. The transmutation of physical into psychic energy was a principle of theosophy in general. Swiney left the precise spiritual aim of League members rather vague. She described it as being to 'touch the stars'. Like J. Ellice Hopkins, Swiney instituted a religious organisation in which men could be trained in self-control to women's benefit. The advantage to women who wished to avoid sexual intercourse of having a religious system which codified the necessity of avoiding it, must have been great. When women could point out that the unwanted activity would be damaging to the 'Higher Self' of both partners it gave them extra authority and influence. A spiritual belief must have strengthened many women in the pursuit of bodily integrity.

Swiney is unusual amongst feminist writers in her forthright declaration of female superiority. She enlisted the names of leading biologists to support the idea that man was a genetic mutation. She stated that life began as female, and in many species when the environmental conditions were in harmony with the maternal organism, she reproduced parthenogenetically and only brought forth males when the conditions of nutrition and temperature were less favourable.

The first male cell, and the first male organism, as an entity separated from the mother, was an initial failure on the part of the maternal organism to reproduce its like, and was due to a chemical deficiency in the metabolism or physique of the mother.[17]

Women's superiority, in Swiney's eyes, extended to having a brain larger and better than men's which made her better at everything including deduction and reasoning. Swiney's ideas on the male mutation could be seen as an extreme feminist version of eugenics in which the whole of the male gender was seen as an avoidable eugenic tragedy.

Swiney also wrote of the sex slavery of women outside marriage. She wrote about prostitution, sexual abuse of children, incest and the white slave traffic. She wanted the age of consent raised for girls to 18 or more. She bewailed the ineffectiveness of the 1908 Incest Act caused by the male bias of juries and magistrates and called for legislation to make the abuse of authority for the purposes of sexual exploitation an offence. She described the effects of the registration of prostitutes as making a woman who worked in prostitution, 'no longer a person with human rights, but a scheduled tool in the inventory of legalised immorality'.

The importance of Swiney's contribution to feminist ideas on sexuality lies in the clarity with which she expressed her central idea, which was that women's oppression was based on and maintained through, sexual subjection, and in the persuasive force with which she uttered it. She was an extremely prolific writer, showed little of the usual Victorian reticence about calling sperm, sperm, and directed a passionate rage and indignation at men which is unsurpassed in the literature of the time. An example of her passionate denunciation of men should suffice to show how powerful her appeal must have been to women who sought an expression for their anger at men:

> Church and State, religion, law, prejudice, custom, tradition, greed, lust, hatred, injustice, selfishness, ignorance, and arrogance have all conspired against her under the sexual rule of the human male. Vices, however, like curses, come back to roost. In his own enfeebled frame, in his diseased tissues, in his weak will, his gibbering idiocy, his raving insanity, and hideous criminality, he reaps the fruits of a dishonoured motherhood, an outraged womanhood, an unnatural, abnormal stimulated childbirth, and a starved poison-fed infancy.[18]

Variations on psychic love

It was common for feminists in this period to praise love and endow it with spiritual, semi-mystical qualities which sound strange to our ears. The ideal of passionate or non-genital love served many purposes. It offered a mental and sometimes, it would seem, physical satisfaction which did not involve sexual intercourse. To the feminists considered here lust meant the male desire for sexual intercourse, imposed on woman against her will, or with indifference as to her consent, with appalling consequences to women in diseases, unwanted pregnancy, and ill-health, and with little or no attention to tenderness, affection or what might give the woman pleasure. Sexual intercourse was seen as an experience which undermined a woman's feelings of self-respect and equality in her relationship with a man. The lauding of psychic love gave women a justification to avoid and disdain male sexual demands and provided a way of achieving those satisfactions which sexual intercourse did not provide. Whilst sexual intercourse could highlight the other glaring inequalities of the relationship in which she was involved, psychic love, which contained a large element of fantasy, enabled these to be disregarded. It seems to have been those women who were actively involved in relationships with men who put most of the energy into promoting psychic love or one of its spiritual equivalents.

There were other potent reasons why the feminists saw it as necessary to devalue sexual activity between men and women. They saw that the sexualisation of woman limited her possibilities and exposed her to abuse. Prostitution, sexual abuse of children and sexual assault, were seen to be inextricably linked with man's view of woman as simply a sexual function and the notion that he could not survive without a sexual outlet. In the nineteenth and early twentieth centuries, many feminists saw the replacement of sexual intercourse with some form of psychic love, as a way of solving these problems. Elmy and Swiney were major figures in the promotion of the ideas of continence and psychic love, but they were by no means alone in holding them. They were representative of mainstream feminist opinion. Other feminists used different tactics and promoted slightly different solutions, but they shared the same basic philosophy.

Margaret Shurmer Sibthorp was a woman who talked, like Swiney, of an individual spiritual satisfaction which women could aspire to if they were able to rise above fleshly concerns. Sibthorp produced, almost singlehandedly, a feminist publication entitled *Shafts*, for a few years in the 1890s. In a review of a book, *The Physiology of Love*, by Henry Seymour, she outlined her philosophy about sex and spirituality. She wrote of the book that:

> Sex is not a state to be worshipped; it is not even a state to linger in, or to dwell upon with that delight of the flesh which is most deadly to spirit life. Sex is a condition which when

dwelt upon and lingered over and searched into after this mode is liable to produce a derangement of the moral tone, and a *MADNESS* on the subject, most disagreeable in its results. Sex is a *phase* through which the spirit passes in order to gain experience and discipline. It calls forth if lived through aright, the very highest purity, the noblest strength and impulses; tending ever to the higher and higher life.[19]

Sibthorp does not seem to have thought that women could entirely avoid sexual intercourse. They could, however, transcend it. Wolstenholme Elmy regarded Sibthorp with some suspicion and remarked upon her in a letter to a friend that she was unsuitable for a panel of suffrage speakers because she would speak about the superiority of women.[20]

Lucy Re-Bartlett wrote copiously about sex relations between women and men in the decade before the First World War. Like the feminists who took to theosophy, she was interested in spiritual development. Her concern started at the same point, with the effects of male sexual demands on the relationship between the sexes. Much of her writing is composed of a glowing eulogy to the suffragettes. To her the women's movement, but particularly the Women's Social and Political Union, represented the spiritual force which would transfrom the way women and men related and impel humankind forward into the 'Coming Order'. She also wrote about Italy and was a member of the Societa Italiana di Sociologica. She was a member of a Swiss and two British prison reform organisations. Her books about sex and feminism were *The Coming Order* (1911), *Sex and Sanctity* (1912) and *Towards Liberty* (1913).

Re-Bartlett wrote that the significance of the suffrage struggle was that it represented the transition of mankind from 'spiritual childhood' to 'spiritual adulthood'. She saw human evolution as divided into three stages of development, the instinctual, the mental and the spiritual. Most human beings were at that time in the second stage which was a difficult period when the 'uncritical simplicity of the instinct' was left behind and the 'peace and wisdom of the spirit not yet gained.' The militant suffragist was the woman of the future and would help mankind to reach the next stage. She agreed with other feminists that 'Sex union in the human being should be limited strictly to the actual *needs of creation*.'[21] If this were so then women would not have to be humiliated by being used against their will, 'Women would no longer need to feel indignity or humiliation if in the act of union they knew they had never given themselves to their husbands only, but always to God and to the race.' Re-Bartlett's words give us an idea of how the women we have been looking at felt when their bodies were used for their husbands' pleasure. It is small wonder they sought to ennoble the experience.

Re-Bartlett's plea for a more spiritually satisfying relationship between men and women reflects all the loneliness and aching dissatisfaction which married middle-class women in the period were feeling at finding that their relationships with men took the form of having to provide their bodies for the satisfaction of male sexual demands. She expressed bitter contempt for the form which marriage took: 'It is often said that marriage exists for the protection of women, but in its present form it is often her prison and her degradation.'[22] Re-Bartlett, like the other feminists considered here, thought that it was vital for motherhood to be a matter of choice for women. This was to be achieved by limiting 'creative action' to 'creative desire', i.e. sexual intercourse only for reproduction. Artificial contraception was anathema to her since this, the use of appliances, allowed the dominance of male sexual demands which the woman had no excuse to avoid:

> those artifical means which in the educated classes are so largely resorted to in order to prevent results leave the animality resulting from the undue use of the sexual act the same as in the populace, adding to it a new element of degradation through the violation of physical nature which in the populace rarely, and in the animal never appears.[23]

Her desire to provide women with dignity and self-respect in their relationships with men through control over their own bodies, coupled with a deeper form of love and communication, could not be achieved by use of a form of birth control which merely meant more sexual intercourse. This was the root of the feminist objection to birth control which was maintained by some feminists well into the 1920s when 'artificial' birth control was officially accepted by mainstream feminists such as the National Union of Societies for Equal Citizenship in 1925. One woman who maintained her resistance, Margery Smith, wrote in a letter to the NUSEC journal in 1925, 'we regard artificial birth control as wrong. We know well that it would open the way to demands from men that would amount to a new tyranny. We do not want more tyrannies, but more practical love.'[24]

To modern ears the words 'free love' are likely to conjure up an image of casual promiscuity. In the 1890s a body of feminists who were rejecting marriage and entering into what they called 'free love' unions with men meant something very different. These women were as enthusiastic about continence and psychic love as any others in the women's movement. The impetus towards 'free love' came from an understanding that the marriage laws constrained women and subjected them to the power of their husbands, particularly in respect of marital rape. 'Free love' seemed preferable because it could give them more power to control access to their own bodies, not because it allowed them to escape from lengthy monogamous unions. Mona Caird wrote of a new ideal of marriage which would suffer no interference from society or the law and which would be based on the full understanding that woman had an obvious right to 'possess herself, body and soul, to give or withhold herself, body and soul, exactly as she wills'.[25] Arabella Dennehy, writing of the 'Women of the Future' in the *Westminster Review*, expressed her reasons for choosing 'free love' in much the same way:

> Is woman to remain the physical and moral slave of man, or is she to determine her own future? Is marriage a mere piece of social mechanism for subjugating women and allowing men to gratify their basest desires while outwardly conforming to conventional regulations? If so, then true morality would lead to this inevitable result – abolish marriage, establish free union in which each sex would have an equal voice, and make love the only law regulating the relationship of the sexes.[26]

Effie Johnson, while debating *Marriage and Free Love* in the same journal, plumped for 'free love' because 'that most effectively leads to the goal towards which both Evolution and Progress press – viz, Spiritually'.[27] Johnson's aim was similar to Wolstenholme Elmy's. It was 'spiritual love which is the apex of all material evolution, the flower which aeons of slowly developing animal organisms at length bear.' Johnson was extremely scathing about the current form of marriage, which after the many forms taken throughout history, had evolved into 'that terrible growth, prostitution, linked with a miscalled Monogamy, which admits a one-sided licentiousness under monogamic laws, truly appalling to contemplate'. She made it clear that she did not see 'free love' as being about unrestrained sexual intercourse. She said that 'free love' did not mean 'excess' and that the women who chose it did so in revolt against the injustice of marriage law for women. 'Real free love', she said, was not the 'indulgence of depraved passion.'

Annie Besant provides a fascinating example of a woman who took up theosophy and celibacy and fell into line with majority feminist opinion on sexuality after having been a 'free love' practitioner and a uniquely strong female propagandist for the vital necessity of sexual intercourse. Besant promoted 'artificial' birth control techniques, mainly the vaginal sponge, in the 1870s whilst the majority of the women's movement were in strong opposition to such techniques. She believed, at that time, that men were incapable of self-control and that prostitution was inevitable; sentiments very different from those of women in the repeal campaign. The fanatical strength of her belief in the necessity of sexual intercourse to health and happiness can only be equalled by the strength of her espousal of celibacy a little over ten years later. In 1877 she was saying that 'until nature evolves a neuter sex celibacy will ever be a mark of imperfection'.[28] According to Besant celibate people died earlier, were less strong than married ones, grew peevish and aged very quickly. She quoted male medical experts to charge celibacy with causing as many ills as Swiney was able to lay at the door of its opposite. Besant quoted figures to show the alarming percentage of lunatics in France who were celibates. Celibacy created a 'long train of formidable diseases' including 'spermatorrhoea in the male, chlorosis and hysteria in the female' and many more.

In 1899 Annie Besant embraced theosophy. It was the third of the major beliefs and campaigns which she took up in her life. The first two were secularism and socialism, and it was at this stage that she adopted 'free love'; in theory, it is suggested, as far as Charles Bradlaugh was concerned, and in practice with Edward Aveling and George Bernard Shaw. Her conversion to theosophy was a source of consternation to her previous associates. One possible explanation for her change of heart is a disillusionment with the realities of the free love lifestyle. Purportedly, after her affair with Shaw, her hair turned grey and many years later Shaw told an interviewer that she had 'absolutely no sex appeal'.[29]

The inner core of the theosophical movement which Besant joined was celibate. She wrote an article for the American free thought magazine *Lucifer* in 1891 which was a recantation of her earlier position. She had come to the conclusion that the cause of the problem of unwanted childbearing was not in the material plane and could not be solved with a material cure. Self-restraint was the answer:

> Now the sexual instinct that he [man] has in common with the brute is one of the most fruitful sources of human misery. . . . To hold this instinct in complete control . . . is the task to which humanity should set itself. . . . It follows that Theosophists should sound the note of self-restraint within marriage, and the restriction of the marital relation to the perpetuation of the race.[30]

Sexuality and the suffrage struggle 1906-14

A determination to transform male sexual behaviour was a predominant theme of the constitutional and militant suffrage campaigners in the intense phase of feminist activity leading up to the First World War. When the vote became a major public issue after 1906 all the concerns which we have seen raised by earlier feminists in the area of sexuality came to the fore. These were the iniquity of the double standard, and the effects of male sexual behaviour on women through prostitution, the white slave traffic and the sexual abuse of children. An issue which came into prominence particularly in this period was that of venereal disease. Whilst the vote was the focus of attention, issues of sexual behaviour were continually raised in the context of reasons why women needed the vote. Suffragists of all shades of opinion made it quite clear that they intended, when the vote was gained, to be able to effect a total change in men's sexual behaviour from a new position of strength. Organisations as different as the Conservatives and Unionist Women's Suffrage Societies, the Church League for Women's Suffrage, and the Women's Social and Political Union, were issuing statements on the double standard and prostitution which were practically identical in tone. The NUWSS, for instance, which was the respectable non-militant wing of the suffrage struggle, stated in a pamphlet that suffrage stood for 'The Cause of Purity – we want to put down the White Slave Traffic, to protect little children from assaults, and to save our boys from hideous temptations.'[31]

In the years before the First World War venereal disease became a public issue. Medical knowledge was advancing by leaps and bounds. The syphilis baccillus was isolated in 1905 and the Wasserman blood test developed to test for it. Doctors were beginning to realise how far-reaching the effects of venereal disease could be in the causation of congenital deformities and the various ills produced in the lifetime of the sufferer. The general public anxiety led to the setting up of the Royal Commission on Venereal Disease in 1912. When Christabel Pankhurst decided to take up the issue in 1913 there was a great deal of information at her disposal. Revelations about the damage which the disease could cause to wives and children when passed on by men were genuinely shocking and provided good inflammatory material.

In an article entitled 'The Virtue of Plain Speaking' in the *Suffragette* in April 1913, she announced and explained her adoption of the issue. She wrote that suffragists had gradually added to their 'armoury of arguments', as they realised the 'greater fullness' of the suffrage cause.

> But there is one – and it is the latest development of the movement – which is going to do far more than all else put together to arouse women to strive for the vote with all their soul and might. It is the realisation that the moral purity and the physical health of the race depend upon votes for women.[32]

She stated that a strong, if not the strongest, force opposed to the enfranchisement of women was the desire of men to carry on indulging in 'sexual vice' and their understanding that votes for women could threaten this.

> Under all the excuses and arguments against votes for women, sexual vice is to be found lurking.
> The opposition argues thus; if women are to become politically free they will become spiritually strong and economically independent, and thus they will not any longer give or sell themselves to be the playthings of men. That, in a nutshell, is the case against votes for woman.[33]

Raising the issue of sexual vice was a final massive effort to inspire women with anger and energy which would gain success in the suffrage campaign. 'We have here', Christabel explained, 'the thing which will appeal to and unite all women.'

Throughout 1913 the *Suffragette* carried articles by Christabel Pankhurst on 'sexual vice', concentrating on venereal disease, which were published as a pamphlet entitled *The Great Scourge and How to end It*, or alternatively, *Plain Facts about a Great Evil*. Her message was that 'sexual disease' caused by men's immorality was transmitted to wives who were usually ignorant of what was wrong with them and would be kept in deliberate ignorance by doctors as to the real nature of their illness, lest their husbands might be embarrassed. The diseases were 'the great cause of physical, mental, and moral degeneracy and of race suicide', she said, and 75-80 per cent of men had gonorrhoea whilst a considerable percentage of the rest had syphilis. The cure for venereal disease was 'Votes for women and chastity for men.'

The feminists of the pre-war period continued to raise the ideas which we have seen voiced by feminists in the 1890s about the general effects on women of the form taken by male sexuality. They saw the general effect as being to institute a system of 'sex-slavery' for women, in which women were seen only in terms of sex and of no other functions. This sexualisation of woman led to her being considered fit for no other career than that of sexual object and affected the opportunites of all women for education, work, and general self-development. Christabel Pankhurst wrote that sexual disease was due to the 'doctrine that woman is sex and beyond that nothing'. Often, she said, this doctrine was dressed up by men into the idea that women were and should be mothers but this was really a deception:

> What a man who says that really means is that women are created primarily for the sex gratification of men, and secondarily, for the bearing of children if he happens to want them, but of no more children that he wants.[34]

The result of male desires had been that 'the relation between man and woman has centred in the physical', and the relationship had become that of 'master and slave'.

Cicely Hamilton, a playwright and member of the Actresses Franchise League, wrote *Marriage as a Trade* in 1909. She defined marriage as a trade because it entailed the exchange of women's bodies for subsistence. She charged men with having emphasised only the sex faculty in woman in order to gratify their desire.

> Sex is only one of the ingredients of the natural woman – an ingredient which has assumed undue and exaggerated proportions in her life owing to the fact that it has for many generations furnished her with the means of her livelihood.
>
> In sexual matters it would appear that the whole trend and tendency of man's relations to woman has been to make refusal impossible and to cut off every avenue of escape from the gratification of his desire.[35]

A contributor to the *Freewoman* magazine made much the same points. The *Freewoman* represented the new sex-reforming tendency within feminism. After writing of sub-human species where the female was not subject to the male, she went on:

> But the human female has lost her great prerogative. As Bondswoman, she must perforce pander to the lusts of her lords and masters. From her infancy she has been sedulously trained for this purpose, though she is strangely ignorant of sex and its functions, and if she would earn an independent livelihood she is handicapped all along the line.[36]

The analysis which these women give, in which they see women as deliberately restricted and prevented from making an independent living so that they will be forced into sexual slavery with men, is very similar to some contemporary feminist writings. Adrienne Rich, a lesbian feminist theorist, expanded upon this theme in her recent article *Compulsory Heterosexuality and Lesbian Existence*.[37] She details the many ways in which women are forced into heterosexual relations with men.

The pre-war feminists also engaged in detailed criticism of the form of male sexuality. In particular they set out to defeat the idea that male sexuality was a powerful and uncontrollable urge. This was more difficult in the pre-war period than it had been in the early 1890s. The movement for sex reform became more organised in the 1890s through the Legitimation League and its journal the *Adult* and acquired two eloquent propagandists in Edward Carpenter and Havelock Ellis. The Legitimation League was founded in 1893 ostensibly to campaign for the interests of children born out of wedlock. Its journal was published from 1897 to 1899 with subtitles such as 'A Journal for the Advancement of Freedom in Sexual Relationships' and 'A Crusade against Sex-enslavement'. The journal was a platform for those who were promoting the idea that sexual intercourse was a vital necessity for men and women. A typical example of the ideas expressed is the following quotation from an article entitled 'Free Thought and Free Love' by Lucy Steward.

> To healthy young adults, a certain amount of sexual intercourse is necessary in order to keep their bodies and minds in the best possible condition. The evil results of abstinence are especially noticeable in women, probably because abstinence is considerably less frequent among men. Undoubtedly it is unsatisfied sexual longing that is responsible

for the greater part of the hysteria, chlorosis, and menstrual disorders which are common among young unmarried women.[38]

The first volume of the *Adult* contained a hostile review of Wolstenholme Elmy's *Phases of Love* by Orford Northcote. Battle was now joined. The distinction between the ideas of the sex reformers and the majority of feminists became ever clearer. Northcote praised *The Human Flower* but was very unhappy at the concentration on psychic love in the later book: 'To exalt the mental sex states over the physical desire to which they are due, as is done in this book, is to rehabilitate the ascetic notions of medievalism, under a new but equally dangerous form.'[39]

A refutation of the uncontrollability of the male sex urge was as vital to the pre-war feminists as it has been to women working around the issue of male violence in the contemporary wave of feminism. If the imperative male sex urge existed then the sex-slavery of women might seem inevitable. Its existence was used then as now to justify men's use of prostitutes, the sexual abuse of children, rape and assault. The feminists argued, as they had been doing since the women's movement began, that the male urge was constructed and not a natural endowment of man. It could, therefore be retrained and transformed. Francis Swiney had scorned the 'large majority of persons, ignorant of physiology [who] still believe in the exploded fallacy of man's necessity for physical sexual expression and the need for its gratification'.[40] She was determined that men could be trained into continence, especially as women were now realising its importance and could educate men. It was important because 'woman's redemption from sex-slavery can only be achieved through man's redemption from sex-obsession.'

Christabel Pankhurst devoted a large part of *The Great Scourge* to refuting the idea that it was men's 'nature' that necessitated the sexual abuse of women. She demanded to know why such 'human nature' arguments were not used to justify killing and robbing and suggested that the idea was invented to shield immoral men. She refused to adopt the idea which she suggested was the only conclusion from men's arguments, 'that woman's nature is some-thing very much clearer, stronger, and higher than the human nature of men.'

'Suffragettes, at any rate,' she wrote, 'hope that this is not really true.'[41] She quashed the argument that sexual intercourse was necessary to men's health by quoting a great many doctors who maintained that continence did not cause men's genital organs to atrophy. She was unable to resist, however, suggesting that they might, on the contrary, atrophy from too much use. Emmeline Pankhurst joined in the debate as fiercely as her daughter. Commenting on a speech by a man who said that there would always be prostitution she wrote:

> If it is true – I do not believe it for one moment – that men have less power of self-control than women have, or might have if properly educated, if there is a terrible distinction between the physical and moral standards of both sexes, then I say as a woman, representing thousands of women all over the world, men must find some way of supplying the needs of their sex which does not include the degradation of ours.[42]

A woman writing to the *Freewoman* magazine echoed Mrs Pankhurst's sarcastic sentiments:

> I deny that self-control in sex matters is incompatible with human nature; the man or woman who is incapable of sexual self-control should be walking about on four legs, and not on two, because lack of self-control is incompatible with human nature.[43]

Christian suffragists took the same line. Ursula Roberts, of the Church League for Women's Suffrage, waxed very indignant on the 'utterly false and pernicious' doctrine that 'prostitution is necessary'. She argued that 'all the authority of modern science goes to controvert the old heresy that chastity is physically harmful to men.'[44]

Feminists found it necessary to explain how the male sexual urge came to take the form it did if there was no inevitable biological difference in this respect between men and women. Christabel Pankhurst's explanation for 'uncontrollable passion' was that erotic thoughts, conversation and literature could provoke over-stimulation. She believed that a natural remedy had been provided for this in nocturnal emissions. Swiney developed a pseudo-biological explanation on the evolutionary principle. Past indulgence, she suggested, had affected men's brains so that they were now inclined to sexual indulgence to a greater extent than ever before:

> The grooves in the brains of men have been, through heredity,

carved out deeper in the sexual desire nature, until an abnormal tendency to indulgence in sex-relations has been engendered quite contrary to and subversive of natural law. Men have made their laws fit in and give license to their stimulated predilections.[45]

Besant tried to account for the phenomenon in a similar way. Speaking of the 'excessive' development of the sexual instinct in man, she wrote:

It has reached its present abnormal development by self-indulgence in the past, all sexual thoughts, desires and imaginations having created their own thought forms, into which have been wrought the brain and body molecules, which now give rise to passion on the material plane.[46]

This refutation of the naturalness of men's sexual abuse of women was potentially revolutionary in its implications for the relations between men and women. The strength with which feminists were still promoting self-control for men suggests that little headway had been made despite the influence of the social purity movement, in fighting the mythology of men's lack of control. The burgeoning of the sex reform tendency which promoted the same old idea had made the struggle doubly difficult. There were other aspects of male sexuality besides uncontrollability which came in for criticism from feminists. One was the brutish insensitivity of men both in sex and in their relations with women in general. Lady Sybil Smith wrote that now that women had more power of selection as a result of machinery bringing about an economic change in the position of women, they would be able to seek the qualitites they really desired in men, not strength alone but 'sympathy, gentleness and self-control'.[47] In future generations of men, according to her analysis, these qualities would become more and more developed. Christabel Pankhurst criticised the tendency of men to seperate sex from loving emotion. She stated that 'sexual intercourse where there exists no bond of love and spiritual sympathy is beneath human dignity'.[48]

The correspondence columns of the *Freewoman* magazine in 1911 and 1912 carried a debate on sexuality between the feminists who were critical of male sexuality and that small group of feminists who had recently embraced sex reform. Stella Browne, a socialist feminist campaigner for birth control and abortion, whom we will come across in the next chapter making a bitter attack on a 'spinster' who criticised male sexuality, was interested in sex reform and a disciple of Havelock Ellis. She proclaimed with enthusiasm in the *Freewoman* in 1912, 'Let us admit our joy and gratitude for the beauty and pleasure of sex.'[49] She meant by sex, sexual intercourse. Other women who did not feel in the least grateful were trying to articulate their discontents and work out what a woman-centred sexuality might consist of.

A woman signing herself a 'grateful reader' wrote in to 'suggest a point of view' which she felt had not been covered in the *Freewoman* debate, 'the absolute indifference or dislike of the sexual act in many women'.[50] This writer was speaking specifically of sexual intercourse, as she made clear when she said that this dislike existed in women who had been 'unwise', i.e. engaged in premarital sexual intercourse and liked 'lovemaking' but 'consistently hated the sexual act itself'. It did not depend on lack of 'sex attraction'. She suggested that it might be due to the girls' ignorance. It might also be due to the fact that men knew 'exactly what they want' and women did not. She suggested a further reason for women's dislike of sexual intercourse, 'I think many women, besides their life-long training in personal modesty, feel instinctively that . . . the man does despise them and hold them in contempt and they despise themselves.' This letter worked towards a critical analysis of women's experience of sexual intercourse and why they might not find it full of 'beauty and pleasure'. This could be because of men's attitudes to women as expressed in that act or because other forms of 'lovemaking' were more pleasure-able. The possibilities offered by this delicate exploration of women's sexual experience could not be followed up towards the creation of a woman-determined sexuality because the propaganda of the male-defined sex reform movement eliminated any feminist critique, as we shall see in later chapters.

The feminist ideas we have been looking at here were applied practically in women's campaigns around sexuality. These campaigns can only be understood in this context. In the absence of any understanding of this feminist perspective, historians have labelled the women campaigners prudes and puritans. In the next two chapters we will look at the massive campaign waged by feminists for forty years against the sexual abuse of girls. Feminists worked also to end the regulation of prostitution, to end marital rape, and the white slave traffic and to transform male sexuality. The campaign against sexual abuse was as extensive and sustained as that around prostitution but has been little documented. Here we will look at some of the details of that campaign from an understanding of the ideas on sexuality which motivated the women campaigners.

CHAPTER 3

'The sort of thing that might happen to any man'[1]

Feminist campaigns and politics around the sexual abuse of children

The history books have paid scant attention to campaigns against the sexual abuse of girls. Where age of consent legislation has been mentioned historians have tended to see it as the result of a reactionary, puritanical, anti-sex lobby. It has been taken out of the context of what was actually a massive, multifaceted campaign on the issue. This campaign included struggles to gain women magistrates, women police and women doctors to deal with abused girls, for reserved playgrounds for children in parks, plus a campaign of public education designed to point out the bias of police, judges and juries and to gain better treatment for the girl victims throughout the legal process and after it.

The feminist indignation at the sexual abuse of girls stemmed from their general concern to protect women and girls from the exercise of aggressive male sexuality and male violence. Sexual abuse of girls was seen specifically as an abuse of power by adult men. This was clear in the campaign from 1885 to 1908 to gain incest legislation. Feminists were determined that all forms of abuse of power to gain sexual gratification would be heavily penalised, so that male relatives would be included in a category which comprised employers, stepfathers, etc.

> We think that not only should there be a special law against incest, but also when an offence is committed by any person in a fiduciary position there should be severer punishment. Guardians, schoolmasters, employers of all kinds, foremen in factories, managers of places of amusement, have a power in their hands over young girls which makes it far more difficult for a girl to resist or protect herself than in ordinary cases.[2]

Concern about the sexual abuse of children rose from the campaign for the abolition of the Contagious Diseases Acts of the 1860s. The raising of the age of consent for sexual intercourse to 16 years in 1885 resulted directly from revelations about juvenile prostitution and the sexual exploitation of young girls. The 1885 Act which raised the age of consent to 16 for sexual intercourse, leaving it at 13 for indecent assault, was passed after a House of Lords select committee reported in 1882 on the law relating to the protection of young girls. The report stated that juvenile prostitution was 'increasing to an appalling extent'.[3] One witness in the report spoke of the effect that the increasing demand for young girls was having – women prostitutes in the West End of London now had to dress as little girls to get any custom.[4] The 1885 legislation was spurred on by the exposure by W.T. Stead, editor of the *Pall Mall Gazette*, of the white slave traffic, based upon the fact that he easily purchased a 13-year-old girl from her mother for the purpose of prostitution. After 1885 feminists campaigned to close loopholes in the Act and to gain further legislation on sexual abuse. Before we look at details of the campaign for legislation we will look at the wider campaign of which the demand for legislation was just one part.

The male bias of the justice system

There was a massive effort to arouse public opinion to the male bias of the male justice system, symbolised by the title quote for this chapter, 'This is the sort of thing that might happen to any man', taken from a judge's summing up of a sexual abuse trial which caused feminist indignation in 1925. Feminists complained that the offence of sexual abuse was not treated as if it was at all serious and that sentences were completely inadequate in comparison with the sentences given for sexual abuse of boys, and minor offences against property. The leniency of sentences and the clear bias of the male judges were backed up by the covering up of offences by the police and the connivance of men of influence in concealing offences.

At a 1914 conference on child assault, a Mrs Crosfield spoke of the difficulties of gaining recognition from the authorities of the seriousness of sexual abuse of girls: 'When we as women tried to meet it [the evil] we found that one of our chief obstacles lay in the difficulty of convincing the clergy and even the magistrates of the magnitude of the danger.'[5] The handling of cases by the judges and the remarks they made in summing up caused particular indignation amongst campaigners. The judges appeared to try to help defendants find excuses as in the following case quoted by Miss Hall, Honorary Secretary for Church Army Rescue Work. She had

> heard of a case of a . . . man who committed an assault on his little step-daughter of 14 or 15. He pleaded guilty, and just as sentence was about to be passed, the judge said, 'Had you any reason to think that she was over 16?' 'Oh yes,' he said, 'I thought she was over 16,' and he was let off. Of course he knew her age perfectly. But there is in some quarters a policy of dealing leniently with these offenders.[6]

Another example was given at the same conference of a judge who clearly showed partiality towards the defendant on the basis of his sex. Mrs Clare Goslett of the Mothers' Union reported, 'We must look to the education of public opinion when a judge says to a jury: "We are all liable to fall, gentlemen; we must be lenient" and they were lenient.'[7] The title quote comes from a case which became quite a *cause célèbre*. It was mentioned in Parliament by Lady Astor in 1923 and helped in the establishment of a Departmental Committee on Sex Offences. It was quoted in the *Shield*, journal of the Association for Moral and Social Hygiene, and in the *Vote*, journal of the Women's Freedom League. The judge gave out a light sentence in the case of sexual assault on a 7-year-old girl by a middle-aged man. As he passed sentence the judge opined that the girl had importuned the man, tempting him. In the *Vote*, Mr Fyfe comments 'Surely a person holding such views, and presumably judging others by himself, is hardly fit to have jurisdiction over his fellow men!'[8]

The AMSH collected evidence on sex offences in its Committee on Sexual Morality in 1919. Several witnesses spoke of their disquiet about police behaviour and their willingness to prosecute. A police magistrate gave the following example:

> Cases have come under my own cognisance where a girl is even pregnant as a result of this [incest] – the eldest girl of rather a large family. The mother was broken-hearted, but the police took the line that the man was a respectable artisan in a good position, and if he were prosecuted it could break up the home, so they took the line of discrediting her story. There is a great deal of that going on, far more than any person would ever believe.[9]

A Miss Costin gave evidence to the same committee about the indifference of the police to the protection of young girls. She was indignant that men were never arrested for solicitation, and told the following story:

> as a young girl living in London she had often been solicited and . . . when she complained to the police they replied . . . she had better go home as the streets were no place for her. The police had told her that when girls complained about being annoyed they had merely remarked that the girl was a little hussy and ought to be in bed.[10]

It was not just the police and the judges who failed to take sexual assaults on children seriously. An NSPCC paper describes how men of influence would use blackmail on the society after a case had been taken up, threatening to withdraw subscriptions to protect their acquaintances. The example given is of a cathedral canon who threatened to withdraw the annual collection for the NSPCC to protect a church organist.[11]

There was much complaint from the campaigners that the sentences given for sexual assault on children bore no relevance to the seriousness of the offence. The fact that sentences for minor offences against property were higher caused particular indignation. Mrs Goslett at the 1914 Child Assault conference was angry that the punishment for father/daughter incest was often less than that for stealing a loaf.[12] A Mrs Rackham at the same conference stated that the real danger of light sentences was that they set the standards for behaviour. The NSPCC complained of light sentences, and the *Shield* took up the issue of sentences again and again.[13]

The feminist approach

Women involved in the campaign against sexual abuse of children included both those who were self-consciously feminist and those who, representing the Church Army and the Mothers' Union, probably were not. The issue of sexual abuse figured largely in two journals representing the militant wing of the suffrage struggle before the First World War. These were the *Vote*, journal of the Women's Freedom League, and *Votes for Women* an independent journal edited by the Pethick-Lawrences after their split from the WSPU in 1912. In the 1920s when the militant stage of the suffrage struggle was over with the achievement of partial enfranchisement for women in 1918, sexual abuse remained a subject of feminist concern for the National Union of

Societies for Equal Citizenship which developed out of the pre-war National Union of Women's Suffrage Societies. Sexual abuse was also a prominant issue in the *Woman's Leader*, the NUSEC journal, in the context of the many equal rights issues around which feminists were fighting. Around such aspects of the campaign against sexual abuse as the male bias of police and courts, the attitudes of professed feminists, women's organisations and women representatives of church and social purity organisations were in close harmony. All saw the justice system as biased against women and saw themselves as fighting for the interests of women and girl children as a group. Such a situation does not exist today, when we are used to non-feminist women campaigners around sexuality in groups such as the National Viewers and Listeners Association and church organisations being overtly anti-feminist and hostile to the idea that there might be a contradiction between the interests of women and the interests of men.

Votes for Women carried a regular feature throughout 1915 entitled 'Comparison of Punishments'. This was designed to highlight the huge disparity between sentences which were being given by the courts for crimes against women and those given for minor offences against property or for offences against boys. In the feature one column would carry three examples of light punishments and the other column would carry three examples of heavy punishments. Under light punishments there would be an example of wife abuse, an example of the sexual abuse of female children and one of cruelty to animals. The 'heavy' column contained examples of petty theft and vagrancy or the sexual abuse of boys. On 1 January the examples of light punishments were: a young man of 19 charged with indecent assault on girls of 8 and 9 received 3 months hard labour, a man charged with cruelty to a horse received a £4 fine, a labourer living apart from his wife who molested her in the street and threw stones at her window received 2 months hard labour. The examples of heavy punishments for comparison were as follows: a 64-year-old pastor of Hackney Mission Hall was charged with assaulting a boy in a picture palace and received 5 years penal servitude, a coster who stole 4 coats received 12 months hard labour, and a man found guilty of fraud on shopkeepers for sums amounting to under £5 received two sentences of 18 and 15 months imprisonment. Each feature carried a comment section and on this occasion it asked why the distinction was made between boys and girls. The writer states that the distinction could not be made on the grounds of the damage caused since young girls could be made pregnant and boys could not:

> Is a boy so much more valuable than a girl? Is the girl so much less rigorously protected? Or is the wickedness of the crime judged on some scale which does not consider the harm inflicted? And if so, why should the fixing of that scale lie exclusively with men?[14]

The comment attached to another 'Comparison of Punishments' feature was entitled 'New Danger to Young Girls'. The 'new danger' was the wave of patriotism in the First World War which, in its admiration for the men who were defending their country, promoted the idea that a soldier could do no wrong. There was a 'tendency on the part of some magistrates and some newspapers to take a lenient view of criminal and other assaults on women and girls, when these are committed by men in uniform, or by men willing to enlist.'[15] The magistrate's remark in the case of a soldier who had attacked four women is quoted, 'You look like a decent young fellow, and you are in uniform. If it were not for that you would go to prison.'[16] The soldier was given a 40 shilling fine.

The writer of the feature did not simply want heavier sentences for all offences. She wanted a reversal of the pattern of sentencing so that offences against the person would always be treated more seriously than offences against property. It is clear from this feature that feminists were not seeing sexual abuse in a vacuum, as a uniquely horrifying offence. They saw it as one of a series of crimes against women which included wife-battering, which were not taken seriously by the male justice system. The title of one comment section, which addressed itself entirely to assault on female children, makes this clear. It is called 'Crimes against Women'.[17] A feminist interpretation from the *Vote* about why wife-battering was not taken seriously by the courts shows that the feminists were not just taking a punitive law and order line. Their concern was with the way in which women were treated as second-class citizens. This writer uses an analogy between race and class oppression to make her point:

> A man recently tried to excuse the conduct of certain white men when dealing with coloured races. He said that an unconquerable and inexplicable aversion arising from the fact that these were subject races – and dark at that – caused the

white man to lose control over his passions and be guilty of abominable and unspeakable cruelties. Perhaps it is the same feeling that they are dealing with a subject race that makes instances of brutality to women on the part of so-called working-men so common that they cause laughter in court and serve as amusement for the magistrate and his officers. There must be something rotten in a judicial system which thinks ill-treating a woman is funny.[18]

The efforts of the feminist press to publish details of sentencing in sexual abuse cases was part of a broad propaganda effort to change public opinion so that sexual abuse would be treated seriously. The NSPCC called for such a campaign, as did several women speakers at the 1914 conference on child assault. A Mrs Hutchinson, at the conference, described how a group of women in her area found out when child assault cases were coming into court, attended and monitored the proceedings so that through publicity and the weight of their presence in the courtroom they might influence sentencing. She suggested that his process should be put into operation throughout the country and the idea was taken up with enthusiasm at the conference. The Women's Freedom League employed a similar practice. Their Miss Edith Watson, close friend of Nina Boyle, pioneer of the Women's Police Volunteers, routinely attended the hearings of sexual abuse cases for the WFL.

Women police

The movement to institute a women's police service was integrally connected to the campaign against the sexual abuse of children and to a general movement to acquire women magistrates, doctors and other officials to deal with women and children. The idea was that women and child victims of sexual offences needed to be looked after by members of their own sex who would support them at the police station and through the courts. Only then, it was felt, could the girl's ordeal be alleviated and enough confidence created for her to give a reasonable statement and evidence in court.

In the 1880s and 1890s organisations such as the National Vigilance Association were mounting public pressure for the institution of women watchers or wardens at police stations and courts, sometimes referred to as 'police matrons'. The resolution they sent to the 1889 women's congress in Paris makes their motivation clear. It spoke of the necessity for police matrons, 'in order to prevent suffering from the possible vice, brutality, or incompetency in illness of male officials'.[19] It is clear that NVA women had no trust in male police and feared, doubtless as the result of their considerable experience, that they might take the opportunity to further assault the victims as well as showing general insensitivity. The call for police matrons was part of a wider demand for the employment of women in all areas where men might cause distress to women and girls. In 1891 the NVA adopted the policy that women and children seeking help should, if an examination was necessary, only see women doctors. The reasons given were very practical. Women and children who had been assaulted by men should not have to suffer examination by another man which could seem like a second assault. It was more difficult to get the police to accept the need for women police doctors. Nesta H. Wells, the first woman police surgeon, started her duties in Manchester as late as 1927. In an article in the *Shield* she stressed the importance of women and girls who had been sexually assaulted being examined by women.[20]

It was in the power of the judge to 'clear the court' in sexual abuse cases. This was usually taken to mean clearing the court of all women including, often, women justices and women jurors. The AMSH of a 1916 survey of the treatment of sex offences in ten towns in Britain, stated:

> It seems to us that cases of indecent assault and criminal assault, above all cases, justify the institution of women police officials. It is appalling to think that a frightened child must stand up in a court full of men to give her evidence, when she ought to be in a woman's lap, with only those officials present who are absolutely necessary.[21]

A 1915 article in the *Vote* stipulated the need for women police for the same reason. In this case the employer of a 13-year-old girl who had seduced her shortly after she went into service was acquitted because the girl was too terrified to give evidence. The writer comments, 'Think of a child taken into a court full of men – her one terrible experience of a man had naturally made her suspicious of all men – and she had been asked questions the meaning of which, in most cases, she could not have understood.'[22]

The women campaigners wanted women magistrates and women jurors as well as women police. A Miss Muller outlined the case at a 1890 meeting of the Moral Reform Union, a strongly feminist social purity organisation. Speaking of sexual abuse cases she said, 'Every case in the *Police News*, as reported in the press, told the same story, – men making and executing the laws, and women tried without one woman to represent them.'[23] She told the story of the maintenance case of a 15-year-old village girl. The girl lived with her uncle whom she cited as the father of her child though he denied it. The court was full of 'jockeys, grooms and low village boys' and the only women present were the girl, Miss Muller, the girl's mother and an elderly friend. The judge ordered the court to be cleared of women though Miss Muller stayed. She commented: 'As a woman was not tried by her peers, – that is, she was only tried by a jury of men – there ought always to be one or two of her own sex in court to give her their moral support.'[24]

In a pamphlet published after the passage of the 1922 Act it is clear that no progress had been made. The writer attacks the policy of clearing the court of women in sexual abuse cases and states, 'There must be women in court. If tried before a jury there must be some women jurors.'[25] She explains that justice could not be expected of men by describing an incident in which, 'two men coming out from such a trial were overheard saying to a woman who deplored that there had been no conviction, "What nonsense! Men should not be punished for a thing like that. It doesn't harm the child." '[26]

A concerted movement to get a women's police force began in 1913 on the initiative of the National Council for Women. The Women's Police Volunteers formed by Nina Boyle of the Women's Freedom League were established in 1915. Their original purpose was to deal with the protection of women and children. Their use was quickly converted in garrison towns to one quite opposite from the original intention. They were used to police women and keep them off the streets after curfew to protect soldiers. This corruption of the function of the women police volunteers led to a serious split in the movement for a women's police force. Some women were able to go along with the wartime function. The Women's Freedom League would not. The first official body of women police was appointed in 1918 and foundations for a service for the whole country were laid in 1920 by the Baird Committee which recommended that there should be women police in all thickly populated districts. The numbers of women police grew until 1922 when they were cut as a result of government economies under Geddes. The fight to improve pay, conditions of service and powers, and to increase their numbers continued to be a feminist concern throughout the 1920s, and 1930s. The early policewomen had no powers of arrest. The Baird Committee saw their functions as follows: investigations under the Children's Act, and Immoral Traffic Acts, inspection of common lodging houses, supervision of parks and open spaces, visiting of licensed premises, prevention of offences by prostitutes and any work in connection with offences by or against women and children. In connection with the sexual abuse of children they were to take statements from children, look after them in the police station, accompany them to court. They were envisaged as having an active part to play in the supervision of parks and open spaces to prevent assaults on children. In the 1920s, feminist journals and women's organisations were pressing for special reserves for children in parks, to which adult men would not be admitted.[27] Another similar project for which feminists pressed and which they eventually acquired, was reserved railway carriages for women and girls with the same object of preventing sexual assault.

Attitudes to the abused child

Much of the contemporary literature on the subject of sexual abuse of children contains a victimological perspective, which places responsibility to a greater or lesser extent upon the child as having participated in, or precipitated the abuse, as acting seductively or looking seductive. In the period 1880–1930 this kind of approach, used by some judges and the press, was strongly criticised by the women reformers.[28] Psychoanalytical assumptions about the child's desire for sexual contact with adults had not as yet affected those concerned with the issue. The period saw a movement away from the early Victorian approach of regarding the abused child as 'fallen' and in need of strict reformatory treatment. The campaigners around sexual abuse saw the child as exploited and in need of sensitive and sympathetic help. However the traditional male Victorian view of women and sexuality lingered on and was used by judges, MPs and the clergy when they wished to excuse the behaviour of adult male offenders against children. This view was that women could be divided into good and bad, pure and 'fallen', innocent or guilty according to whether they had had sexual connection outside marriage. This dichotomy was used to protect adult men from any responsibility for their sexual use of women and girls. The women who 'fell' were guilty and thereafter deserved no consideration or protection. The campaigners around sexual abuse fought these attitudes, though they were sometimes unable to reject them without ambivalence because the dominant sexual ideology left its residues within them.

The women campaigners argued fiercely against allegations, by magistrates and judges and in the press, that the abused children were seductive. Lady Astor in the House of Commons fulminated against a judge's conclusion that a little girl of 7 had encouraged the assault upon her. 'Nobody can say that a little girl of 7, 8, 9 or 10 could lead a man on,' she asserted.[29] The *Shield* frequently carried expressions of indignation at this form of victim-blaming. As late as 1937 the editorial was still making the same point. Amidst anger that girls of under 16 years were being described as a danger to men, and the fact that they could get three years' detention in a home whilst the man was acquitted or bound over, it stated:

> We wish judges would not encourage people to think that decent men are morally defenceless creatures against the wiles of unscrupulous girls under 16, and that their seduction by the girl, even if they themselves are over 30, is mainly the girl's iniquity.[30]

Votes for Women in 1915 in one of its 'Comparison of Punishments' features gave a strong feminist reaction to victim-blaming. The writer roundly criticised the press for saying little girls are to blame: 'the practice of putting the blame for these discreditable outrages upon the child or the young woman is an abominable one, and would not be tolerated in any country where women are regarded with honour and respect.'[31]

The way the child victim was treated by the authorities depended upon the attitudes of clergy and social workers towards her. The women campaigners were engaged in a struggle to combat the view that the 'fallen' child was evil and corrupting. Examples of this latter attitude came from representatives of the church at the 1914 Child Assault conference. The chairman, the Lord Bishop of Ely, gave a viewpoint which was significantly lacking in Christian charity:

> It [sexual abuse] is a crime degrading and terrible in itself and has the worst effect on the rising generation. These poor

children ought to be precluded from association with other children, for without any fault of their own they are moral lepers.[32]

The Reverend Thomas G. Cree backed up the Bishop dutifully:

As you, My Lord, said, each of these children is really a leper. She is a source of the most awful danger to all the children with whom she is brought into contact. In the few homes we have for these cases, children have to be watched carefully night and day. It is never safe to leave them together, because their minds are so full of evil thoughts that they will talk about these things and spread them. . . . Another case I know of – a school where one child had been criminally assaulted, no steps were taken to isolate the child and it spread the complaint in that school to a terrible extent.[33]

The women at the conference contradicted these cruel attitudes. Mrs Nott-Bower said that she and her fellow guardians had not had to deal with any corruption emanating from children who had been abused. She seemed to wish to assert some conformity to the views of the members of the cloth by admitting that 'corruption' could be a problem in 'children who have been the victims of corrupt practices for months and years'.[34] Mrs Goslett argued even more strongly against the 'corruption' idea:

I would like to plead against calling these children lepers. They are *not* lepers. They have been injured; they may even talk of the injury; but we grown-up people have such a different outlook from the little child. A little child who has been hurt sometimes does not even know what has been done to her, and we dare not class her with the girls who have participated in the wrong willingly, or at least consciously.[35]

Mrs Goslett in the last few words, like Mrs Nott-Bower above, remains ambivalent. The idea that girls could be corrupting or 'evil' clearly contradicted the experience that these women had had of working with girls. None the less they were unable to separate themselves completely, despite their brave efforts, from the prevailing ideology of the church. They clung to the idea that if the girl was 'willing' or had been abused over a long period, then she could be a source of danger.

The idea that abused children could be a danger to other children lingers on throughout the period. An AMSH report in

1916 described a detention home into which the victims of sexual assault were placed, 'but the supervision appeared to be very inadequate. Child victims of criminal assault are sent here pending trial, and mix freely with the other children, who thereby run the risk of contamination.'[36] In 1925 the report of the Departmental Committee recommended that schoolteachers should be told of offences so that 'contamination' of other children could be prevented.[37] The idea lying behind such statements is, presumably, that the 'contaminated' children would go out and seduce men. It is another form of victim-blaming which removes responsibility from adult men.

The reformers were anxious to end the punitive forms of care traditionally given to the child victims. The practice at the time was to remove the assaulted child to a detention home pending trial and possibly for some years thereafter. This form of treatment effectively punished the child. It was strongly criticised by the NSPCC. In reply to the idea that victims should be put in a home, a 1926 NSPCC paper states, 'It appears to me that as the child assaulted is the *victim* not the offender the course suggested indicates an altogether wrong view.'[38] Mrs Nott-Bower at the 1914 conference showed grave doubts about sending the victims to industrial schools. She asked whether there was no other way to deal with them, and suggested state guardianship and adoption. Her main concern was that the child should not have to mix with thieves just because it had been the victim of 'outrage'.

The NSPCC suggested that the girl should remain at home with her mother; 'a girl's best friend is her mother and . . . she should remain with her at home.'[39] The Departmental Committee was of the same opinion. The report stated that some witnesses had recommended that all victims go to institutions for care and training, to avoid neighbourhood gossip, strain on the child and the perpetuation of 'bad habits' from the offence.[40] The report was categorically of the opinion that victims should not be removed from their parents save in exceptional circumstances. Removal to a home, it said, was an extra hardship for the victim, especially in cases which the writers had heard of, where children with good homes were removed for years because their parents were persuaded that such action was necessary. If removal was necessary in a particular situation, the report recommended boarding-out rather than a home. The report was remarkable for its lack of punitive attitudes and criticised some rescue homes which it described as being like 'old-fashioned penitentiaries' and quite unsuitable to receive victims of abuse.

A particularly sympathetic, child-centred approach is described in a *Shield* article on 'Protective Work among Children'. Here Evelynne Viner writes of what some children's workers did do in the case of criminal assault. The worker would send the child for a long change to a country cottage and meantime persuade the mother to move so that the child could come back to new surroundings. The worker would change the child's school to one where the teachers would be sympathetic and extras like music and swimming were encouraged. She would get the teacher to take a special interest in the child, make her a monitress so that her free time was occupied and her self-respect restored. The worker would try to get the confidence of the mother and advise her as to the best way of helping the child forget the past, watch the child as she grew older and help her when starting work.[41]

No distinction is made in these writings between sexual abuse outside the home and abuse by male relatives in the home. The latter would obviously create special difficulties if the male offender was not removed and the girl was supposed to stay at home with her mother.

The causes of sexual abuse

The feminists explained sexual abuse of children in terms of the power of adult men over girl children, particularly in the family. They saw it as being encouraged by the lack of seriousness with which the offence was treated by police and courts. They saw it as a symptom of the double standard of sexual morality which protected men's sexual use of women in prostitution and of female children by blaming the women and girls and covering up offences. They saw sexual abuse of female children as one of a series of crimes against women by men which resulted from the second-class status accorded to women.

There were other non-feminist forms of explanation of sexual abuse mentioned in the literature at the time though little attempt was made to discover causes and there was certainly no vigorous examination of them. In the first half of the period the commonest of these to be mentioned were overcrowding, poverty, low moral example and ignorance. After the First World War there was more and more concentration on the 'medical model': the tendency to see offenders as 'sick' and in need of treatment. By the 1930s this was the dominant form of explanation. The adoption of the medical model did not take place without resistance from feminists, as we shall see.

The forms of explanation which tied sexual abuse into overcrowding, poverty and ignorance can be seen as a scapegoating of the working class. The *Vigilance Record*, for instance, described incest as 'a standing menace to the homes of many of the poor of this land'.[42] The following quotation from an AMSH enquiry associates incest with the general immorality of the lower orders:

> Incest is not uncommon; there is much illegitimacy; and there is said to be a good deal of drug-taking to procure abortions. . . . There is a good deal of overcrowding and of back-to-back housing with insufficient lavatory accommodation. But even in good-sized houses, people will confine their sleeping accommodation to one or two rooms. Sexual promiscuity is rife among the lower classes, and grown women will sell themselves for a glass of beer.[43]

The Bishop of Ely thought along similar lines: 'It will not be possible to dwell on the causes of this evil – the low state of parental example, for instance, or over-crowding.'[44] Ignorance was blamed for the fact that parents did not know that offences should be reported or that they were even illegal:

> It has been one of the evidences of the low moral understanding of many parents that in many cases of incest the fathers have claimed a right to their actions, and in others the mothers have acquiesced in what was being done.[45]

The NSPCC suggested that the ignorance of the children could be remedied by teaching about incest in schools.

Overcrowding was a popular form of explanation. The Departmental Committee linked overcrowding with incest and also pointed out that the practice of taking in lodgers by working-class families to help pay the rent, led to assaults on children.[46] Parr of the NSPCC described the effects of overcrowding thus: 'The most private acts of some members of the family are witnessed by others and this low standard of living is invariably accompanied by a habit of speech on sexual matters which has the worst possible effect on children.'[47]

Surprisingly enough the main opposition to the idea that sexual abuse offenders came from the lower classes came from the NSPCC. Parr followed the statement above on overcrowding with the comment that 'Men of all classes are among the offenders, those of good education and of bad; those whose character has never been called in question, as well as those of no reputation.'[48] Certainly those organisations which dealt first hand with cases of sexual assault would have had difficulty in assigning offenders to the working class. The NVA detailed innumerable cases involving Indian princes, school teachers, workhouse superintendants, and various clergy. Clergymen seem to have been a particular target for the campaigners. Whilst trying to prove that drink was not a main factor in sexual abuse the NSPCC gave details of what it considered to be 'temperate' offenders: a Baptist minister who assaulted five girls, a Presbyterian minister who assaulted three members of his Sunday school, a clerk in holy orders, numerous other clergymen and a Sunday school teacher who interfered with three girls in his Band of Hope. Josephine Butler in her earlier onslaught on the double standard had been particularly keen to expose the behaviour of men of her own class. It seems that this tradition continued.

Other causes which got an occasional mention were: lack of self-control, association with semi-nude dancing, the fact that boys would become violent, promiscuous and without self-restraint because they had been initiated by middle-aged women in their youth, evil men, and 'debased passion and brutal lust.'[49]

The 'medical model' came into use as a form of explanation in the 1920s. There is a suggestion at the 1914 Child Assault conference by Miss Evelyn Fox of the Central Association for Care of the Mentally Defective that offenders in sexual abuse cases might come into the category 'moral imbecile' under the recent Mental Deficiency Act and require permanent treatment rather than prison. The suggestion did not go down very well. Parr of the NSPCC thought medical checks for offenders might be a good idea because it would serve as a deterrent, not because he saw the offenders as 'moral imbeciles'. 'It would be a serious check on a good many people if they knew they had to be examined, with the possibility of being put into a home for Mental Defectives.'[50] When the medical approach began to get off the ground, as it did in the *Shield* from 1923 onwards, it was a very signifcant departure in the debate on sexual abuse. The argument that sex offenders against women are 'sick' is rejected by contemporary feminists, and by many contemporary academic researchers, particularly when applied to incest offenders.[51] It is a simple, reassuring kind of explanation which eliminates the need to look for any social or political dimensions to sexual abuse.

Feminist explanations around the double standard, and male power, were irrelevant to it.

The *Shield* published the findings of a report in 1923 which supported its growing determination that offenders were sick. This report found that all but 17 out of 76 offenders in cases of indecent assault and indecent exposure were mentally defective.[52] A parliamentary discussion of the same year in which the two women MPs, Lady Astor and Mrs Wintringham, took this line was reported in the *Shield*. Mrs Wintringham said she believed that offenders were mentally deficient, not just insane and wanted machinery set up for the examination of offenders whom she described as 'moral degenerates'. Out of this discussion the Departmental Committee on Sex Offences was set up. The Committee's report was not sympathetic to the idea that offenders were sick. Large numbers of witnesses had apparently recommended mental examination, but the committee had not, after carefully studying the evidence, found the experts to bear out the opinion that many offenders were insane or defective. Of the 108 men remanded to prison in the three years to the end of March 1924 for indecent assault, incest and carnal knowledge of a girl under 16, none could be certified insane and only 8 mentally deficient. The report recommended appointment of skilled medical examiners to the courts, that all indecent exposure offenders be examined and other sex offenders only where there were previous convictions for sex offences or where the court suspected disease or defect. It also recommended the possibility of prolonged detention in suitable institutions of repeated offenders.[53]

In 1932 the *Shield* carried an article on 'Sexual Offences against Young Children'. The introduction asked, 'When are we going to take effective measures for the better protection of little children from assaults by *unbalanced and degenerate* men?' The article stated the aim of the AMSH that a man who was not certified insane or feeble-minded but who had committed three offences should be deemed a 'moral imbecile' and detained indefinitely.[54] The AMSH with three other societies drafted a Bill which provided for the medical examination of all offenders against children under 13 years plus all indecent exposure offenders, and the indefinite detention of offenders after three convictions. In October 1931 the *Shield* was urging that all attention should be diverted from the age of consent and the abolition of the reasonable cause to believe clause to concentrate on this Bill. In November the AMSH convened a conference in London which agreed to appoint a committee consisting of a nominee from each of fourteen societies to promote the limited Bill.

The medical approach was not universally popular with campaigners, particularly the feminists. In a letter entitled 'When Crimes are not Crimes' in the *Woman's Leader* in 1926, Miss F.K. Powell describes the storming of brothels in Strasbourg by several thousand boys who were at a youth conference, on three successive nights. She suggests that it is social attitudes which create phenomena like this mass rape, not mental illness:

> There is no need to imagine that people who criminally assault young persons and children are mentally abnormal, as what is right to buy is also right to have without buying, whether it is human beings or any other merchandise.[55]

When men's attitudes to women were so degraded that they could simply buy women in prostitution, she considered, then rape was explained. A chattel can be either stolen or bought.

The development of the 'medical model' as an explanation for men's sexual abuse of girls contributed significantly to the decline of the feminist campaigns as we shall see in the next chapter which describes the battle for legislation on incest and the age of consent.

CHAPTER 4

'Henpecking'

Women's campaigns to gain legislation against the sexual abuse of girls

It was the National Vigilance Association, an organisation founded directly from the indignation aroused by W.T. Stead in the *Pall Mall Gazette*, which was most influential in the campaign to gain legislation against sexual abuse of girls after 1885.

Many feminists joined the NVA in its early years as they redirected their energies from the Contagious Diseases campaign after these Acts were abolished finally in 1886. Josephine Butler gave her support at first until she became disillusioned in the 1890s over the enthusiasm of some NVA members to legislate against women engaged in prostitution instead of protecting them. Millicent Fawcett of the National Union of Women's Suffrage Societies chaired the Rescue and Preventive sub-committee which was concerned with rescuing women and girls from prostitution and sexual exploitation. The National Vigilance Association fought not only sexual abuse of children but many other forms of sexual exploitation and harassment of women. The Association or its branches provided solicitors to conduct prosecutions in innumerable cases of rape and attempted rape, sexual assault and indecent exposure to adult women, against senders of obscene letters to girls, against sexual harassment of women and girls in the street. Soliciting by men was not an offence and the NVA took non-judicial action in such cases. An entry in the executive minutes in 1902 reads,

> A lady, living in Grosvenor Road, had written asking for assistance with regard to her servants, who were annoyed by workmen opposite her house. The secretary had seen the lady and her servants, and subsequently interviewed the foreman of the works.[1]

The servants were likely to have been young teenage girls. An entry for 1904 records that the help of the Association was asked by a clergyman for Annie Cleverley, a Sunday school teacher, who was pestered by a man on the way to and fro. An NVA officer warned the man off.

From its inception the NVA was anxious to have soliciting by men made an offence. The very first set of minutes records that some members were in favour of applying the solicitation laws to men.[2] The entry mentions the activities of a 'well-known barrister in Westbourne Grove' and the 'action of soldiers at the entrance to Hyde Park'. The NVA proposals for 1886 for the amendment of the criminal law included making it an offence 'for a man or woman to molest or annoy any person in a public place'. The NVA saw the solicitation laws as discriminating against women as a petition heading shows:

> That your petitioners are deeply impressed by the inefficiency, inequality and injustice of the law as regards the sexes in matters relating to morals, and that in particular the law with regard to solicitation and molestation needs considerable amendment.[3]

There was a recognition by the NVA in its early years that sexual exploitation of women and especially young girls was facilitated by the positions of economic power and authority which men often held. One of the proposals suggested that to amend the criminal law was to 'make provision to meet the case of immoral offences committed by persons in authority'. It was the NVA's Mrs Percy Bunting who, at a conference of women workers at Nottingham in 1895, demanded a law to protect girls from sexual exploitation by Guardians, schoolmasters and employers as well as fathers. The NVA's concern was founded upon their own experience of innumerable cases of servants impregnated by their masters and then abandoned, and of men abusing other positions of trust and authority, such as clergymen, the US Vice Consul, the steward of the Liberal Club, Kilburn, and the chaplain of a Dublin Maternity Hospital.

The Association for Moral and Social Hygiene took up the campaign against sexual abuse in the later period from the First World War onwards. It was founded in 1913 from the amalgamation of the Ladies National Association for the Abolition of the Contagious Diseases Acts and the Men's National Association. The two earlier associations were set up by Josephine Butler in

1870 to launch the Contagious Diseases campaign. They were almost wholly concerned throughout their lifespan with the fight against state regulation of prostitutes which was also the main focus for the AMSH. Alison Neilans, who became secretary of the AMSH in 1913 and remained so for 25 years, had been a militant suffragette in the Women's Freedom League and had been imprisoned three times. Her obituary in the *Guardian* in 1938 stated that she had 'manfully [?] stood for the fundamental unity of the moral law and ideal for all persons, races and sexes, and the great principle underlying her work had been the equality of the moral law as applied to both sexes'.[4] Though the main work of the AMSH was to campaign against the state regulation of prostitution in Britain and abroad (it was the British branch of the International Abolitionist Federation), much of its activity was directed towards gaining legislation which would ensure that the clients of prostitutes were prosecuted and towards making it an offence for any man to solicit or annoy any woman in the street. Both the organisations, the NVA and the AMSH, which were to lead the campaign against sexual abuse were founded upon the desire to eliminate the double standard of sexual morality and its injustices for women. Their biases were different, as we shall see. The AMSH was concerned to protect the civil rights of women at all times whereas the NVA, in its later years, was prepared to be punitive towards women at the sacrifice of their civil liberties.

The campaign to amend the 1885 Act

The experience of putting the 1885 Act into effect for the protection of girls, convinced the organisations involved, particularly the NVA, that the Act had serious deficiencies which required remedy and the campaign to amend it began almost immediately. Mrs Fawcett outlined the amendments she wanted in a paper to the 1892 conference of women workers among women and children. These were changes in the time limit and in the law on affiliation, the abolition of the reasonable cause to believe clause, legal punishment for incest and severer punishment for men who abused positions of authority. The reasonable cause to believe clause, which decreed that believing a girl was over 16 was a defence to age of consent charges, and the time limit clause, which required that prosecutions must be got under way within three months of an offence being committed, were believed by NVA members to have been introduced into the Act to protect men against prosecution. As Mrs Fawcett pointed out in her paper, they were both exceptional in law. There was no time limit for the commencement of proceedings in other offences such as felony or murder, and no such thing as a defence of reasonable cause to believe in other offences which concerned the age of the victim. The explanation for such innovations in the law lay with the attitudes of the male MPs who made clear in the debates in Parliament that they wished to protect men, particularly young ones of their own class, from the operation of the law.[5]

The minutes of the NVA legal sub-committee are littered with examples of cases they could not proceed with because of the time limit. The fact that no action could be taken in such cases caused considerable anger and frustration to those who came across them.[6] Many cases only came to light when the girls were obviously pregnant or were delivered of babies and at that stage the only action which could be taken was to seek affiliation orders, for maintenance, against the fathers of the children. This was a situation which the NVA found particularly galling when the man involved was the girl's father and incest was not recognised as an offence.

Benjamin Waugh, founder of the National Society for the Prevention of Cruelty to Children, was deeply concerned about sexual abuse of children, and his interest led to the NSPCC being strongly focussed on the issue throughout the 1890s and the early twentieth century. In 1886 he asked the NVA to consider trying to get the reasonable cause to believe clause removed. The NVA also sought to make children's evidence more acceptable in court. Many of their cases were reported to have failed because of lack of evidence or corroboration. In 1886 the NVA proposed that the depositions of young children, taken before a magistrate while the matter was still fresh in the child's mind, should be allowed to be used in court. Another proposed amendment in the same year was to raise the age of consent for indecent assault from 13 to 16. There were also moves to raise the age of consent beyond 16 and in 1889 the NVA sent a resolution to the women's congress in Paris for the raising of the age of consent to 18.[7] At various times over the next 30 years, organisations or individual women within them called for the raising of the age of consent to 17, 18, 19 or even 21. Such moves, presumably motivated by women's lack of enthusiasm for male sexuality, aroused tremendous alarm in men who saw themselves being deprived of sexual access to women. In 1924 one anti-feminist writer accused feminists of wanting to raise the age of consent to the menopause.[8] Another aim of the NVA was to take the custody of children away from the person against whom proceedings were taken for indecent assault, such as father or guardian. The draft bill of 1892 omitted the raising of the general age of consent because the NVA thought that public opinion was not yet ripe for such a move. It included raising the age for indecent assault from 13 to 16, severer penalties for offenders in positions of authority, making incest a crime, providing for the taking of children's evidence without oath, extending the time limit clause to 12 months. When it became clear that all but the incest clauses were meeting with tough opposition in the House, a separate Incest Bill was constructed and the other clauses were turned into Bills which did not find sponsors and had to wait until after the Incest Bill was passed in 1908 to be reintroduced.

Two of the NVA's aims were realised as parts of other Acts before the concerted campaign that led up to the 1922 Criminal Law Amendment Act. In the Children's Act of 1904, the time limit was increased from 3 to 6 months, an improvement, but by no means all that the reformers wanted and the campaign for further extension continued. The Children's Act of 1913 allowed children to give evidence without taking the oath and the jury was left to decide how useful such evidence was.

Incest

Up to the 1908 Punishment of Incest Act there was no penalty for incest in civil law in England. In Scotland incest was punishable by death up to 1887 and the same punishment applied in several American states. Cromwellian England had imposed the death penalty for incest but this was swept away at the Restoration. Thereafter incestuous marriage but not incestuous sexual intercourse was punishable only under canon law, by penance, until the church courts were virtually abolished in 1857.

Throughout the nineteenth century the subject of incest among the poor was referred to directly and obliquely by medical officers of health, evidence to Royal Comissions and private investigations, but ignored by the legislators. Whenever the housing of the poor was described, a connection was made between overcrowding and incest. It was mentioned by Engels, Mayhew, Sir John Simons, Shaftesbury, the Association of Medical Officers of Health meeting in 1868, the Reverend Andrew Mearns in *The Bitter Cry of Outcast London*. Mearns's evidence came from prison officers, sanitary officials, slum clergymen and inspectors of schools. Mayhew and Acton both connected incest with the path to prostitution, as did the Rescue Society who were dedicated to rescuing girls and women who were involved in prostitution.[9] The subject of incest stretched the Victorian talent for euphemism to its limits with phrases such as 'promiscuous herding' and 'unnatural outrage and vice'. Silence reigned in the media. Even the *Lancet* for 1885 stated, 'There are things done in secret which should not so much as be named in family circles or in newspapers which have entrance into private houses.'[10] The subject was introduced to the House of Lords Select Committees on the 'Protection of Young Girls' (1882), and the 'Sweating System' (1888), but not followed up. The Royal Commission on the 'Housing of the Working Classes' (1884–5) responded with detailed examination of witnesses and a call for further investigation. Some of the reluctance to take action seems to have been based on the idea of the sanctity of the home and the desirability of domestic activities being safe from state intervention. The idea of the sanctity of the family is still used today to protect men from any interference in their right to abuse women and girls within the family.[11] In the late nineteenth century, government inspection of homes was seen as a great vice. Shaftesbury said that physical cruelty to children was too private and domestic and beyond the reach of legislation.

The NVA from its inception drew attention to father/daughter incest and pressure for legislation built up from the foundation of the NSPCC in 1889. The NSPCC and the NVA were both involved in large numbers of prosecutions of fathers. In the absence of incest legislation they had to prosecute offenders under other statutes such as rape or age of consent. A Mrs Heyworth, writing to the NVA in 1901, gave an example of this process whilst offering help to the association in its campaign around the Incest Bill:

> She [Mrs Heyworth] stated that she had been informed on good authority that in such cases, up to the age of 18, judges hold and juries find, the outrage of a father on his child amounts to rape, the parental authority being considered equivalent to violence or threats, and that a mere assertion by the girl that she submitted through fear, is practically enough to secure a conviction for rape.[12]

In 1887 a Bill was drafted to make incest a crime and was

submitted to the parliamentary committee of the NVA for consideration. The necessity for incest legislation was seen by the NVA to be in the same category as the need for legislation to outlaw the seduction of young girls by those in positions of authority over them, such as employers. Mrs Fawcett, who ran the Rescue and Preventive sub-committee, had precisely this approach. She stated that incest was 'by no means extremely uncommon' but if a girl was over 16 so that no other statutes applied, nothing could be done whilst incest was not an offence. As an explanation of the absence of legislation of the subject, she placed incest into the context of the general 'subjection of women':

> Now this may very probably be a survival of the old evil doctrine of the subjection of women and the absolute supremacy of the head of the family over all members of it. . . . In all nations of progressive civilisation the history of their progress has consisted in the gradual emancipation of sons, servants, daughters and wives from their former subjection.[13]

The emancipation of sons and servants was accomplished, she considered, but not that of women. She said she was in favour of parental authority but such authority entailed obligations,

> and when a father towards a child, a guardian towards a ward, a master towards a servant, is guilty of using the position of authority the law gives him to induce the child or servant to commit immoral actions, the offence ought to be recognised and punished as having a special degree of gravity.[14]

One of her recommendations for the revision of the criminal law was therefore as follows: 'To provide legal punishment for incest, and as a corollary to this, to visit with special severity all abuse of the authority which the law vests with the father, guardian or employer.'[15]

In 1895 the NVA had a draft bill for which they were seeking a sponsor in Parliament. The bill dealt not merely with incest but with several of the other amendments which the NVA sought in the criminal law. Despite having 'received petitions from all parts of the country, containing thousands of signatures in its favour', the NVA was unable to find a sponsor during 1895.[16] In 1896 Mr H.J. Wilson MP agreed to take charge of the Bill.

The Criminal Law Amendment Bill was blocked many times in Parliament in 1896, but the incest clause was not as strongly opposed as the rest. Therefore the NVA decided to draft a Bill dealing only with incest in the hope that it would have an easier passage. An Incest Bill was introduced in 1889 and again blocked, and in 1903 the Incest Bill got as far as the House of Lords. In the Lords the Lord Chancellor, Lord Halsbury, rejected the Bill on the grounds that there was no need for legislation on the subject despite the hundreds of meetings organised by the NVA which had sent resolutions in support. The Bill was reintroduced in each session by its sponsor, Colonel Lockwood, until in 1908, as a result of receiving favourable consideration from the government, it got through both Houses and became law. The Punishment of Incest Act 1908 was a much narrower measure than the feminists had campaigned for. It applied only to biological relatives, and did not protect girls from sexual exploitation from other males in positions of authority. It stated 'any male person who has carnal knowledge of a female person known to be his grand daughter, daughter, sister or mother is guilty of a misdemeanor and liable to penal servitude of not less than 3 years, and not more than 7 years.' The Act also fell short of the feminists' aims in stating that a 'female over 16 was also guilty if she consented'. They had wanted an age limit of 18. The Act also stated that an offender would lose all 'guardianship' for the offence. The Act has remained substantially the same to the present day.

The campaign for the 1922 Act

After the Punishment of Incest Act was passed, attention turned once more to the need for an Act amending the 1885 Act. In 1912 a committee was formed to further such legislation entitled the 'Pass the Bill' Committee which changed its name within the year to the 'Criminal Law Amendment' Committee. In a 1912 leaflet entitled *The Age of Consent* the committee urged the necessity of a national campaign to: raise the age of consent to at least 18 for girls, to protect girls up to 21 from seduction by employers or guardians, to repeal the reasonable cause to believe clause, to protect boys up to 16 (or 18) from seduction by women, and to extend the time limit from 6 to 12 months. Supporters were given tips on how to help with campaigning: 'Arrange meetings in drawing rooms, or in public, circulate petitions to parliament, send a deputation of local people to the MP who represents your town or district and distribute these leaflets where they are needed.'[17] The committee included some well known feminist names such as Mrs Fawcett, Miss Emily Davies, Lady Strachey,

Miss Alison Neilans, Miss Maude Royden as well as Lady Bunting of the NVA and Miss Helen Wilson of the AMSH. Seventy-two supporting societies were named including the Ladies National Association, the National Organisation of Girls' Clubs, the National Union of Women Workers among Women and Children (which later became the National Council for Women), the United Girls School Settlement, the National Women's Labour League, the Women's Freedom League and many other suffrage organisations.[18] A conference was held in 1913 and in 1914 a Bill known as the Bishop of London's Bill was introduced into the Lords. The clauses were to raise the age of consent to indecent assault for either sex to 16, to raise the age of consent to sexual intercourse for a girl to 18, to extend the time limit to 12 months and remove the reasonable cause to believe clause. The Bill reached as far as the committee stage in the Lords and was changed into the Criminal Law Amendment Bill for introduction in 1917.

The 1917 Bill included clauses making it a criminal offence to engage in sexual intercourse when suffering from venereal disease and clauses dealing with brothels and indecent advertisements. The Bill was amended in committee to include a clause which provoked considerable controversy and illustrates the growing differences between the organisations involved over their attitudes to the civil liberties of women. Clause 3 gave power to the courts to order the detention of girls under 18 in certain cases; where the girl was convicted of loitering or importuning, for an offence under the Vagrancy Act, i.e. wandering or behaving in a riotous manner, and an offence under the Incest Act or any offence under the proposed 1917 Act itself. Subsequently the offence of being a common prostitute was added to the list. The detention was supposed to be a way of protecting the girl from sexual misadventure and was considered to be in lieu of punishment. The girl was to be detained until she was 19 or for any period less than that as the court might direct, in an institution or home. Rather than being in lieu of punishment, this clause would have introduced a very effective punishment for any girls who behaved in ways which the courts disapproved of. The spirit of this idea is practised today as girls who act out sexually (but not boys) are incarcerated in homes, supposedly for their own safety. Unfortunately this punitive and anti-woman clause gained much support, pratically from the NVA. The NVA commented: 'Already those who have been accustomed to co-operate in all matters relating to the care and protection of girls, find themselves in opposite camps.'[19] The AMSH was in the opposite camp. The *Vigilance Record* summed up their arguments by saying that the opposition was based upon the idea that:

> the liberty of the subject is at stake; that no citizen, especially girls between the ages of 15 and 18, ought to be at the mercy of the arbitrary and tyrannical power that could be exercised by one police constable, or should be consigned to detention in a Home for 2 or 3 years at the discretion of one magistrate.[20]

The NVA rejected these quite reasonable arguments based upon feminist and civil libertarian premises and argued: 'Surely the law only steps in when liberty is dethroned and license reigns!'[21] The NVA was still formally dedicated to the establishment of an equal moral standard but clearly this had been abandoned in all but name. The NVA seems at this time to have lost all feminist influence. The supporters of clause 3 wanted to eliminate prostitution and venereal disease through the sacrifice of women's civil rights. This was a far cry from the ideal with which the NVA had started out, of implementing an equal law on soliciting.

The executive committee of the National Union of Women Workers (later the National Council for Women) was completely divided over the issue of detention. The rescue and preventive sub-committee wanted it whilst the others saw it as a threat to a girl's liberty. The NUWW had passed unamimous resolutions in favour of equal moral standards for men and women in society and before the law, but on this occasion some members were quite unable to see the contradiction. The Joint Select Committee eventually decided against clause 3. The differences of opinion here show how uneasy the alliance was at this time between feminists and those who favoured compulsion despite their common aims around the age of consent and other amendments to the 1885 Act.

The Joint Select Committee was considering a new Bill of 1918, the 'Sexual Offences Bill', as well as the Criminal Law Amendment Bill. The new Bill embodied the principle of compulsion in another guise. One clause allowed for the compulsory medical examination of those suspected of having engaged in sexual intercourse whilst suffering from venereal disease. The report of the committee in 1920 recommended the abolition of the reasonable cause to believe clause but not the raising of the age of consent above 16. The AMSH was concerned that elements of compulsion, particularly any version of clause 3, would find their way into any Bill that was presented as a result of the Select Committee's report. They published a manifesto and convened a conference in the Women's Institute building in January 1921 to discuss the Bill, and promote their own model Bill.

The AMSH favoured a limited Bill calling only for clauses raising the age of consent for boys and girls to indecent assault and sexual intercourse, the abolition of the reasonable cause to believe clause, extension of the time limit, and increased penalties for brothel keeping. The Bill of 1921 was streamlined to the AMSH recommendations to make it non-controversial and introduced into the House of Lords. The government said it was willing to give facilities for the Bill provided it would pass through all its stages as an agreed Bill. The Bill was defeated because of the addition at third reading stage in the House of Commons of a lesbian amendment.

The AMSH sent a letter to some peers including the Law Lords making their views on the amendment, which was modelled on the Labouchere amendment of 1885 which criminalised male homosexuality, known. They said they accepted no responsibility for the new clause which had not been before any parliamentary standing committees and had not been considered by any of the 59 national societies which supported the Bill.[22] The AMSH did not wish to express any opinion on the subject matter of the amendment but protested the way in which it had been added. They saw the amendment as an attempt to destroy the Bill for which they had worked for so long. The new clause was rejected when the Bill was sent back to the Lords and the Bill was defeated since it was no longer an agreed Bill. The AMSH issued a memo on the defeated Bill to the press and to the co-operating societies:

> The CLA Bill was wrecked in the House of Commons last night, and the impression has been given that it was wrecked by amendments made to the Bill by the House of Lords. This is quite a wrong view. The Bill was deliberately wrecked by those in the Commons who are determined not to give girls under 16 effective protection against seduction.[23]

The Bill was adopted the next year as a government Bill. It was again violently attacked in the Commons and only allowed to proceed by the Home Secretary promising to accept an amendment retaining the reasonable cause to believe clause for men under the age of 23. The Bill received the royal assent on 24 August 1922. The result of the Act was immediately to create an anomalous situation whereby the retained clause applied to carnal knowledge (sexual intercourse) but not to indecent assault, so that an offender had a defence for the major charge but not for the minor one. None the less the main aims of the campaigners had been achieved. The age of consent was levelled up to 16 for both offences, and the time limit was extended from 6 to 9 months.

The debate on the Bill in the House of Commons makes it clear that this was seen to be an issue on which men's and women's interests were in opposition. There was a strong vein of sexual antagonism, with male MPs defending their interests against what they clearly saw as the terrifying strength of women and hurling insults at women's organisations and feminists. The House of Commons and suffrage had been all male until 1918. The frustration of male MPs at the change in their fortunes, the fact that they might have to take notice of women's opinions, was evident in the debate. The pressure from women's organisations was described by Lieutenant Colonel Moore-Brabazon as 'henpecking'. He asked why there had been a government measure: 'Has it been done because of the great pressure of women's organisations in this country? If so, then it seems to me to be a sad confession on the part of the home secretary of henpecking.'[24] Major Sir George Hamilton was virulently antifeminist:

> Do men, especially young men, for whom I am speaking, go about hunting for girls to seduce? That seems to be the argument of these various societies. Is that really the feminist outlook on males? I have always been against feminism. I loathe feminism and the whole of that aspect of the feminist mind that looks on man as a corrupt creature, hunting about to seduce someone is all wrong. I am confident of this, that the average decent woman, especially if she is a mother, is just as much against feminism as I am.[25]

One MP was prepared to contradict himself totally in his attempt to protect the right of men to have sexual access to young girls. To protect men who used girls under the age of 16 he argued, in common with many other MPs that men could not defend themselves against the tremendous seductive powers of young girls:

> She sets to work to throw allurement after allurement over

him. She uses all the artifices of her sex to achieve her object. She gradually sees him being lashed into the elemental and aggressive male, and when that point is reached he is like a runaway horse; his control has gone. He pursues and he succumbs.[26]

He used the argument frequently used today to defend men against charges of rape and sexual abuse, that male sexuality is uncontrollable. It was precisely this idea that feminists were challenging most fiercely. But, despite this uncontrollability, and the fact that the male had the 'instinct of pursuit', he was prepared to assert that 'modest' women had nothing to fear.

sex attraction is one of the elemental things of life, and it will be agreed that when you get down to the instincts which move men and women in sex matters, the outstanding instinct of the male is pursuit. . . . The instinct of the female is resistance, reserve, followed, if she is won, by surrender, but broadly speaking, she has the reserve, and the resistance . . . and the most potent individual force that makes for sexual morality in a community is woman's modesty.[27]

This is a very complicated prescription. Women had the instinct of reserve, yet sometimes, as we have seen, they led men on. They also had instincts of both resistance and surrender which sounds tricky. The important message from all this deliberate confusion is that woman was always to blame and men need take no responsibility for their sexual behaviour at all.

The 1922 Act was the last occasion on which major legislation on sexual offences passed through parliament before the late 1950s. There was, though, a special piece of legislation in 1928 which extended the time limit to 12 months.

Why did the massive wave of female indignation over the sexual abuse of girls die away? From the 1930s to the present wave of feminism, the subject of sexual abuse, and particularly incest, has been confined to academic journals rather than being in the forefront of public consciousness, and has not been seen as a crime against women by men. It was feminist energy which fuelled the campaign at its height and the general decline of militant feminism in the 1920s must have played its part in undermining the campaign. Some of the campaigners' demands were satisfied in the 1922 Act, but many, especially those concerned with the treatment of the child victim by police and courts and the validity of children's evidence, were not.

Virtually all those practical goals that the campaigners had been fighting for were recommended by the Departmental Committee report in 1925. They could have been implemented by statute or government directive, but no action was taken. The AMSH put pressure on the government to implement the recommendations right up to the Second World War as well as producing abortive Bills of its own. It seems likely that public concern over sexual abuse was waning and the report came too late.

The change in attitudes to sexual abuse which weakened the strength of the campaign resulted from a change in the dominant sexual ideology as much as from the decline of feminism. These two phenomena were closely connected as can be seen in Chapters 7 and 8. The scientific mystification of sexuality and sexual aggression towards women which issued from the work of the male sexologists, psychologists and pschoanalysts placed the initiative firmly in the hands of the professionals. It became less easy for women to approach the problem of sexual abuse simply from their own experience and feminist theory. The development of the 'medical model' had two significant implications. Women's anger against men was deflated when responsibility was taken away from the male offender and attributed to his 'disease'. 'Sick' offenders could be seen as exceptions whose behaviour had little relevance to that of men in general. The issue of sexual abuse was removed from the context of crimes against women. Despite dissentient voices, the move to see offenders as sick had taken over from the fiercely indignant largely feminist campaign against sexual abuse by the 1930s. In this current wave of feminism, feminists have had to demolish the 'wisdom' of the scientific establishment and rely again on their own experience and judgement in reestablishing a campaign against the sexual abuse of girls.[28]

In Chapters 7, 8 and 9 we will look in detail at the work of the sexologists and their impact on feminism. In the next two Chapters we look at the effects upon women's lives and relationships of the new sexual demands and categories being created for women by the sex reformers and the sexologists. Spinsters and lesbians were prominent in the feminist campaigns around sexuality before the First World War as they are today. By the 1920s both categories of women were being subjected to bitter attack from sex reformers and even other feminists. The attack upon spinsters and lesbians who had been so important in the campaigns was yet one more factor which helped to undermine the feminist challenge.

CHAPTER 5
Spinsterhood and Celibacy

Spinsters provided the backbone of the feminist movement in the late nineteenth and early twentieth century. Rosemary Auchmuty, in her unpublished doctoral thesis 'Victorian Spinsters', points out that most of the Victorian feminists we read about in modern history books, were married women, such as Mrs Elizabeth Garratt Anderson, Mrs Josephine Butler, and Mrs Millicent Garratt Fawcett. She argues that in our own time

> feminist movements have tended to address themselves chiefly
> to the middle-class wife and mother, so that feminist
> historians searching for their Victorian antecedents have
> naturally picked out what they see as 'oppressed' married
> women for the modern liberated lady to identify with.[1]

Appended to her thesis is a short 'Who's Who' of about 200 Victorian spinsters notable for their achievements in various fields. Auchmuty suggests that it would be hard to find a similar number of married feminists or married women with similar achievements in that age. She attributes the nature and content of Victorian feminism to the fact that it was 'led by Victorian spinsters on behalf of Victorian spinsters'.[2]

The importance of Victorian spinsters has been neglected by contemporary comentators, living in a society in which nearly all women marry. In the late Victorian period almost one in three of all adult women were single and one in four would never marry.[3]

The 1851 census revealed that there were 405,000 more women than men in the population.[4] They were described in the press as 'excess' or 'surplus' women and in the 1860s to 1880s the 'problem' of 'surplus' women caused great alarm amongst male commentators. Those men who saw women as being superfluous if they were not servicing men, suggested emigration as a solution:

> We must restore by an emigration of women that natural proportion between the sexes in the old country and in the new ones, which was disturbed by an emigration of men, and the disturbance of which has wrought so much mischief in both lands. . . . The first difficulty is chiefly mechanical. It is not easy to convey a multitude of women across the Atlantic, or to the Antipodes by any ordinary means or transit. To transport the half million from where they are redundant to where they are wanted, at an average of fifty passengers to each ship, would require 10,000 vessels, or at least 10,000 voyages.[5]

This quotation from W.R. Gregg gives an idea of the total contempt for women who failed to perform their life's work of servicing men, which the Victorian spinster had to confront. Women who fail to relate to men are still socially disapproved of today. If anti-spinster feeling is declining a little at present this could be because there are so few spinsters today that they are not seen to constitute so serious a threat. The Victorian feminists fought the idea that woman was simply man's appendage and the very notion that women could be surplus; surplus to the needs of men.

The demands of feminists in the 1850s and 1860s were aimed at dealing with the problem of 'surplus' women in ways which served women's interests. They were mainly concerned with the plight of the middle-class spinster who was restrained by Victorian notions of respectability from leaving home, or engaging in the trades open to working-class women. She was left dependent and without vocation. The campaign for women's employment and education stemmed largely from such concern. Most of the commentary of the time, including that of feminists, saw 'surplus' women as a problem of the middle classes. We have no good reason to suppose that there were vastly more unmarried women amongst the middle class, though it is suggested that the reluctance of middle-class men to undertake the expense of marriage when they could gain the services much more easily through the use of mistresses or servants, may have exacerbated the plight of the middle-class spinster. Unmarried women from the working classes did have access to work and the vast majority of them were absorbed in the domestic servant industry which relied almost entirely on unmarried women.

When the plight of the middle-class spinster is written about in the history books, it is generally posed as the excruciating difficulty felt by women who were desperate for husbands. This is not an accurate picture. Numbers of spinsters, at least until after the First World War, made a positive choice not to marry. They made such a choice, either because they regarded marriage as a form of humiliating slavery and dependence upon men, or because they wanted to pursue a career and fulfill their potential in a way which would not have been allowed to them by husbands. Maria Grey and Emily Shirreff wrote in 1871:

> A woman should be reminded . . . that in marrying she gives up many advantages. Her independence is, of course, renounced by the very act that makes her another's. Her habits, pursuits, society, sometimes even friendships, must give way to his.[6]

Florence Nightingale is one of these women who refused to marry. She comments that there were women who sacrificed marriage, 'because they must sacrifice all their life if they accepted that . . . behind *his* destiny woman must annihilate herself.'[7]

Judging by their own statements and the fuss made about them in the press and by anti-feminists, some feminists were choosing before the First World War not to have any sexual relations with men. They were taking this decision in protest against the form taken by male sexuality, the way that women were oppressed in their relationships with men, and because some of them believed that the position of all women could only be improved in a society where there was a large class of celibate women. It would be very difficult to judge the size of this revolt or precisely what it meant to all the women involved. However the fact that feminists and others considered the phenomenon to exist and were either very enthusiastic or hysterically alarmed about it, is interesting and demands examination even if the number of women involved was fairly small.

There is no doubt that the proportion of women relative to men in the population was increasing in every census or estimate from 1821, when there were 1,036 women to every 1,000 men, to 1901 when there were 1,068. In 1911 the proportion remained at the 1901 figure. The year 1911 also represents a peak for the number of women in each age group from 25 upwards who remained single. After the First World War, the proportion of women to men rose to 1,096 to 1,000 in the 1921 census. It was still 1,088 to

1,000 in 1931. However the rate of marriage rose in every age group after the war. So though 1911 did not represent the all-time high in the proportion of women to men in the population it does seem to have represented the time at which marriage was least popular between 1801 and 1931. The 'fuss' about spinsters continued in the press and other publications through the 1920s and into the 1930s.

Developments which gave women slightly more choice about marrying before the First World War were the expansion of higher education for women combined with the beginning of the opening up of the professions to women, and the massive expansion in white-collar employment in the period after 1880, into which women could be drawn. Much of the impetus of the early women's movement had come from or been directed towards helping spinsters, against the double disadvantages of their position. In the period immediately before the First World War spinsters were fighting back against the prejudices which created difficulties for them in finding a livelihood, social life and relationships outside marriage. Undoubtedly some women were deliberately choosing to remain single and were articulating their decision in political terms.

Christabel Pankhurst stated categorically that spinsterhood was a political decision, a deliberate choice made in response to the conditions of sex-slavery: 'There can be no mating between the spiritually developed women of this new day and men who in thought and conduct with regard to sex matters are their inferiors.'[8] Christabel Pankhurst's stand represents a significant new strand in the reasons women were giving for remaining unmarried. She asserted that it was men's sexual behaviour which made them unsuitable for intimacy with women. As we have seen in the previous chapter, the period 1906–14 was one of increased intensity in the campaign by feminists to control male sexual behaviour and protect women from abuse. It should not surprise us that some of these women involved in the campaign should live out in their private lives, their total rejection of the form taken by male sexuality. It can be reasonably assumed that Christabel Pankhurst was not alone in her views in the Women's Social and Political Union, since 63 per cent of members in 1913, when her statement was made, were spinsters, and many of the rest were widowed.

Lucy Re-Bartlett saw the Women's Social and Political Union as the harbinger of a desirable new social order, and was, unlike many social commentators of the time, entirely enthusiastic about it. She saw the phenomenon of celibacy amongst feminists and other women as a positive decision to refuse to enter into relationships with men until the animal nature of men was transformed and a new spiritual form of relationship between the sexes was possible. In *Sex and Sanctity*, after speaking of the 'horrors of the White Slave Traffic' and 'the ruin of little children', she describes the 'new social conscience' arising in militant and non-militant women alike, in Britain and in other countries. These women, she declared:

> feel linked by their womanhood to every suffering woman, and every injured child, and as they look around upon the great mass of men who seem to them *indifferent*, there is growing up in the hearts of some of these women a great sense of *distance*. . . . In the hearts of many women today is rising a cry somewhat like this . . . *I will know no man, and bear no child* until this apathy is broken through – these wrongs be righted.[9]

She wrote that both married and single women were feeling and acting thus, 'It is the "silent strike" and it is going on all over the world.'[10] She refers to press articles which talk of celibacy increasing among women and attribute it to degeneracy and dislike of motherhood. In fact, she said, it represented a 'newly awakened conscience' and a 'far deeper motherhood' lay behind it. The strike was only a 'temporary protest – an appeal' and not a revolt against men but against 'certain false social conditions'.

In a chapter entitled '*Feminine Celibacy: its Meaning Today*' Re-Bartlett seeks to explain how the phenomenom arose. She writes that it was 'engaging the attention of a considerable number of people today' but its deepest causes were undefined. Women were definitely positively refusing marriage, she asserts, since if it was husbands they wanted, they could emigrate and there was little interest in that. She saw education as an important factor since it was 'training girls to think with a clearness' which had never been approached in the past. As a result women were becoming critical. The 'modern' schoolgirl imbibed the ideal of 'women's independence, women's dignity, women's value'. Meanwhile there was no corresponding change in the education of boys so that the men produced by it were just not 'good enough' and the girls turned to face college and freedom. The new independent women's struggle was described as a battle against succumbing to sexual relationships with men!

> When because of those beating wings in her soul (beating free from the lower level where the dominion of sense brings bondage), woman fights desperately with herself and with men: fights her own vanity and man's appeal to it – fights smallness and domination, and all passion which is just the blood, because so soon as any of those things touch her, she feels the new wings within her droop and cease to beat. And their beating has become as very life – life which must be defended even at the cost of human life, if need be. And she stands away from man until he understands.[11]

This new 'warrior maid' according to Re-Bartlett, was now all over the world.

Whilst writing about the celibate militant suffragettes Re-Bartlett defends them against the accusation of their critics that they showed 'great bitterness towards men'. She explains that such a period of withdrawl from men was necessary and the women's anger was necessary also. She writes that a

> period of this kind must needs be passed through before the old relations between men and women be set aside and the new and nobler ones established. Woman cannot truly struggle for the new order, until she hates the old.[12]

In contrast with the suffragettes' attitude towards men, she praises at length the wonderful 'solidarity' which she saw spring up between women of the new type. She criticises the tendency of pre-suffragette women to seek approval from men by denigrating other women. Re-Bartlett states that the 'new' woman 'loves instinctively her sister woman' and that this phenomenon was to be seen most frequently among the suffragettes.

Some spinsters in the period proclaimed the necessity of creating a large class of spinsters who were making a positive choice to be so, as a political tactic to improve the general lot of women. Cicely Hamilton is one of these. Her book *Marriage as a Trade* is a lengthy exposition of why women wished to be spinsters, the ploys used against them and her belief in the political necessity of spinsters to the women's revolution. She sought to explain the 'uncompromising and brutal attitudes' which men had always adopted towards spinsters. She considered the attitude of married women merely 'servile and imitative' of that of men. It was adopted partly to force women into marriage and prevent economic competition. The attitude was not merely contempt for a 'creature [who] was chaste and therefore inhuman' but active dislike which she felt could only arise from 'consciousness that the perpetual virgin was a witness, however reluctantly, to the unpalatable fact that sexual intercourse was not for every woman an absolute necessity'.[13] The spinster was by her very existence a living reproach to men as to the form of their sexuality. Hamilton's reason for being a spinster was specifically a rejection of the conditions of marriage. Since she saw marriage as a trade she saw the conditions of marriage as a wife's conditions of work and considered them insupportable. They included total lack of payment, sexual subjection and occupational hazards for which no warning or compensation was given. She likened venereal disease to the risk of lead poisoning in a pottery or the danger of combustion in a dynamite factory.

Hamilton considered that in recent history nothing was more striking than the improvement in the position of the spinster. She said that the lack of a husband was no longer a reproach and 'some of us' were proud to be fighting their way in the world without aid from any man's arm even though they were often assured that thay had lost the best that life had to offer. Man's dream was still of 'someone smaller than him who asks him questions while he strokes her hair' and the average wife was still a person 'who is willing to submit to be patronised'.[14]

The importance of spinsters was that only they could help advance the cause of women as 'any improvement as has already been affected in the status of the wife and mother has originated outside herself, and is, to a great extent, the work of the formerly contented spinster'.[15] As the spinster improved her position so she steadily destroyed the prestige of marriage and the conditions of marriage would only be improved if there was a viable alternative to marriage open to women. She attributed the institution of chivalry to the fact that there had been a socially approved alternative lifestyle open to women in the middle ages which offered a choice instead of compulsory marriage. This was the conventual life. She connected the end of chivalry at the reformation with the downfall of the conventual life. She attributed the witch-burnings unequivocally to the masculine policy of repressing deviations from the type of wife and mother. If marriage was voluntary and not enforced, she thought, men would have to pay for the work they got for nothing and men would have to exercise self-control instead of seeing 'one half of the race as sent into the world to excite desire in the other half'.[16]

A contributor to the *Freewoman* magazine, E. Noel Morgan, also argued that a celibate class of women was necessary for the 'task of raising the fair sex out of its subjection'. She saw the existence of such a class as a deliberate strategy on the part of 'nature' which intended to emancipate women rather than as the result of a positive choice by women not to marry:

> Now the existence of this unhusbanded class of women seems to me to be deliberately planned by nature for a specific purpose. We find that wherever women are admitted to sex intercourse to such a degree that the celibate class is practically non-existent, there the position of women socially, economically, and intellectually is of a low order.[17]

She believed that women needed the passion they would otherwise use in sex to fight for the emancipation of women.

Opposition to the spinsters

The development of a class of spinsters proud to proclaim that they were happy, fulfilled, had made a deliberate choice and were vital to the political struggle of women met with serious opposition. It was not just men who wanted to deride and undermine the position of these women. Some feminists also went into the attack. The *Freewoman* magazine gave the opposition its platform. Its founder and editor was Dora Marsden who had been in the Woman's Social and Political Union and broke away to found the *Freewoman* because she considered the Pankhursts too autocratic. She had been imprisoned for her work in the suffrage struggle. She had also tried the Women's Freedom League after leaving the WSPU, but resigned from that too. The 'Notes of the Week' in the first issue demonstrate Marsden's political philosophy:

> Our journal will differ from all existing weekly journals devoted to the freedom of women, in as much as the latter find their starting-point and interest in the externals of freedom. They deal with something which women may acquire. We find our chief concern in what they may become. Our interest is in the Freewomen herself, her psychology, philosophy, morality, and achievements, and only in a secondary way with her politics and economics.[18]

She said that women had to be spiritually free and stressed that she did not see the vote as even a symbol of freedom. She was most critical of the reasons that suffrage fighters gave for wanting the vote:

> These reasons have been culled out of an unthought-out and nebulous feminism, and at most have amounted to nothing more than half-hearted and sentimental allusions, to prostitution, sweating, child-assault, race-deterioration, and what not. But all real understanding of what these things mean, and discussion as to how they are to be remedied have been systematically discouraged.[19]

There are in fact no further references to the above topics in the *Freewoman*. Marsden showed no understanding of the effect that what she called 'externals', which could also be called material realities, had on the practical ability of women to achieve their freedom. She believed that women could be free inside their heads no matter what was happening in the outside world:

> There comes a cry that woman is an individual and that because she is an individual she must be set free. It would be nearer the truth to say that if she is an individual she *is* free, and will act like those who are free.[20]

The direction in which her politics were leading can be seen from the contents and history of the journal. The content from the beginning was very much concerned with freedom of speech and thought and many, if not the majority, of contributors were men. The overall impression is of a literary magazine with a strongly Bohemian tone. There were articles on removing restrictions on women's freedom to relate sexually to men, through marriage law reform, the promotion of unmarried love and criticisms of monogamy. There were also articles on uranism (male homosexuality). Not surprisingly the subtitle *A Feminist Review* changed in May 1912 to *A Weekly Humanist Review*, and the editorial policy was described as being to 'show that the two causes, man's and woman's are one'.[21]

The spinster-baiting in the *Freewoman* was conducted alongside a protracted propaganda campaign against the WSPU. The assault on spinsters started in the very first issue. In an article entitled 'The Spinster' written 'By One', a sketch is drawn giving a destructive twisted character to the class of women depicted in the title. The opening lines are particularly insulting:

I write of the High Priestess of Society. Not of the mother of sons, but of her barren sister, the withered tree, the acidulous vestal under whose pale shadow we chill and whiten, of the Spinster I write. Because of her power and dominion. She, unobtrusive, meek, soft-footed, silent, shamefaced, bloodless and boneless, thinned to spirit, enters the secret recesses of the mind, sits at the secret springs of action, and moulds and fashions our emasculate society. She is our social nemesis.[22]

The writer attributed great power and influence to the spinster and scapegoated her for all the ills of society. She is seen as converting her desperate disappointment and frustration at being cheated of a man and motherhood after being reared to expect such things, into a cold-blooded puritanism with which she squashed out the life-impulse in literature and the theatre and in the children she taught. Examples of the busy spinster's activities are as follows:

In the auditorium of every theatre she sits, the pale guardian. . . . She haunts every library. . . . In our schools she takes the little children, and day by day they breathe in the atmosphere of her violated spirit.[23]

The conclusion of the article requests compassion for the dreadful plight of the spinster and calls for the removal of the savage restrictions which condemn unmarried women to celibacy. The article is in fact far from sympathetic in tone. It is a vicious indictment of the spinster along lines which were to become more familiar after the First World War, when the appellation 'prude' was directed at all feminists, spinsters and women who offered any critique of men's sexual behaviour. In subsequent issues of the *Freewoman* articles appeared purporting to describe how different varieties of spinsters emerged. One, on the college-educated woman, spoke in disapproving tones of her growing lack of interest in clothes, lack of 'sex attraction' and indifference to men. The *Freewoman* writers were united in alarm at the spinster, even when they were spinsters themselves.

Central to the first article was the argument that sexual activity with men was vital to the health of women and that without it she became either bitter and twisted or gushingly sentimental. The invention of an imperative sexual instinct which once thwarted led to nameless, but serious ills, and some nameable ones such as haunting libraries, was an argument from the sexological ideology of compulsive heterosexuality. Some spinsters resisted this enforcement of sexual intercourse. A debate began in the letters page on the subject of the harmfulness of abstinence (from sexual intercourse) for women. A feminist spinster, Margaret Hill, fired the first salvo on behalf of the spinster:

> But it is Society that has wronged women and not Nature. She, indeed, has well fitted the female for the part she was intended to take, for woman is physically complete. Though she is a necessity to man, he is not necessary to her. In single life she retains health, strength, and vitality, and her functions are unimpaired. It is inconceivable that the female could hold her position if she were craving for motherhood. Maternal love comes like her milk when the babe needs it.[24]

Kathryn Oliver wrote to the *Freewoman* attacking the 'new morality which would permit for women the same degrading laxity in sex matters which is indulged in by most of the lower animals, including men', saying that she was neither a prude nor a puritan but an 'apostle of the practice of self-restraint in sex matters'.[25] She denied absolutely that celibacy was dangerous to the health of women:

> I am an unmarried woman, nearly 30 years of age, and have always practised abstinence, and although not a powerful person, I enjoy the best of health, and have never troubled a doctor since I was six years old. My married women friends, on the contrary, have always some complaint or something wrong. Who has not seen the girl married at twenty almost immediately degenerate into a nervous wreck? I deny absolutely that abstinence has any bad effect on my health.[26]

'New Subscriber' who later revealed herself to be Stella Browne, entered into an individual debate with Kathryn Oliver in which we see her taking up the cudgels against spinsters as she did against lesbians (see chapter 6). Browne replied in the next issue that Oliver must belong to the class of women who are 'sexually anaesthetic' and 'cold-blooded', but there were other varieties of women. She assured readers that many women's health, happiness, social usefulness and mental capacity were 'seriously impaired and sometimes totally ruined by the unnatural conditions of their lives' if they were celibate.

Oliver replied by accusing 'New Subscriber' of being of the 'male persuasion' and stated that from her observation of unmarried girls and women whom she had known intimately there were no grounds to suppose they were adversely affected by complete chastity. She suggested that the idea of a sex relationship seldom entered the thoughts of most women until they loved and if it did it appeared 'repulsive' rather than attractive. She protested that she was in fact 'normal' and had experienced sexual desire occasionally after she 'fell in love' at about twenty. She again proclaimed the desirability of self-control and the ruling of instincts and desires by intellect and reason, capacities which, in her opinion, raised women 'miles above and beyond men'. 'New Subscriber' wrote again accusing Oliver of being 'of cold temperament sexually' and bewailing the effects of such women as she on the women's movement in much the same vein as the original spinster article:

> It will be an unspeakable catastrophe if our richly complex
> Feminist movement with its possibilities of power and joy,
> falls under the domination of sexually deficient and
> disappointed women, impervious to facts and logic and deeply
> ignorant about life.[27]

These comments fit into Browne's campaigns to get women to participate enthusiastically in sexual intercourse. Those women showing the greatest resistance meet with her strongest disapproval.

Christabel Pankhurst also addressed the attacks on spinsters' thwarted instincts. In reply to 'some men' who said that women not mated with men suffered and became a problem because of their 'unsatisfied desires', she stated that unmarried women had lives of joy and interest. In reply to those who apparently said that 'women's ideas of chastity are the result of past subjection', she said that the subjection of women had therefore brought women one great gain which was 'the mastery of self and sex' and women had no intention of giving that up.

There were two fronts to the battle against the spinsters. One was to declare against all evidence to the contrary that spinsters suffered from thwarted desire which turned them into vicious and destructive creatures. This was a good way to discredit and undermine the vast quantity of work which celibate women were then doing in the women's movement, much of it directly opposed to male sexual behaviour. Another was to promote sex freedom. If sexual intercourse with men was vital and there was a surplus of women, then marriage would be no solution to the spinsters' problems. 'Sexual freedom' was another possibility, and was being promoted by some feminists in the *Freewoman* magazine. Christabel Pankhurst was very suspicious and hostile to the 'new morality' proponents. 'Sex freedom' was being heralded as the way to eliminate prostitution, an idea which is still popular today. The argument is that men's use of women in prostitution is the result of women's sexuality being repressed so that men have difficulty finding partners. 'Sex freedom' and prostitution in fact manage to coexist very happily side by side. The argument transfers responsibility for men's use of women in prostitution from men to women. Christabel summed up the argument thus:

> It would seem that certain men are alarmed by the dangers of prostitution, and, of course, they find it expensive. At any rate, we detect a tendency in some quarters to preach to women the observance of a looser code of morals than they have observed hitherto. 'You are asking for political freedom,' women are told. 'More important to you is sex freedom.' Votes for women shoud be accompanied, if not preceded, by wild oats for women. The thing to be done is not to raise the moral standard of men, but to lower the moral standard of women.[28]

Women, she said, replied with a firm negative to this suggestion: 'When women have the vote, they will be more and not less opposed than now to making a plaything of sex and of entering casually into the sex relationship.'[29]

A woman writing to the *Freewoman* spoke of her worry over the paper's tendency to glorify 'freedom in all that concerns sex impulses', and expressed fear of the anti-social effect of allowing 'sex impulses' to run riot. There were many aspects of the new morality of which she approved, such as changing women's position in marriage so that she could 'unite herself with the man she loved', and so that her children might be hers in the eyes of the law, and divorce was facilitated, but she had grave reservations. She warned that people should not be encouraged to think that a 'satisfactory' society could be built on the 'basis of a complete freedom in sex matters', because the 'sex instinct' was unstable and unreasonable when separated from 'any idea of duty, honour, or spiritual-mindedness'.[30] Several correspondents took the line that sex should be connected to emotion, attachment and responsibility and saw 'sex freedom' as threatening this. The model they had before them of male sexual behaviour, based heavily on the use of prostitutes and therefore divorcing sex entirely from the context of loving relationships, did not look at all suited to what they saw as the interests of women:

> I do not think that to make our morality on a plane with men's would improve our position, or that anything but a lasting tie would satisfy a woman. When she marries she gives so much more than a man that she must have a hold on him. . . . As for being merely the instrument of pleasure, a woman's desire is, in general, no mean second to a man's.[31]

'Cailin Dhu', the writer of the above letter, in fact believed that women were naturally monogamous whilst men were polygamous. The very practical reasons lying behind women's need for lasting ties, such as the fact that they bore children and were not in a position to earn a reasonable living, would suggest that women's 'monogamy' was socially rather than naturally constructed.

One correspondent, with great foresight, attributed the propounding of a 'new morality' to the fact that men feared that when women got the vote, their sex freedom under the double standard might come to an end. The solution was to encourage women to something called sex freedom, however illusory, so that the single standard that came into being would be that which men wanted and not the alarming vision being propounded by most feminists:

> It is noteworthy how anxious men are to safeguard their incontinence in the coming age of the Freewoman. They are expecting trouble, as your columns show, and by paying heed to them, Freewoman will be leaving the frying-pan for the fire.[32]

She was quite right. There was no question of an equal standard of sexual morality in a society in which the sexes were not equal. When it looked as if the feminists might carry out their threat to enforce chastity on men, a new code of sexual morality developed which ensured that men retained the advantage. Some feminists suggested that 'sex freedom' gave man more advantges even than they had enjoyed under the double standard. There is no doubt that in any system of free enterprise, including a sexual one, those with the greatest material advantages benefit most from the system and often at the expense of those who are not so advantaged. But in 1911, though they did not know it, the celibates were swimming against the tide.

It cannot be assumed that those spinsters who were defending their right not to engage in sexual intercourse with men, were sexually inactive. The attack on the spinster was integral to the attack on the lesbian. Whilst the 'spinster' and 'women's friendships' were respectable, then love between women could flourish in a variety of different forms. A new 'respectibility' was being created by the sex reformers, based upon a woman's enthusiastic participation in sexual intercourse in or out of marriage. New categories were being created based upon sexual contact. Instead of the married woman and the spinster, there were now the actively heterosexual woman and the lesbian.

In the period immediately before the First World War, the women's movement was deeply divided over the issue of sexuality. There can have been no other issue which so clearly separated feminists into two opposite camps whose ideas and practice were at total variance. Feminists were divided about the correct tactics for the suffrage struggle — some espoused and some eschewed violence against property. But at least there were degrees of militancy and the goal was the same. Between Kathryn Oliver and Stella Browne, over sexuality, there was not merely a difference of tactics but a difference of aim. One camp advocated the joys and necessity of heterosexual intercourse in or out of marriage without any serious attempt to criticise the form of male sexuality and its effects on women, presumably because such criticism would have detracted from the strength of their campaign. The other camp pointed out that many women received no joy from sexual intercourse, suggested that there were large differences of interest between men and women over the issue of sexuality, launched a major critique of the form of male sexuality, and advocated non-cooperation with the sexual desires of men.

It is important to remember here that many women in the latter group loved women and were involved in passionate relationships with their own sex. They did not identify themselves as lesbian either because this would have been seen as invalidating their ideas — lesbians within feminism today remain silent for like reasons — or because they did not see themselves as 'lesbians'. The sexological category of 'lesbian' was not yet accepted. Any attack on the spinster is inevitably an attack on the lesbian. Women's right to be lesbian depends upon our right to exist outside sexual relationships with men. When lesbians are stigmatised and reviled, so, also, are all women who live independently of men. In the following chapter we will look at how the anathematising of the lesbian developed from the work of the sexologists in the 1890s on to the 1920s.

CHAPTER 6

Women's Friendships and Lesbianism

In the eighteenth and early nineteenth centuries many middle-class women had relationships with each other which included passionate declarations of love, nights spent in bed together sharing kisses and intimacies, and lifelong devotion, without exciting the least adverse comment. Feminist historians have explained that the letters and diaries of middle-class women in America in the first half of the nineteenth century frequently contain references to a passionate same-sex friendship.[1] Lillian Faderman's book *Surpassing the Love of Men* details innumerable such friendships between women which met with such social approval that a woman could cheerfully write to the male fiancé of the woman she loved, saying that she felt exactly like a husband towards her and was going to be very jealous.[2] Women so involved with one another might, if they got married, refuse to be parted from their loved one, so that the husband would have to honeymoon with two women instead of one. Such friendships were seen by men as useful because they trained women in the ways of love in preparation for marriage.

These women wrote about their feelings to each other in ways which would nowadays seem quite inappropriate to same-sex friendship. Faderman describes the friendship between Jane Welsh Carlyle and the novelist and spinster Geraldine Jewsbury. Jewsbury sought to sustain her friend through her difficult marriage to the foul-tempered philosopher Thomas Carlyle. In their correspondence they expressed their passionate emotional attachment. The following extracts from Jewsbury's letters show how she felt:

O Carissima Mia . . . you are never out of either my head or my heart. After you left on Tuesday I felt so horribly wretched, too miserable even to cry, and what could be done? (July 1841); I love you my darling, more than I can express, more than I am conscious of myself, and yet I can do nothing for you. (October 29 1841); I love you more than anything else in the world. . . . It may do you no good now, but it may be a comfort some time, it will always be there for you. (May 1842); If I could see you and speak to you, I should have no tragic mood for a year to come, I think, and really that is saying no little, for I have had a strong inclination to hang myself oftener than once with the last month. (c.1843)[3]

Historians could not fail to notice the expression of such sentiments. They have tried to ignore them or explain them away so that they could not be allowed to challenge their heterosexual account of history. The commonest approach has been to say that such romantic expressions were simply the normal form of friendship at that time. They say that it was fashionable to be effusive. Precisely the same explanation has been given for the romantic emotional expression between men of the sixteenth century. In this way historians have tidied away what they found incongrous and wiped the history of homoeroticism from the slate of heterosexual history.

The American feminist historian Carroll Smith-Rosenberg has given passionate friendships between women the attention they deserve in her essay '*The Female World of Love and Ritual*'.[4] She does not underestimate the importance of passionate friendships but by concentrating on explaining why women might have found such friendships necessary at the time she implies that such expression between women is somehow deviant and needs more explanation than heterosexuality. She explains that such relationships between women were a vital support for women who were likely to marry virtual strangers, for whom they were unlikely to feel great emotional or physical attachment. She sees these women as having needed the comfort of female friends through the difficult and gruelling lives of constant childbearing. She explains that men and women were brought up in quite separate, homosocial worlds so that women were most likely to rely on same-sex relationships for support and nurturance. The implication of such an explanation might be that such same-sex friendships are obsolete today. It is not the existence of love between women that needs explaining but why women were permitted to love then in a way which would encounter fierce social disapproval now.

The feminist historians who have been uncovering these relationships have assumed that they were devoid of genital sexual expression on the grounds that the repression of women's genital sexuality in the nineteenth century would have made spontaneous genital expression unlikely. Whether or not these women expressed themselves genitally there is no doubt that physical excitement and eroticism played an important part in their love. This is clear from the way Sophia Jex-Blake describes her relationship with Octavia Hill in the following quotation from her diary of 1860. The two women are negotiating the spending of a holiday together:

> Told Octa about Wales, – sitting in her room on the table, my heart beating like a hammer. That Carry [Sophia's sister] wanted to go to Wales and I too, and most convenient about the beginning of July, so . . . 'Put off my visit?' said Octa. 'No, I was just going to say . . . if you wish to see anything of me, you must come too, I think and not put off the mountains until heaven.' She sunk her head on my lap silently, raised it in tears, and then such a kiss.[5]

It is not a platonic peck on the cheek which is being described here. On the grounds of the absence of genital contact alone, some contemporary feminist writers have sought to establish a clear distinction between these passionate friendships, even in the case of spinsters like Jex-Blake and Hill who were in passionate friendships with women all their lives, and 'lesbianism'.[6] Such a distinction is very difficult to draw. The conventions which govern the expression of erotic love may change, but the emotions and the physical excitement may have felt the same.

Today intense emotional and sensual interaction between women friends in the West is not seen as socially acceptable. Faderman illustrates this change with an experiment which was carried out at Palo Alto High School in 1973:

> For three weeks the girls behaved on campus as all romantic friends did in the previous century: They held hands often on campus walks, they sat with their arms around each other, and they exchanged kisses on the cheek when classes ended. They expressly did not intend to give the impression that their feelings were sexual. They touched each other only as close, affectionate

friends would. But despite their intentions, their peers
interpreted their relationship as lesbian and ostracised them.[7]

In contemporary society women are only expected to feel a
controlled and non-physical level of fondness for their women
friends and to wonder if they are 'lesbian' if they feel more. Why
and how did this change occur?

Faderman explains that women's same-sex friendships came to
be seen as a threat in the late nineteenth century as the women's
movement developed to challenge men's dominance and new
social and economic forces presented middle-class women with
the possibility of choosing not to marry and be dependent on men.
She sees the sexologists who classified and categorised female
homosexuality, including within it all passionate friendships, as
having played a major role in discouraging love between women
for all those who did not want to adopt the label of homosexual
ity. Another American feminist historian, Nancy Sahli, shows
how the outlawing of women's friendships was put into
operation.[8] In American women's colleges up until the late
nineteenth century, the practice of 'smashing', in which young
women would pursue their beloveds with gifts and declarations
until their feelings were returned and they were 'smashed' was
perfectly acceptable. These friendships were gradually outlawed
and rendered suspicious by college heads who were often living
with women they loved in passionate unions themselves. By the
1890s it was seen as necessary to root out these friendships as
unhealthy practices.

Lesbianism

As part of their self-imposed task of categorising varieties of
human sexual behaviour, the sexologists of the late nineteenth
century set about the 'scientific' description of lesbianism. Their
description has had a momentous effect on the ways in which we,
as women, have seen ourselves and all our relationships with
other women up until the present. They codified as 'scientific'
wisdom current myths about lesbian sexual practice, a stereotype
of the lesbian and the 'pseudohomosexual' woman, categorising
women's passionate friendships as female homosexuality and
offered explanations for the phenomenon. Male writers of gay
history have tended to see their work as sympathetic and helpful
to the development of a homosexual rights movement since they
explained male homosexuality in terms of innateness or used

psychoanalytic explanations which undermined the view of male homosexuality as criminal behaviour.[9] Female homosexual behaviour was never illegal in Britain, though there were attempts to make it so in 1921, so the sexologists' contribution cannot be seen as positive in that way.

Havelock Ellis provided a classic stereotype of the female homosexual in his *Sexual Inversion* (1897):

> When they still retain female garments, these usually show some traits of masculine simplicity, and there is nearly always a disdain for the petty feminine artifices of the toilet. Even when this is not obvious, there are all sorts of instinctive gestures and habits which may suggest to female acquaintances the remark that such a person 'ought to have been a man'. The brusque energetic movements, the attitude of the arms, the direct speech, the inflexions of the voice, the masculine straightforwardness and sense of honour, and especially the attitude towards men, free from any suggestion either of shyness or audacity, will often suggest the underlying psychic abnormality to a keen observer.
>
> In the habits not only is there frequently a pronounced taste for smoking cigarettes, often found in quite feminine women, but also a decided taste and toleration for cigars. There is also a dislike and sometimes incapacity for needlework and other domestic occupations, while there is some capacity for athletics.[10]

The importance of his description is that it classified as 'homosexual' precisely those forms of behaviour for which spinster feminists, the 'New Women' of the 1890s were criticised by anti-feminists. In the 1890s some women were trying to escape the 'effeminate' stereotype of woman. These feminists were neatly slotted into a picture of lesbian women who were really pseudo-men. Using the accusation of lesbianism to subvert women's attempts at emancipation is a form of attack with which women involved in the contemporary wave of feminism are all too familiar. Ellis's *Sexual Inversion* was the first volume in his *Studies in the Psychology of Sex*. Contemporary male gay historians have seen him as performing a service to male homosexuals by breaking down the stereotype that they were effeminate. For women the service he performed was quite the reverse.

Havelock Ellis was not the first to create such a stereotype of lesbians, and it could be argued that some lesbians at the time at which he was writing did have the characteristics he describes. None the less it is likely that the majority of women who loved women at that time, when there was a poorly developed lesbian sub-culture, did not. The masculine stereotype which provided a model for later generations of lesbians was not in wide circulation. Ellis included within his six case studies of lesbians, women who had had no overt sexual contact with other women, who were in fact involved in 'passionate friendships' which, as we have seen, were not previously considered bizarre or out of the common experience of women. He also included in the case studies his wife, Edith Lee Ellis, who does not seem from other descriptions, to have matched up to his stereotype.

Pseudohomosexuality

As a counterpart to the 'butch' masculine stereotype of the lesbian which the sexologists were creating, they provided a model for the 'pseudohomosexual'. They made it clear that their concern about the pseudohomosexual stemmed from what they saw as the spread of homosexuality within the feminist movement. Edward Carpenter expressed in 1897 his alarm at the phenomenon of lesbianism within the women's movement, combined with a quite obvious horror at the extent to which feminists were abandoning the constraints of the feminine sex role:

> [feminists were] naturally drawn from those in whom the sexual instinct is not preponderant. Such women do not altogether represent their sex; some are rather mannish in temperament; some are 'homogenic', that is inclined to attachments to their own sex rather than the opposite sex; such women are ultra-rationalising and brain-cultured; to many , children are more or less a bore; to others, man's sex-passion is a mere impertinence, which they do not understand, and whose place they consequently misjudge. It would not do to say that the majority of the new movement are out of line, but there is no doubt that a large number are; and the course of their progress will be correspondingly curvilinear.[11]

Edward Carpenter, like Havelock Ellis, is currently seen as a founding father of sexual enlightenment, and as a male homosexual who, in writing about men's love for each other positively, was an inspiration to the burgeoning male homosexual rights movement. In the light of his reputation as a homosexual revolutionary, as well as a friend to feminism, such comments on lesbians and feminists strike a rather discordant note. What they suggest, like the rest of his writings, is that his view of women's emancipation was that women should have equal rights so long as they remained different, feminine and passionately attached to men. The radical socialist circles in which Carpenter and Ellis moved in the 1890s, such as the 'Fellowship of the New Life', seem to have had a vision of womanhood similar to that of the 'emancipated', long-skirted and beaded 'hippy chick' of the late 1960s, for whom men were still supposed to be the pivot of existence.

Iwan Bloch is one of the three sexologists who, together with August Forel and Havelock Ellis, were pinpointed at the 1929 Sex Reform Congress in London as the founding fathers of sexology.[12] Bloch connects quite clearly the burgeoning of lesbianism in the women's movement and the 'problem' of 'pseudohomosexuality':

> there is no doubt that in the 'women's movement' – that is, in the movement directed towards the acquirement by women of all the attainments of masculine culture – homosexual women have played a notable part. Indeed according to one author, the 'Women's Question' is mainly the question regarding the destiny of virile homosexual women. . . . For the diffusion of pseudohomosexuality the Women's Movement is of great importance, as we shall see later.[13]

The pseudohomosexual was characterised as a woman who did not necessarily fit the masculine stereotype, had been seduced by a 'real homosexual' and led away from a natural heterosexuality, to which it was hoped that she would return. Real homosexuality was seen to be innate, and pseudohomosexuality a temporary divergence. Ellis described pseudohomosexuality as a 'spurious imitation':

> These unquestionable influences of modern movements cannot directly cause sexual inversion, but they develop the germs of it, and they probably cause a spurious imitation. This spurious imitation is due to the fact that the congenital anomaly occurs with special frequency in women of high intelligence who, voluntarily or involuntarily, influence others.[14]

The pseudohomosexual is shown to be not just easily led but intellectually inferior which should be enough to discourage women from 'imitation'. Bloch informs us that 'original' homosexuality is much less common amongst women than amongst men, 'Whereas in many women even at a comparatively advanced age, the so-called "pseudohomosexuality" is much more frequently met with than it is in men.'[15] This pious hope that women are somehow more innately heterosexual than men, he supports with the explanation that heterosexual women are inclined towards 'tenderness and caresses' which make it easy for 'pseudohomosexual tendencies' to arise.[16]

For Bloch, as for the other sexologists, male homosexuality was defined by genital contact and their lack of other kinds of physical contact with each other prevented men from straying from the heterosexual path. Through the defining of any physical caresses between women as 'pseudohomosexuality' by the sexologists, the isolation and stigmatising of lesbianism was accomplished, and women's friendships were impoverished by the suspicion cast upon any physical expression of emotion

What lesbians do in bed

In order to fit women's passionate friendships into the category of lesbianism, it was necessary to categorise the forms of physical expression quite usual in these relationships as homosexual behaviour. So Ellis asserted that the commonest form of sex practice between women was 'kissing and embracing' and that genital contact was rare:

> Homosexual passion in women finds more or less complete expression in kissing, sleeping together, and close embraces, as in what is sometimes called 'lying spoons' . . . mutual contact and friction of the sexual parts seems to be comparatively rare. . . . While the use of the clitoris is rare in homosexuality, the use of an artificial penis is by no means uncommon and very widespread.[17]

We notice that whilst describing the rarity of genital contact Ellis found it necessary to cite the use of the 'dildo'. The use of dildos is likely to have been as rare between women in the nineteenth century as it is in lesbian practice today. The use of dildos has always been a common motif of men's sexual fantasies about lesbians and figures largely in nineteenth-century male pornography, as it does today. It is probably from this source that Ellis derives his inspiration. It is possible that some of his other ideas, such as the masculine stereotype, which clearly does not derive from his case studies, come from a similar source. There are other examples in the sexological literature of men's sexual fantasies about lesbian sexuality. Krafft-Ebing invented a form of ejaculation for women: 'The intersexual gratification among these women seems to be reduced to kissing and embraces, which seems to satisfy those of weak sexual instinct, but produces in sexually neurasthenic females ejaculation.'[18] A form of ejaculation in women is another common motif of contemporary men's pornography.

Women defining themselves

One of Ellis's case studies illustrates how this confusion around self-definition was operating amongst women at the time that Ellis was writing. The case study is of a woman who specifically denied herself genital sexual expression with the woman she lived with and loved in order to avoid having to fit herself into the definition of homosexuality being offered in the sexological literature of the 1890s. She writes that her woman friend had been having a 'tryng time' and moved into her bed on the advice of a doctor so that she would not have to sleep alone:

> One night, however, when she had had a cruelly trying day and I wanted to find all ways of comforting her, I bared my breast for her to lie on. Afterwards it was clear that neither of us could be satisfied without this. . . . Much of this excitement was sexually localised, and I was haunted in the daytime by images of holding this woman in my arms. I noticed also that my inclination to caress my other women friends was not diminished, but increased. All this disturbed me a great deal. The homosexual practices of which I had read lately struck me as merely nasty; I could not imagine myself tempted to them.[19]

The woman continues by saying that she consulted an older man friend who advised her to be very careful and not give in to her impulses. She told her friend of her anxiety and of her decision, which was clearly to forego genital sexual expression. The friend was unhappy, none the less they went on sleeping together. The result is that they continued to have a passionate emotional and physical relationship which merely omitted genital contact:

> in the day when no one was there we sat as close together as we wished, which was very close. We kissed each other as often as we wanted to kiss each other, which was many times a day.

110

The results of this, so far as I can see, have been wholly good. We love each other warmly, but no temptation to nastiness has ever come, and I cannot see now that it is at all likely to come. With custom, the localised physical excitement has practically disappeared, and I am no longer obsessed by imagined embraces. The spiritual side of our affection seems to have grown steadily stronger and more profitable since the physical side has been allowed to take its natural place.[20]

This woman's precautions did protect her from being classified as a true invert in Ellis's studies. It would be interesting to see how contemporary lesbians would define this woman today. The case study demonstrates the effect which sexological literature was already having upon what was in the 1890s probably only the very small group of women who had access to this literature. These women were having to make choices and instead of living out their love for other women in whatever ways seemed appropriate to them, they had to decide whether they were female homosexuals or just friends.

The social and economic background

American lesbian feminist historians suggest that female homosexuality and all strong emotional expression between women was stigmatised by the sexologists in the late nineteenth and early twentieth century in response to a concatenation of social and economic circumstances which offered a real threat to men's domination over women.[21] Increased job opportunities for middle-class women in the steadily growing spheres of education, after the 1870 Education Act in Britain, in clerical work and shop work, provided opportunites for women to maintain themselves independently of men. Changes in social attitudes allowed for single women to live together outside their families without being regarded with suspicion. Suitable living space in the form of rooms and flatlets was becoming available in the 1890s. Here, a spinster novelist, Rhoda Broughton, looks back on her youth in the 1850s:

That a couple of girls would find an affinity in each other which their own family circle did not provide, and 'forsaking all other', betake themselves to a joint flat, to maintain which their own industries should furnish the means, was an idea which would have consigned the holder of it to Bedlam. For one thing, there were no flats, and if there had been, for any

111

female thing under fifty to occupy one without a chaperon would have condemned her to utter ostracism.[22]

A section in Radclyffe Hall's *The Unlit Lamp* in which she describes a circle of women engaged in passionate friendships with each other living in rooms in London in the 1890s, suggests that opportunities for women to live together existed at that time.

We have seen in the chapter on spinsters that the number of women in excess of men in the population was steadily rising in the last half of the nineteenth century. When this 'surplus' of women had the possibility of living and working outside the structures of heterosexuality they became a threat to the maintenance of men's control. This threat was particularly serious when independent women were engaged in passionate friendships with each other and were in a position to form a strong female network which could bond against men. It was this last danger that the development of a strong feminist movement appeared to be creating in the late nineteenth century. It is clear from the writings of the sexologists that they were far from enthusiastic about feminism, and particularly its lesbian manifestations. An attack upon passionate emotional involvement between women served to undermine the link between them and dilute their potential strength. As we have seen in the earlier part of this chapter, American historians of women's friendships have suggested that it was precisely women's lack of any possibility of an independent life which made their passionate friendships acceptable as no threat to the heterosexual structure in the early nineteenth century.

Explanations for lesbianism

Two explanations for homosexuality were advanced in the period. One form of explanation was to attribute homosexuality to a hereditary, unchangeable cause. Havelock Ellis saw homosexuality as innate, Krafft-Ebing cited a hereditary taint and Edward Carpenter favoured the theory of a third or intermediate sex. The other form of explanation, developed in the work of the psychoanalysts from Freud onwards, was to see homosexuality as a result of childhood trauma. Lillian Faderman explains how the first form of explanation was more attractive to lesbians in the period, because if offered no possibility of a 'cure', and attributed no blame or individual responsibility. She suggests that, as a result, those women who were determined to assume a lesbian identity, based upon the sexological definitions, could do so and demand public tolerance on the grounds that they could not help themselves. As an example of this process Faderman cites Radclyffe Hall's *The Well of Loneliness* as an impassioned plea for tolerance in which the heroine is fashioned into a 'masculine' homosexual as in Ellis's definition. In the novel, sexological works such as that of Ulrichs, which the heroine's father has read, enable him to have pity for his teenage daughter's condition. Radclyffe Hall makes it clear that she is making a public demand for this pity in the following last few words of the novel, in which Stephen addresses her dead father:

> You knew! All the time you knew this thing, but because of your pity you wouldn't tell me. Oh, Father – and there are so many of us – thousands of miserable unwanted people who have no right to love, no right to compassion because they are maimed, hideously maimed and ugly. God's cruel; He let us get flawed in the making.[23]

Some historians suggest that explanations in the form of innateness helped in the formation of a proud self-conscious homosexual sub-culture in the post-First World War period. But we must remember that the necessity for this form of 'defence' was the result of the sexologists' work in stigmatising and isolating the lesbian in the first place.

The lesbian amendment
The changing climate in attitudes to lesbianism is illustrated by the way in which female homosexuality was almost made illegal in 1921. An amendment to the bill to make the age of consent 16 for indecent assault was added in committee and subsequently passed in the house. The amendment read as follows: 'Any act of gross indecency between female persons shall be a misdemeanour and punishable in the same manner as any such act committed by male persons under section 11 of the Criminal Law Amendment Act 1885.'[24]

The amendment failed to pass into law because the bill to which it was attached was an 'agreed' bill, meaning that the government would only find time for it if it was not significantly altered. The amendment destroyed the bill. The debate gives us an opportunity to sample the attitudes of MPs towards lesbianism at this time. All who spoke purported to be equally disturbed at having to mention such a noxious subject, and they were united in their condemnation. Those who opposed the amendment did so on the grounds that making lesbianism illegal would only spread the offence by giving it publicity. Colonel Wedgwood declared, 'it is a beastly subject, and it is being better advertised by the moving of this Clause than in any other way.'[25] Lieutenant Moore-Brabazon suggested that there were three possible ways of dealing with the 'pervert'. The death penalty would 'stamp them out', and locking them up as lunatics would 'get rid of them' but the third way, ignoring them, was best:

> The third way is to leave them entirely alone, not notice them, not advertise them. That is the method that has been adopted in England for many hundred years, and I believe that it is the best method now, these cases are self-exterminating. They are examples of ultra-civilisation, but they have the merit of exterminating themselves, and consequently they do not spread or do very much harm to society at large. . . . To adopt a Clause of this kind would harm by introducing into the minds of perfectly innocent people the most revolting thoughts.[26]

Lesbianism, then, did not escape legal penalty in Britain for so long simply because of Queen Victoria's fabled refusal to believe lesbians existed, or because the legislature regarded lesbianism as less 'beastly' than male homosexuality. Lesbianism was an alarming phenomenon to these MPs because they thought it would spread like wildfire if women even heard of it. Silence, and every attempt to make lesbianism invisible, was the only effective weapon.

One reason the MPs gave for the great dangerousness of lesbianism was its purported role in destroying civilisations:

> These moral weaknesses date back to the very origin of history, and when they grow and become prevalent in any nation or in any country, it is the beginning of the nation's downfall. The falling away of feminine morality was to a large extent the cause of the destruction of the early Greek civilisation, and still more the cause of the downfall of the Roman Empire.[27]

It could, according to another MP, cause 'our race to decline'.[28] Another reason given was the danger posed to husbands who might lose their wives to the 'wiles' of the lesbian. Most cogent of all was the fact that lesbianism 'saps the fundamental institutions of society' since 'any woman who indulges in this vice will have nothing whatever to do with the other sex'.[29] The MPs were aware that the spread of lesbianism could undermine the institutions of marriage and the heterosexual family through which male dominance over women was maintained.

It would be a shame to leave this debate without mentioning the great solicitude shown by ex-public school MPs towards their colleagues in the Labour party. Colonel Wedgwood explained, 'I do not suppose that there are any members of the Labour party who know in the least what is intended by the Clause.'[30] Wedgwood claimed that they would not know because they would not have studied the classics, and it was only from such study that MPs could know anything of homosexuality.

The women sex reformers and lesbianism

Stella Browne and Marie Stopes are two women who are recognised as having made very significant contributions to the history of sex reform. Stella Browne was a socialist feminist who campaigned for birth control and abortion from the period immediately before the First World War to the 1930s. She was a member of the British Society for the Study of Sex Psychology founded in 1914, and involved with what is regarded by some historians, like Sheila Rowbotham, as the radical, progressive wing of the sex reform movement.[31] Marie Stopes began her carreer in the writing of sex advice books and the promotion of birth control information with the publication of *Married Love* in 1918. Both women helped to popularise the ideas of the male sex reformers. Stella Browne constantly reiterates her debt to Havelock Ellis. Marie Stopes engaged in a detailed study of sexological literature in the British Museum before writing *Married Love*. They both promoted an ideal of heterosexual love which fitted the sexological prescriptions. The promotion of heterosexuality by sex advice writers was invariably combined with the stigmatising of lesbianism. If women were to be encouraged into active participation in heterosexual sex then they had to be persuaded that there was no reasonable alternative by the negative portrayal of love between women. Stopes and Browne both exhibited great anxiety about lesbianism and sought, with great difficulty, to distinguish between innocent affectionate friendships and inversion. There are indications that both these women had experience of passionate friendships with women which they felt forced to redefine or reject when they adopted the ideology of the male sexologists.

Browne's paper 'The Sexual Variety and Variability among Women' is described by Sheila Rowbotham as having a 'very modern relevance in what she says about love and women's sexual feelings'.[32] Her discussion of lesbianism is described as 'dated' and much to be expected in its 'specific historical context'. In fact the promotion of heterosex to women in which Browne was involved required the denigration of lesbianism. The two cannot be separated and both emerged from a 'specific historical context'. Then, as now, the construction of compulsory heterosexuality for women has been based upon the stigmatising of lesbianism. Browne distinguished between pseudohomosexuality and real lesbianism: 'Artificial or substitute homosexuality – as distinct from true inversion – is very widely diffused among women, as a result of the repression of normal gratification and the segregation of the sexes, which still largely obtains.'[33] She further distinguished between pseudohomosexuality, which she went so far as to say might be 'entirely platonic', and 'true affectionate friendship' between women: 'Sometimes its only direct manifestations are quite noncommittal and platonic but even this incomplete and timid homosexuality can always be distinguished from true affectionate friendship between women, by its jealous, exacting and extravagant tone.'[34] Browne gives women a clue about how to classify the nature of their feelings for other women. Homosexual love is 'jealous, exacting and extravagant', i.e. unpleasant. She offers no clearer distinction and it would not be surprising if women remained confused. The dividing line between friendship and pseudohomosexuality is clearly artificial given that pseudohomosexuality can be 'platonic' anyway. She compounds the confusion by saying that women need not doubt their heterosexuality even if they experience no attraction towards men until late in life and have felt devotion and intense desire for women friends:

> Also many women of quite normally directed [heterosexual] inclinations, realise in mature life, when they have experienced passion, that the devoted admiration and friendship they felt for certain girl friends, had a real, though perfectly unconscious, spark of desire in its exaltation and intensity; an unmistakable, indefinable note, which was absolutely lacking in many equally sincere and lasting friendships.[35]

It is possible to infer from the way in which Browne writes about passionate friendships between women that her sympathetic knowledge comes from her own experience. If Browne did have such relationships and felt it necessary to repudiate them in the light of the stigmatising of lesbianism and the promotion of the heterosexual imperative by male sexologists such as Ellis, this would explain the extravagance of her anti-lesbianism. She was determined that women should have 'real' love only for men and her own possible guilt and ambivalence might have led her to overcompensate in favour of men:

> Careful observation and many confidences from members of my own sex, have convinced me that our maintenance of outworn traditions is manufacturing habitual auto-erotists and perverts, out of women who would instinctively prefer the love of a man, who would bring them sympathy and comprehension as well as desire. I repudiate all wish to depreciate or slight the love-life of the real homosexual; but it cannot be advisable to force the growth of that habit in heterosexual people.[36]

She backs up her assertion that women require men with a list of the dreadful physical consequences which will befall them if they are independent:

> I would even say that after twenty-five, the woman who has neither husband nor lover and is not under-vitalised and sexually deficient, is suffering mentally and bodily – often without knowing why she suffers; nervous, irritated, anaemic, always tired, or ruthlessly fussing over trifles; or else she has other consolations, which make her so-called 'chastity' a pernicious sham.[37]

Stella Browne remained interested in lesbianism after the war. In 1924 she presented a paper to the British Society for the Study of Sex Psychology entitled 'Studies in Feminine Inversion'. This fascinating paper tends to confirm that Browne had experience of homosexuality. She explains that her case studies 'would probably be much more illuminating had they been recorded by an observer who was herself entirely or predominantly homosexual'.[38] The careful wording here leaves plenty of room for Browne to see herself as at least partly homosexual. She describes the five cases, four single and one couple, as well-known to her, and since she did not have clients and was not in the medical profession, it is tempting to conclude that these women were her friends or at least close acquaintances.

She assumed that most of her subjects did not engage in genital sexual expression or see themselves as homosexual. The evidence she advanced for these women's homosexuality was in some cases bizarre and did not include any suggestion of emotional let alone physical feelings for women. Case D is labelled homosexual because of her appearance and habits and because she was fond of children. She is described as follows:

A decided turn for carpentry, mechanics and executive manual work. Not tall; slim, boyish figure; very hard, strong muscles, singularly impassive face, with big magnetic eyes. The dominating tendency is very strong here, and is not held in leash by a high standard of either delicacy or principle.[39]

Her fondness for children which one might have expected to be used to prove her maternalism and absence of homosexuality, is here used, rather surprisingly, to demonstrate that she is homosexual:

Is professionally associated with children and young girls, and shows her innate homosexual tendency by excess of petting and spoiling, and intense jealousy of any other person's contact with, or interest in the children. I do not definitely know if there is any physical expression of her feelings, beyond the kissing and embracing which is normal, and even, in some cases conventional, between women or between women and children. But the *emotional tone* is quite unmistakable; will rave for hours over some 'lovely kiddy', and injure the children's own best interests, as well as the working of the establishment, by unreasonable and unfair indulgence.[40]

Browne seems here to be confusing lesbians with child molesters.

Browne was prepared to go further than any other writers of her time in prescribing that these women should engage in overt sexual expression with other women. But what looks at first sight like a radical and progressive suggestion, turns out on examination to be based on Browne's horror of feminists, particularly their lack of enthusiasm for heterosexual sex, and on her fear that lack of genital sex caused women to be hostile to men. She wrote of the dangers of repression thus:

No one who has observed the repressed inverted impulse flaring into sex-antagonism, or masked as the devotion of daughter or cousin, or the solicitude of teacher or nurse, or perverted into the cheap, malignant cant of conventional moral indignation, can deny its force.[41]

Suffragists were singled out for attack. 'I am sure that much of the towering spiritual arrogance which is found, e.g. in many high places in the Suffrage movement . . . is really unconscious inversion.'[42] She thought that it was repressed inversion which fuelled feminism, and that the women's feminist zeal would be undermined if they had sexually fulfilling relationships with each other.

Browne remained seriously confused about lesbianism. At one point in the article she writes of 'inverted impulse': 'Let us recognise this force, as frankly as we recognise and reverence the love between men and women.' In the neighbouring paragraph she rails against the social pressures, i.e. the 'repression and degradation of the normal erotic impulse' which forced women of 'strong passions and fine brains' into relationships with women which were 'makeshifts and essentially substitutes, which cannot replace the vital contact, mental and bodily, with congenial men'.[43] It seems that Browne was in a real agony of mind. She was unable to condemn love affairs between women, perhaps because she was one of the women of 'fine brains' who were forced into them, but she saw them as really inferior to heterosexuality. She could only justify such relationships on the grounds that genital contact was involved so that they might serve to undermine the aggressive feminism which she saw as based on women's frigidity.

Marie Stopes was a fervent missionary in the cause of heterosexual love and sex. Her biographer, Ruth Hall, shows her importance, by pointing out that her most famous book *Married Love* was accorded sixteenth place out of twenty-five in a list of the most influential books of the previous fifty years by a group of American academics in 1935. It was placed just behind *Das Kapital* and Ellis's *Psychology of Sex* but ahead of Einstein's *Relativity*, Freud's *Interpretation of Dreams* and Hitler's *Mein Kampf*. Stopes invested heterosexual sex and specifically sexual intercourse, with mystical, religious exultation in a book she wrote when she had not even experienced sexual intercourse herself (*Married Love*). One might well be tempted to think that the lady did protest too much. Ruth Hall points out that Marie was indifferent to men and formed intense emotional relations with women until well into adult life. Hall suggests that her vigorous repudiation of homosexuality in all its forms in her writings resulted from a flight from her own inclinations:

> Her attraction towards other women remained for at least
> part of her adult life, making still more difficult the
> establishment of normal relationships with men, and resulting
> in a total rejection of homosexuality either male or female, all
> the more violent for her own unacknowledged penchant.[44]

Married Love was written after Stopes engaged in a detailed study
of sexological literature through which she hoped to find the
answer to the frustrations she felt in her unconsummated marriage. From that literature she would have received an alarming
picture of the dangers of intense female friendship from the
sexologists' classifications and vilifying of lesbianism.

Stopes exposed the intensity of her anxiety about lesbianism in
Enduring Passion in 1928. She was worried because she believed
women would prefer lesbian sex if they tried it, and might
abondon their marriages:

> If a married woman does this unnatural thing she may find a
> growing disappointment in her husband and he may lose all
> natural power to play his proper part. . . . No woman who
> values the peace of her home and the love of her husband
> should yield to the wiles of the lesbian whatever her
> temptation to do so.[45]

She considered that lesbianism was spreading, especially among
'independent' women, and was moved to exclaim, 'This corruption spreads as an underground fire spreads in the peaty soil of a
dry moorland.'[46] Having already admitted the strong and possibly superior attractions of lesbian sex, she was forced to find a
reason for the importance of sexual intercourse which had nothing to do with enjoyment. Stopes believed, though no scientific
proof was forthcoming for her hypothesis, that secretions from
the man's penis were necessary to women's bodily health, and
that these passed through the walls of the vagina during sexual
intercourse. She explained, 'The bedrock objection to it [lesbian-
ism] is surely that women can only *play* with each other and
cannot in the very nature of things have natural union or supply
each other with the seminal or prostatic secretions they ought to
have.'[47] This was bad news for celibate women and women
whose male lovers wore condoms as well as for lesbians. Stopes
was forced to invent a mythical dependence of women on sexual
intercourse for their physical health for want of any more cogent

arguments against lesbianism. Women were asked to have faith and carry on with heterosexuality.

The writings of Stella Browne and Marie Stopes, since they are by women at a time when the vast majority of literature prescribing how women should relate to men was by men, could be seen as validating the prescription of the sexologists. Stopes and Browne could be regarded as promoting what women 'really' wanted, what was 'really' in women's interests. This cannot be a realistic picture. They were writing at a time which was a watershed in the history of the construction of women's sexuality. It was a time when the male sexologists were calling upon women to repudiate their love for each other and pour their energies into men. Browne and Stopes form part of a generation of women who had to twist themselves into knots by rejecting their own experience of loving women. From this time on the sex reformers would have had a less difficult task. In later generations women's love for women would not appear as a conceivable choice, which they would then have to reject.

Women's friendships and lesbianism in British novels in the 1920s

As with any other set of ideas, there seems to have been a gap between the promotion of sexological theories on lesbianism and their filtering across to a more general readership. Some 1920s novels by women indicate that this was the period in which these ideas gained public acceptance. What we see in 1920s novels is a process by which passionate friendship between women, which was still being written about as unexceptional in the early 1920s is transformed by the intrusion of the lesbian stereotype. Radclyffe Hall's *The Unlit Lamp* (1924) and Winifred Holtby's *The Crowded Street* (1924) have as their theme the plight of middle-class unmarried daughters who seek to escape the stifling atmosphere of the family and find some means of personal fulfilment. In both books the spinster heroines engage in passionate friendships with other women. The most powerful and lengthy of such relationships is that between Joan and Elizabeth described in *The Unlit Lamp*. The relationship remained unfulfilled in terms of commitment because, despite Elizabeth's efforts, she cannot separate Joan from her mother in order to live with her. The relationship is described as one of intense emotional attachment, which includes physical caresses. There is no suggestion in the novel that any genital sex took place. Neither of the main characters is described in terms of the masculine stereotype, though in one minor scene where the heroines are visiting Joan's sister in London where she is involved in a circle of women living in rooms and engaged in passionate relationships with each other, a minor character, imbued with some of the characteristics of that stereotype, is portrayed.

In *The Crowded Street* Muriel becomes passionately attached to a school friend Clare, although the attachment is not reciprocated, and Clare eventually marries. Holtby indicates her awareness of the social constraints that were developing to create a climate in which passionate friendships between women were regarded with suspicion. Muriel comments:

> The world was alright. It was she who was wrong, caring for all the wrong things. She could not, however hard she tried, stop herself from loving Clare, though passionate friendships between girls had been firmly discouraged by the sensible Mrs Hancock.[48]

Mrs Hancock, the Headmistress, is described here as reacting towards girls' friendships in the same way as the Principals of United States colleges are described as implementing a changed attitude in the 1890s.[49] Mrs Hancock's reasons are described thus:

> Their intimacy, she considered, was usually silly and frequently disastrous. If carried too far, it even wrecked all hope of matrimony without offering any satisfaction in return. Love was a useful emotion ordained by God and regulated by society for the propagation of the species; or else it inspired sometimes the devotion of a daughter to a mother, or a parent to a child. It could even be extended to a relative, such as a cousin or an aunt. Or in a somewhat diluted form it might embrace Humanity, engendering a vague Joan-of-Arc-Florence-Nightingale-Mrs-Beecher-Stowish philanthropy, to which Muriel aspired faintly, but without much hope of realisation.[50]

These sentiments indicate how far removed the attitudes of the early 1920s were from the early nineteenth century acceptance that love between two women was good and proper and to be admired, and might even be expected to help a young woman by training her in love which she could then direct to a man. Muriel's conclusion rules out for her the possibility of strong emotional attachment to women: 'But love between two girls was silly sentiment. By loving Clare, Muriel knew that she had been guilty of extreme foolishness. And she wanted so much to be good.'[51]

Muriel continues throughout the novel to be unable to develop any strong involvement with men. At the end she is rescued from her family and sterile spinsterhood by what is portrayed as simply a friendship with another woman, based on practical arrangements. Muriel moves to London to keep house for Delia and the novel ends with both women engaged on fulfilling political careers.

Both novels depict passionate friendships between women and give some indication of how social attitudes were beginning to change. What is significant about both of them is the absence of a lesbian stereotype, and in Hall's novel in particular, the 'innocent' pleasure of the relationship between Joan and Elizabeth. Holtby's novel is directly related to what was happening in the world outside the novels. Holtby acknowledges in the introduction to the book that the relationship between Muriel and Delia reflects her own relationship with Vera Brittain, with whom she lived for several years. It is clear from Vera Brittain's account of her friendship with Holtby that Winifred loved her very much and was desolated by Vera's marriage.[52] Holtby's feelings about Vera are made clear in the letter she sent shortly after Vera's marriage in 1924:

> I am happy. In a way I suppose I miss you but that does not make me less happy. . . . I find you in all small and lovely things; in the little fishes like flames in the green water, in the furred and stupid softness of bumble-bees fat as laughter, in all the chiming radiance of warmth and light and scent in the summer garden. . . . When a person that one loves is in the world, then to miss them is only a new flavour, a salt sharpness in experience. It is when the beloved is unhappy or maimed or troubled that one misses with pain. But even pain is perhaps not wholly undesirable.[53]

In her book *Testament of Friendship*, which she wrote after Holtby's untimely death, Vera Brittain sets out to stress the importance and intensity of her relationship with Winifred. Because of the suspicions which had accumulated by the time of writing (1940) around the whole idea of women's friendships, she finds it necessary to deny quite explicitly that she and Winifred were involved in a lesbian relationship:

Those years with Winifred taught me that the type of friendship which reaches its apotheosis in the story of David and Jonathan is not a monopoly of the masculine sex. Hitherto, perhaps owing to a lack of women recorders, this fact has been found difficult to accept by men, and even by other women. Some feminine individualists believe they flatter men by fostering the fiction of women's jealous inability to love and respect one another. Other sceptics are roused by any record of affection between women to suspicions habitual among the over-sophisticated.

'Too, *too* Chelsea!' Winifred would comment amiably in after years when some zealous friend related the newest legend current about us in the neighbourhood.[54]

David and Jonathan have been reclaimed by contemporary gay men as homosexual lovers. We can only surmise that Vera Brittain made no such assumption. She saw their relationship as the epitome of innocent friendship, and is careful to record her own scorn and that of Winifred of the 'suspicions' of the 'over-sophisticated', which were presumably that the two women were lesbian.

Rosamund Lehmann's novel *Dusty Answer* (1927) provides us with an interesting halfway house. It portrays a passionate emotional involvement between two young women, Jennifer and Judith, who engage in physical caresses and who are obviously 'in love' with each other. The young women are portrayed as reluctant to make a formal acknowledgement of their love affair. This relationship is interrupted by the intrusion of Geraldine, who casts the spell of explicit sexual attraction over Jennifer, and sweeps her away into a lesbian affair. Geraldine is described according to a stereotype of the masculine, powerful, and slightly wicked lesbian. Judith describes her thus:

At last it confronted her, the silent-looking face, watching behind its narrowed eyes. The hair was black, short, brushed straight back from the forehead, leaving small beautiful ears exposed. The heavy eyebrows came low and level on the low broad brow; the eyes were long slits, dark-circled, the cheeks were pale, the jaw heavy and masculine. All the meaning of the face was concentrated in the mouth, the strange wide lips laid rather flat on the face, sulky, passionate, weary, eager. She was not a young girl. It was the face of a woman of thirty or more; but in years she might have been younger. She was tall, deep-breasted, with long, heavy but shapely limbs. She wore a black frock and a pearl necklace, and large pearl earrings. . . . Her voice was an insolent voice.[55]

It is made clear that Geraldine is a 'real' lesbian. It is significant that she is described as having irresistible and dangerous powers of attraction which bring Judith also under her spell:

That broad heavy face and thick neck, those coarse and masculine features, that hothouse skin; what taste Jennifer must have to find her attractive! . . . Oh no, it was no good saying that. In spite of all, she was beautiful; her person held an appalling fascination.[56]

Thus a stark contrast is drawn between 'innocent' friendship and lesbianism. The book could even be seen as providing us with the moral that too intense an involvement might lead to the danger of succumbing to the repulsive and appalling powers of a 'real' lesbian. Lesbianism is not seen as a positive choice for Jennifer. She suffers a breakdown and drops out of university under Geraldine's influence.

The culmination of this process of differentiating between innocent friendship between women and fully fledged lesbianism according to the sexological prescription occurs in Radclyffe Hall's *The Well of Loneliness* (1928). The book follows so closely the sexological writings, that we are presented with not only a carefully crafted masculine stereotype of a lesbian in Stephen, but also a model of the 'pseudohomosexual' in Mary Llewellyn. Mary is never attributed any of the characteristics of the masculine stereotype. She is gentle and feminine. Stephen has to renounce her love for Mary after the onset of their affair. She arranges for a man to court Mary and carry her off. This is all done to protect her from the horrors of the lesbian sub-culture. Mary is shown to be not a 'real' congenital lesbian, but a basically heterosexual woman who is temporarily diverted from her path. She falls in love with a woman who is depicted as a substitute man. The book shows how the cogenital versus pseudolesbian distinction could rigidify in later years into the stereotypical roles of butch and femme.

Writers like Havelock Ellis and Stella Browne saw themselves as progressive in their attempts to separate off lesbianism, which included passionate friendship, from 'innocent' women's friendships. Once lesbianism was an isolated phenomenon it provided a much clearer target for attack and by the early 1930s the climate for women's love was becoming increasingly hostile. *Loveliest of Friends* (1931) by G. Sheila Donisthorpe, an American novel, seems to have been popular in Britain, and went through three editions here in as many months. In the novel the innocent Audrey becomes involved in a passionate and exciting relationship with Kim. Very soon it turns sour and Audrey twice attempts suicide. At the end of the book, when the affair is over, Donisthorpe turns to pure propaganda and concludes, about the forsaken Audrey:

> This, then, is the product of lesbianism. This the result of dipping the fingers of vice into a sex-welter whose deadly force crucifies in a slow, eternal bleeding.
>
> And yet there are those who hug as a martyrdom these sadistic habits, who clamour for the recognition of the sinister group who practise them, those crooked, twisted freaks of Nature who stagnate in dark and muddy waters, and are so choked with the weeds of viciousness and selfish lust that, drained of all pity, they regard their victims as mere stepping stones to their further pleasure. With flower-sweet finger-tips they crush the grape of evil till it is exquisite, smooth and luscious to the taste, stirring up a subconscious responsiveness, intensifying all that has been, all that follows, leaving their prey gibbering, writhing, sex-sodden shadows of their former selves, conscious of only one ambition, one desire in mind and body, which, ever festering, ever destroying, slowly saps them of health and sanity.[57]

To make the message absolutely clear, the dedication of the book reads 'To all the contemplating Audreys of this world the message in this book is offered'.

Through looking at novels by and about women, we can see the effect which the sexological injunctions were having on women's relationships with each other. Once women's relationships might have spanned a continuum from casual friendship through intense emotional and physical involvement, to, in those cases where it seemed appropriate to the women concerned, relationships involving both lifelong commitment and genital sex. By the late 1920s a distinction had been clearly drawn between an acceptable level of friendship and lesbianism. The middle ground had been cut out. Women were no longer in a position to engage in passionate involvements with each other without being aware that they were on the edge of a precipice which might plunge them into the stigmatised world of the lesbian. Women's novels later than the 1920s do not provide us with portraits of love between women which is devoid of suspicion until the advent of lesbian feminist writing in the 1970s.

CHAPTER 7

Antifeminism and Sex Reform before the First World War

The birth of sexology in the period from the 1890s to the First World War enabled antifeminists to mount an onslaught upon feminism with all the authority of 'science'. The claims of 'science' were still relatively new and there was no healthy scepticism abroad to protect women from 'scientific' assertions. The introduction to the printed papers of the 1929 Sex Reform Congress, cites Havelock Ellis, Iwan Bloch and August Forel as the founding fathers of the new 'science' of sexology.[1] The work of the sexologists and their popularisers introduced a whole new way of thinking and talking about sex. The superstitions and prejudices of the sexologists were given, under the cloak of science, a spurious objectivity. Their ideas were directly at variance with those of the feminists involved in the campaign to challenge the construction of male sexuality.

The works of Havelock Ellis are an example of the way in which sexology undermined feminism. His work is important because of its fundamental influence on British sex advice literature throughout the twentieth century.[2] In his lifetime he had an international reputation and was widely quoted and referenced by sexologists in Europe and America. He is presently being reclaimed as a guru of the sexual revolution by contemporary historians and commentators. He has been given the reputation of a sexual revolutionary. Edward Brecher writes of 'the first of the yea-sayers' who inaugurated 'the gradual convalescence of our culture from a debilitating sexual disease'.[3] Ellis's biographer, Phyllis Grosskurth, described him as 'one of the seminal figures responsible for the creation of a modern sensibility'.[4] Jeff Weeks writes, 'His work is one of the springs from which the broad stream of sexual liberalism has flowed with apparent ease.'[5] As the mythology of the sexual revolution was created, Ellis was given the reputation of having attacked and made inroads into the puritan sexual morality of the nineteenth century, for having proclaimed that sex was good and enjoyable, for having destroyed the myth of woman's sexual anaesthesia and for having established her right to pleasure. From a feminist perspective his contribution does not look so positive. Ellis promoted three ideas which were to be crucially important in the debate around sexuality in the early twentieth century. He did not invent these ideas. Lillian Faderman explains in her book *Surpassing the Love of Men* (1981) that the sexologists incorporated in their work ideas which had been staple motifs of men's pornography for centuries.[6] Ellis's views can be recognised as staples of antifeminist ideology today.

The first of these ideas was Ellis's assertion that there were innate biological differences between the sexes, particularly in the area of sexuality, which were immutable. The second was to prescribe that sexual relations between women and men should take the form of male dominance and female submission. The third was to create an ideology of the 'ideal' woman, which was represented as a form of feminism, and consisted of the glorification of motherhood.

The assertion of innate biological differences formed the bedrock for his later work, and they were explained in his first substantial work *Man and Woman* in 1894. In his introduction to the 1934 edition he explained that the book: 'Was put forward as the study of the secondary sexual characters intended to clear the ground, and so act as an introduction, for the seven volumes of the *Studies in the Psychology of Sex*.'[7] After examining the evidence for sex differences in what purported to be an objective fashion, Ellis was able to conclude:

> Woman's special sphere is the bearing and the rearing of children, with the care of human life in the home. Man's primary sphere remains the exploration of life outside the home, in industry and inventions and the cultivation of the arts.[8]

In this way Ellis was able to justify the status quo and raise a serious obstacle for those feminists and spinsters who had been working for fifty years to break down the idea that there should be separate spheres for men and women. Since the very basis of Ellis's work was in contradiction to the principles of feminism, it

129

should not surprise us to discover that the whole force of the sexual philosophy that he promoted was to be a sledgehammer blow at the heart of women's movement for emancipation.

Ellis carried his idea of innate differences straight into the realm of sexual behaviour, saying that man was sexually active and woman passive. His explanation of the form taken by male/female sexual relations is an evolutionary one rather than a strictly biological one. He writes that the courtship behaviour of early humans, like that of animals and birds, arose from the needs of reproduction. Ellis explained that contemporary sexual relations were simply a continuation of this process:

> the primary part of the female in courtship is the playful, yet serious, assumption of the role of a hunted animal who lures on the pursuer, not with the object of escaping, but with the object of being finally caught . . . [the male] will display his energy and skill to capture the female or to arouse in her an emotional condition which leads her to surrender herself to him, this process at the same time heightening his own excitement.[9]

Ellis has been seen as a sexual enlightener because he asserted not merely woman's capacity, but also her right to sexual pleasure.[10] But the form of pleasure which woman was to recieve was strictly circumscribed. In courtship she must be hunted, must be captured and surrender. In sexual activity itself she must be entirely passive. The male was to practise foreplay upon her until she was aroused and then sexual intercourse was to take place: 'the woman's part is, even biologically, on the surface the more passive part. She is, on the physical side, inevitably the instrument in love; it must be his hand and his bow which evoke the music.'[11]

The notion of foreplay, called by Ellis the 'art of love', was to provide the rationale for twentieth-century sex advice literature. Behind it lies the idea that women are rather slow and difficult in terms of sexual arousal, and that complex techniques had to be mastered by the man. These techniques, for preparing the woman for the man's preferred sex practice of sexual intercourse, are still the stuff of contemporary sex manuals. In Ellis's case it is particularly surprising that he should have laid such great stress on sexual intercourse being the main event in sexual interaction since he seems to have found that particular practice very difficult, if not impossible, himself. His preference was urolagnia, i.e. gaining pleasure from watching a woman urinate as an end in itself. His sexual preference is clear from his autobiography.[12] He wrote a eulogy to urolagnia in poetic form which contains the immortal lines:

> My lady once leapt sudden from the bed,
>> Whereon she naked lay beside my heart,
>> And stood with perfect poise, straight legs apart,
> And then from clustered hair of brownish red
> A wondrous fountain curve, all shyness fled,
>> Arched like a liquid rainbow in the air,
>> She cares not, she, what other women care,
> But gazed as it fell and faltered and was shed.[13]

Ellis pronounced that aggression was an innate part of sexuality. This is an idea that dies hard. It is a crucial motif of that bible of the most recent wave of the 'sexual revolution', Alex Comfort's *Joy of Sex* (1973). Comfort quotes Ellis in the 'bondage' section of the book which seeks to reassure women that being tied up and gagged for a man's sexual pleasure is a normal enjoyable part of sexual interaction: 'Any restraint upon muscular and emotional activity generally', wrote Havelock Ellis, 'tends to heighten the state of sexual excitement.'[14] Ellis stated that it was almost or quite normal for men to take pleasure in inflicting pain upon women, and 'certainly normal' for women to delight in experiencing pain:

> While in men it is possible to trace a tendency to inflict pain, or the simulacrum of pain, on the women they love, it is still easier to trace in women a delight in experiencing physical pain when inflicted by a lover, and an eagerness to accept submission to his will. Such a tendency is certainly normal.[15]

The examples he gave to support the idea that women enjoyed receiving pain included cases of women enjoying, according to Ellis, being battered by their husbands in Russia, Hungary, amongst the Indians of South America and in the East End of London, along with cases of French prostitutes who 'enjoyed' being beaten up by their pimps.

Ellis's conclusions did not go unchallenged. He explained that he was able to write in such detail about women's feelings because so many women were in correspondence with him telling him precisely what they felt. The women who wrote to him were representative of women in general, he said, unlike the women who wrote books, who were not. He quotes copiously from his women correspondents and on one occasion from one who plainly disagreed. She admitted to masochistic fantasies but asserted that the idea of pain was very different from its actuality, whereas men, she considered, actually wanted to inflict pain:

> As regards physical pain, though the idea of it is sometimes exciting, I think the reality is the reverse. A very slight amount of pain destroys my pleasure completely. . . . No woman has ever told me that she would like to have pain inflicted on her. On the other hand, the desire to inflict pain seems almost universal among men. I have only met one man in whom I have never at any time been able to detect it. . . . Perhaps a woman's readiness to submit to pain to please a man may sometimes be taken for pleasure in it. Even when women like the idea of pain, I fancy it is only because it implies subjection to the man, from the association with the fact that physical pleasure must necessarily be preceded by submission to this will.[16]

Ellis does not demur. His conclusion is still 'That the idea or even the reality of pain in sexual emotion is welcomed by women,' so long as the pain was small in amount and subordinate to the pleasure which was to follow.[17] To illustrate the point he mentioned an anecdote of the nymphomaniac who had an orgasm when the knife passed through her clitoris, presumably during a clitoridectomy operation designed to cure her 'nymphomania'.

Ellis, who professed himself to be pro-feminist, proclaimed that the differences between men and women, particularly that of woman's masochism, did not interfere in the least with her capacity for emancipation. He seems to have been hurt by the fact that feminists insisted on quarrelling with his conclusions and defends himself thus:

> I am well aware that in thus asserting a certain tendency in women to delight in suffering pain – however careful and qualified the position I have taken – many estimable people will cry out that I am degrading a whole sex and generally supporting the 'subjection of women'. But the day for academic discussion concerning the 'subjection of women' has gone by. The tendency I have sought to make clear is too well established by the experience of normal and typical women – however numerous the exceptions may be – to be called in question. I would point out to those who would deprecate the

influence of such facts in relation to social progress that nothing is gained by regarding women as simply men of smaller growth. They are not so; they have the laws of their own nature; their development must be along their own lines, and not along masculine lines.[18]

Ellis's prescription of such sexual differences between men and women undermined the feminist arguments that the form taken by male sexuality was the result not of biology but of social influences. Another way in which he undermined the work of the feminists who were campaigning against male sexual abuse of women and children, was to promote ideas diametrically opposed to theirs on the subject of sexual offences. Having pronounced that women enjoyed pain and being forced to surrender it is not surprising that Ellis had difficulty believing that rape or sexual assault to which women did not consent and which they did not want, could exist at all. He thought that such offences must be extremely rare and that false accusations and lies made up the vast majority of reported cases. He quoted with obvious approval an experiment carried out by one Lawson Tait who examined 70 charges of sexual assault upon girls under the Criminal Law Amendment Act of 1885. Tait was able to advise prosecution in only 6 cases and in these cases convictions were obtained, whereas in 7 other cases where the police decided to prosecute there was either no conviction or a very light sentence. In 26 cases, according to Tait, the charge was clearly trumped up. The average age of the girls was 12 and what seems to have worried Tait most about them was that they used 'sexual argot' (slang) in describing what had happened to them. The fact that they were able to give 'minute and detailed descriptions' helped Tait to reach the conclusion that the children had not in fact been assaulted. He was horrified that they were not sheltered and innocent according to the stereotype of the young middle-class girl of the day. Ellis extended Tait's conclusion about the rarity of genuine cases of assault to cover the rape of adult women. He explained that women probably raped men just as often as the reverse. He doesn't explain how. He considered that the cry of rape was used to cover up women's voluntary sexual exploits:

> There can be little doubt that the plea of force is very frequently seized upon by women as the easiest available weapon of defence when her connection had been revealed. She has been so permeated by the current notion that no 'respectable'

woman can possibly have any sexual impulses of her own to gratify that, in order to screen what she feels to be regarded as an utterly shameful and wicked, as well as foolish, act, she declares it never took place by her own will at all.[19]

Ellis's third important contribution to the anti-feminist platform was the glorification of motherhood. Ellis's ideas on motherhood reflect a general concern in Britain and in other imperialist nations in the first decade of the twentieth century with the health and quality of the nation's children. From the 1880s onwards, those concerned for the future of the empire had been worried about the declining birthrate and increasing infant mortality rate. Concern for the health of older children developed after the introduction of compulsory education led to revelations about the poor physical condition of schoolchildren. The disastrous military performance of Britain in the Boer War, combined with the high rejection rate of recruits on account of physical disability, increased the national alarm. The British Empire was seen to be under threat at this time from the economic competition of rival nations such as Germany, the USA and Japan. As Anna Davin points out in her work on both official and voluntary efforts to rehabilitate the nation's children, there was a 'surge of concern about the bearing and rearing of children – the next generation of soldiers and workers, the Imperial race.'[20] The responsibility for the health of the nation's children was attributed to the mothers. Mothers had to be taught to produce better offspring. Davin explains how the work of the eugenicists, those who sought to improve the 'race' by selective breeding, helped to reinforce this concentration on motherhood since 'good motherhood was an essential component in their ideology of racial health and purity.'[21]

In his book *The Task of Social Hygiene* (1913) Ellis redefined the purpose and form of feminism in the service of his concern for motherhood. The term the 'Woman' movement which was used by some writers at this time in place of the term 'women's' movement is symptomatic of the redefinition that was taking place whereby a concern for the perfection of 'womanhood' took the place of an interest in the emancipation of women. The main task of social hygiene, according to Ellis, was to be the 'regeneration of the race' and the 'evolution of a super-mankind'. He explained that the difference between 'social hygiene' and 'social reform' was that 'social hygiene' would utilise the understanding of eugenics and instead of 'painfully struggling to improve the conditions of life' it would deal adequately with the conditions of life because it has 'its hands on the sources of life'. In his youth Ellis is seen as having had socialist ideals. By this time socialism had certainly given way to genetic engineering in his blueprint for change. Ellis set out to reinterpret the aims of the 'woman' movement totally to fit in with his project of improving the race. His new model for this movement was that of an organisation of mothers seeking to help in the creation of a 'selectively bred race':

> The breeding of men lies largely in the hands of women. That is why the question of Eugenics is to a great extent one with the woman question. The realisation of eugenics in our social life can only be attained with the realisation of the woman movement in its latest and completest phase as an enlightened culture of motherhood, in all that motherhood involves alike on the physical and the psychic sides.[22]

In a chapter entitled 'The Changing Status of Women' he proceeded to attack and brush aside the form taken by feminism at that time in favour of his new prescription. The description of the new equality he envisaged as the result of the changing status of women is very different from that for which most feminists were fighting – could be called 'complementarity' but hardly equality:

> It is necessary to remember that the kind of equality of the sexes towards which this change of status is leading, is social equality, – that is, equality of freedom. It is not an intellectual equality, still less is it likeness. . . . Even complete economic equality is not attainable. Among animals which live in herds under the guidance of a leader, this leader is nearly always a male; there are few exceptions. In woman, the long period of pregnancy and lactation, and the prolonged helplessness of her child, render her for a considerable period of her life economically dependent.[23]

A strange sort of equality this, in which women were always to be followers and men leaders. He criticised the women's movement in Britain for having always confined itself to 'imitating men and to obtaining the same work and the same rights as men', and for having aimed to 'secure woman's claims as a human being rather than as a woman'. Ellis proclaimed that this was only half the task of the women's movement since: 'Women can never be like men, any more than men can be like women . . . woman's function in life can never be the same as man's, if only because women are the mothers of the race.'[24]

Ellis called his redefinition of feminism the 'new phase of the woman's movement'. For an example of this new phase in action he directed his readers to Germany where he claimed that there was a new movement of German women 'fundamentally emotional in character' crying for 'emotional' as well as political rights which had spread through the German Empire and even to the Dutch and Scandinavians. The object of the agitation was the 'demands of the mother' and the new movement bore a 'decisive unlikeness' to the earlier movement. Where the earlier movement was based on 'the perpetual assumption that women must be allowed to do everything that men do' the new teutonic movement was based on what 'marks the woman as unlike the man'. The title of this new movement was 'Mutterschutz' and it was connected integrally to the movement for sexual reform in Germany and supported by recent developments in German science particularly in the field of sexual pathology, according to Ellis. 'Mutterschutz' was originally the title of a 'Journal for the reform of sexual morals' established in 1905 and edited by Helene Stoecker of Berlin and which was by 1913 called *Die Neue Generation*. The journal discussed 'all questions that radiate out from the sexual function' including love, prostitution, sexual hygiene and sex education. The journal was originally the organ of an association for the protection of mothers, more especially unmarried mothers, entitled the 'Bund für Mutterschutz'.

Ellis's connection of his new ideal form of feminism with the Mutterschutz presages the development in the British women's movement in the 1920s of the movement for the endowment of motherhood which, as we shall see in the next chapter, drew connections between eugenics and feminism and exalted motherhood at the expense of other feminist concerns. The exaltation of motherhood by the Mutterschutz tallied neatly with the developing fascist ideal of woman's destiny in Germany of the 1920s and 1930s. Ellis pointed out that the older women's rights movement held aloof from the Protection of Mothers and Sexual Reform Congress which was held in Dresden in 1911 in connection with a great exhibition of hygiene. At the Congress an international union was set up of those interested in sexual reform based upon the recognition of the importance of motherhood which covered Germany, Austria, Italy, Sweden and Holland. Ellis directed readers who wanted to understand the ideals underlying the movement to the work of Ellen Key who believed in the fundamental differences between the sexes and considered it foolish to put women to do 'men's work'.[25] Ellis's overall ideal was the 'desire to breed a firmly-fibred, clean-minded, and self-reliant race of manly men and womanly women'.[26]

In his writings in the 1930s Ellis expressed his relief that the kind of feminism in which women had sought 'equality' with men was dead. As Ellis enthused about the death of feminism he made his concept of the 'new feminism' really clear:

> Those who propagandised this now rather antiquated notion of the 'equality' of the sexes, in the sense of resemblance if not identity, were justified in so far as they were protesting against that superstition of the inferiority of women which had proved so influential, and, as many of us think, so mischievous in its applications within the social sphere. But the banner of Equality under which they fought, while a wholesome and necessary assertion in the social and political realms, had no biological foundation.[27]

He believed in 'equivalence' not equality. This meant that the 'two halves of the race are compensatory in their unlikeness'.[28] He saw the two sexes as having quite separate biologically determined roles. Woman's role was that of wife and mother. Ellis was alarmed at the idea that women should have 'the same education as men, the same occupations as men, even the same sports'.[29] This idea he described as 'the source of all that was unbalanced, sometimes both a little pathetic and a little absurd, in the old women's movement'.[30] Ellis has gained something of a reputation for being pro-feminist because he frequently denounced the idea that women were 'inferior' and their historical 'subjection' to men. Ellis wanted to remove legal inequalities and he wanted women to have 'economic independence'. This independence was to be achieved by the endowment of motherhood, i.e. paying women to fulfil their role as mothers. Ellis wanted to remove the unsightly and obvious symbols of women's subjection, whilst maintaining men's power through the doctrine of 'separate spheres' for men and women.

One of the rewards for women's fulfilment of their separate sphere was that they were to be eroticised, i.e. have the right to sexual pleasure. The sexualising of woman in the context of heterosexual intercourse, a development in which Ellis played an important part, can be seen as a token compensation for all she was to lose, rather than a step forward into sexual freedom. What she would lose was the right to be a spinster, to engage in passionate relationships with women unless they took the form dictated by his lesbian stereotypes, to compete with men for jobs and opportunities and to challenge male sexual behaviour.

The movement for the glorification and protection of motherhood which spread across Europe from Germany was promoted by male sex reformers and incorporated the ideas of sex reform whilst representing itself as being part of the movement for the emancipation of women. What was the connection between the motherhood movement and sex reform? A look at the literature from Germany disabuses the reader of any notion that sex reform or even the promotion of sexual pleasure for women was necessarily in the interests of women. Two German works translated into English in 1908 and 1909 are recognised as landmarks in the history of the sex reform movement. Iwan Bloch's *The Sexual Life of Our Time* was translated by Eden Paul, member of the Independent Labour Party, a prominent voice in the birth control movement in Britain, and later a leading member of the British Society for the Study of Sex Psychology and contributor to the London congress of the World League for Sex Reform in 1929. Like other sex reformers Bloch assumed that there were basic biological and psychological differences between men and women. He used the symbolism of the activities of sperm and ova to illustrate these differences and wrote, 'Spermatozoa and ova are the original representatives of the respective spiritual natures of man and woman.'[31] He acknowledged his debt to Ellis's *Man and Woman* in the development of his ideas. Bloch described the sexual difference thus: 'The nature of man is aggressive, progressive, variable; that of woman is receptive, more susceptible to stimuli, simpler.'[32]

From Bloch's work we get an insight into the meaning of the link between sex reform and motherhood. He quotes the author of 'Splitter' who he says, has 'well characterised woman's extended sexual sphere':

Women are in fact pure sex from knees to neck. We men have concentrated our apparatus in a single place, we have extracted it, separated it from the rest of the body, because prêt a partir [ready to go]. They [women] *are* a sexual *surface* or target; we *have* only a sexual arrow. Procreation is their proper element, and when they are engaged in it they remain at home in their own sphere; we for this purpose must go elsewhere out of ourselves. In the matter of time also our part in procreation is concentrated. We may devote to the matter barely ten minutes; women give as many months. Properly speaking, they procreate unceasingly, they stand continually at the witches' cauldron, boiling and brewing; while we lend a hand merely in passing, and do no more than throw one or two fragments into the vessel.[33]

Bloch was strongly associated with the Bund für Mutterschutz and was on the 1907 committee of that organisation. The link between motherhood and sex reform can be seen from this quotation to consist in a conflation of reproduction with sexuality in women. Woman is represented as totally a reproductive organism, no more no less, and therefore as totally sexual. This is a different picture from the Victorian one in which woman was allowed to be reproductive but not sexual in her own right, merely a sexual receptacle for the male. However the fact that woman was proclaimed and exhorted to be sexual and even to have the right to sexual pleasure was seen to be an extension of her natural role and sphere in motherhood. Woman was to continue to be a reproductive organism with a natural sphere separate and distinct from that of man but she was to receive physical gratification from the fulfilment of her functions.

Forel's work *The Sexual Question*, translated and published in an American edition in 1908, shows how the rhetoric of equality can be incorporated into what appear to be ideas totally opposed to the struggle for women's emancipation. Forel was later to be one of the presidents of the World League for Sex Reform along with Magnus Hirschfeld and Havelock Ellis. He too believed in the natural physical and mental differences between men and women. Writing of women's taste in sexual partners he said:

Her smaller stature and strength, together with her passive role in coitus, explain why she aspires to a strong male support. This is simply a question of natural phylogenetic adaptation. This is why a young girl sighs for a courageous, strong, and enterprising man, who is superior to her, whom she is obliged to respect, and in whose arms she feels secure.[34]

In a section entitled 'The Emancipation of Women' Forel explained that the emancipation of women was necessary because an inequality of the rights of the two sexes created 'sexual anomalies'. His description of what he meant by emancipation showed that he was concerned for the maintenance of a totally separate sphere for womanhood but a recognition of the importance of her work in this sphere, motherhood, through the removal of legal disabilities. He did not envisage any real change in woman's lifestyle or opportunities:

> The emancipation of women is not intended to transform them into men, but simply to give them their human rights, I might even say their natural animal rights. It in no way wishes to impose work on women nor to make them unaccustomed to it. . . . It is our duty to give them the independent position in society which corresponds to their normal attributes. . . . Their sexual role is so important that it gives them the right to the highest social considerations in this domain.[35]

Women should be given equal rights, he declared, so that they could 'react freely according to their feminine genius'.

This new version of feminism clearly had its attractions for women, even some who had been associated with what Ellis called the 'old women's movement'. Mrs Gasquoigne-Hartley was one of those who was seduced by it. She promoted an ideal of womanhood based upon woman's role as mother and her responsibility to the race. She acknowledged the importance of Ellis and Ellen Key in her thinking and her book, *The Truth About Woman* (1913), is a good example of the way in which sex reforming ideas were propagated and used to support a full-scale attack on the form taken by feminism at that time. Her book was considered important enough to be reviewed in nearly every feminist publication, though not with universal enthusiasm.

Gasquoigne-Hartley wrote with all the fervour of a one-time sympathiser with feminism making a complete renunciation. She included in the introduction an apology for her earlier views about women which seem to have been straightforwardly feminist. She says that she began work as the headmistress of a school for girls. She was young and inexperienced and 'believed that [she] was able to train up a new type of woman':

> For a long time I wandered in the wrong path. My desire was to find proofs that would enable me to ignore all those facts of woman's organic constitution which make her unlike man. I stumbled blindly into the fatal error of following masculine

ideals. I desired freedom for women to enable them to live the same lives that men live and to do the same work that men do. I did not understand that this was a wastage of the force of womanhood; that no freedom can be of service to women unless it is a freedom to follow her own nature.[36]

Gasquoigne-Hartley made this change of heart and was doubtless educated in the error of her ways on her marriage to Walter Gallichan who was a populariser of sex reform ideas and editor of the *Free Review*, a magazine which carried progressive sex re-forming ideas. He was, as we shall see, an accomplished anti-feminist. Gasquoigne-Hartley recognised that feminists would oppose her new model of feminism in which women's main task was to be motherhood and service to the race. In answer to the expected criticism she reiterated her opposition to the oppression of women:

And this I contest against all the Feminists; the real need of the normal woman is the full and free satisfaction of the race-instinct. Do I then accept the subjection of the woman. Assuredly not! To me it is manifest that it is just because of her sex-needs and her sex-power that women must be free.[37]

Gasquoigne-Hartley opposed the idea that women should com-pete with men at work. Woman's real work, she maintained, was motherhood and women might only do work which was in accordance with their nature and that which men wanted them to do.

Why did women who saw themselves as progressive embrace what we now see to be a form of antifeminism? A moving force behind antifeminism in women throughout the ninteenth and twentieth centuries seems to have been a desire to validate the roles of wife and mother which they felt themselves to have freely chosen. The glorification of motherhood enhances the status of woman's reproductive role and appears to give women respect for an activity which women rightly deduce as being a badge of inferiority under male domination. When there is little alternative offered to the occupation of wife and mother and any other choice means a very difficult struggle for women, praise for motherhood must have offered reassurance. Just before the First World War the appeal of the motherhood ideal was reinforced by all the authority of 'science' and the whole of the new discipline of sexology. It could be perceived then, as radical rather than

141

reactionary. For a woman like Gasquoigne-Hartley the propaganda of the sexologists must have made the idea of being an eternal spinster schoolmistress seem unattractive. Spinsterhood, as we saw earlier, was associated with sterility, destructiveness and anti-life values. There was little possibility at the time of combining motherhood with a career and had Gasquoigne-Hartley wanted a child, for whatever reason, the new ideology of motherhood would have legitimised her choice. It is possible, too, that the upsurge of militant feminism and the spinster suffragettes, combined with the savage anti-spinster onslaught that greeted their activities might have caused fainthearted feminists to waver and seek an alternative.

At the same time as Gasquoigne-Hartley lauded motherhood she felt compelled to launch a savage critique of feminism. The grounds she used for her attack are those which form the recurent motifs of post-First World War antifeminism. One source of alarm was that feminists were 'anti-men'. Another was the feminist challenge to male sexuality which Gasquoigne-Hartley singled out for attack. She delivered scornful tirades against the renunciation by feminists of sex with men, and the feminist idea that men were responsible for the abuse of women in prostitution, even though she had once, as she points out, held these views herself:

> I must in fairness state that I have been compelled to give up the view held by me, in common with most other women, that men and their uncontrollable passions are chiefly responsible for this hideous traffic [white slave traffic]. It is so comfortable to place the sins of society on men's passions.[38]

Another important ground on which she based her attack on feminists was the denunciation of spinsters. This was to be the most popular line of attack for antifeminists for the next twenty years. In a chapter on biology in *The Truth About Woman* she explained what can be learned about the relations of the sexes in human beings from looking at the organisation of the beehive. She described the worker bees who are infertile females as being ike 'surplus women', both those who could not and those who chose not to marry. The book presents a horrifying vision of the influence that such women would have on society. She pointed out that the poisoned sting of the worker bee was formed from the transformation of the ovipositor (egg-laying tube). Spinsters would 'in giving up the power of life' be 'left the possessor of the stinging weapon of death'.[39]

The virulence of pre-war antifeminism can perhaps best be explained as a reaction to the success of the militant suffrage movement. Walter Heape's *Sex Antagonism* is an antifeminist classic of the period. Heape was a biologist who sought to explain how sex antagonism developed at different periods of human history by looking at the growth of civilisation from primitive society to his own time. His major cause for concern about the women's movement of the time was the way that feminists were speaking of male sexuality and his reply was that women must accept the biological inevitability of the form taken by male sexuality:

> It is the fashion to talk glibly of the need for the suppression of brutal sexual instincts, of the control of sexual passion, and so forth. Such demands are made by woman and addressed to man as a perverted creature, as an abnormal product of civilisation. The fact is that woman's sexuality is on quite a different plane to that of man; she is wholly ignorant as a rule of man's normal requirements, and her virtuous demands, essentially designed for her own benefit as she conceives, are opposed to natural law.[40]

A recurring theme of Heape's book, and of the work of later anti-feminists, is the technique of divide and rule. He states that the 'two classes of women', the wife and the spinster, have 'quite different aims in life'. He forecast a deep division between these two classes:

> Privileges which the spinster most desires the wife is indifferent to, and concessions to the sex which would be a gain to the former would prejudice the interests of the latter. Truly, if the woman's question begins with inter-, it is likely to end in intrasexual strife'.[41]

His alarm at spinsters stemmed from the fact that 'the bulk of those who take an active part in the [women's] movement are undoubtedly spinsters; a dissatisfied, and we may assume, an unsatisfied class of women.'[42] He was appalled at the prospect of women gaining the vote since he foresaw that it would be spinsters who would use the vote to their own advantage by gaining legislation to secure their interests. They would, he declared, use the power of the vote 'most freely' presumably because they would not be under the restraining influence of a husband. They were dangerous partly because if elderly they were

143

likely to be mad as a result of not having used their reproductive organs. He does not admit to being worried lest the spinsters use political power in a way which would decrease men's privileges, but claims that his concern is for the wife and mother since her interests, which were so different from those of the spinster, would be damaged by the spinster vote:

> Thus extended power given to women threatens to result in legislation for the advantage of that relatively superfluous part of the population, and since their interests are directly antagonistic to the interests of the woman who is concerned in the production of children, legislation enacted on their behalf will tend to be opposed to the interests of the mothers themselves.[43]

Heape allowed no useful place in society to unmarried women and described them as the 'waste products of our female population'.[44] One of his answers to the problem of feminism which was responsible for literature 'freely exposed for sale' in London in which 'man, as a sex, is held up to execration as the brute beast', was to prophesy and in doing so to help foment, a deep division in the ranks of women between the spinster and the wife and mother.

Walter Heape's main interest in his book *Sex Antagonism* seems to have been antifeminism rather than sexology though he used sexological arguments to support his ideas. Walter Gallichan, on the other hand, was genuinely concerned to popularise sex reforming ideas which happened to be antifeminist in content. His other main obsessions were bird-watching and fly-fishing. He was a contributor to many journals and a prolific writer on the topics of morality, marriage and sex reform from the 1890s to 1930. In 1909 he contributed to the antifeminist platform with a book entitled *Modern Woman and How to Manage Her*. He described the antagonism between the sexes as 'an age-long conflict' and gave a graphic picture of the 'man-hating' woman: 'The present is the era of the man-condemning, man-hating woman. There is not a woman's club in London wherein you will not hear avowed dislike of men among a fairly large number of the members.'[45] He considered that the man-hating women were fighting a losing battle against the laws of nature and tried to belittle the phenomenon though he recognised that it was currently increasing:

> Among the great army of sex, the regiment of aggressively
> man-hating women is of full strength, and signs of the times
> show that it is being steadily recruited. On its banner is
> emblazoned, 'Woe to Man'; and its call to arms is shrill and
> loud. These are the women who are 'independent of men', a
> motley host, pathetic in their defiance of the first principle of
> Nature, but of no serious account in the biological or social
> sense.[46]

The man-hating was associated with a dislike of sex. He explained
that the 'cold woman frequently becomes a militant man-hater,
and especially so when she is beautiful.'[47]

He was worried that marriage seemed to be out of fashion and
looked forward to a time in the future when marriage would be
more attractive to celibates. The solution to 'man-hating' was to
overcome women's dislike of sex and ensure that they married.
Several of his later works are devoted to sex education and
particularly solving the problem, as he saw it, of female frigidity.
In his works Gallichan constantly acknowledged his debt to
Havelock Ellis. The solution he offered to the 'surplus women'
problem is suggested by the title of his 1914 book *Woman Under
Polygamy*. He suggested that women were actually freer and
happier under the various systems of polygamy he reviewed in the
book, than anyone had supposed in the west. It is clear that he saw
the introduction of polygamy, or concubinage, as being a way to
defuse the threat posed by spinsters to British society. He explained:

> Spinsterhood, and the 'right to live one's own life', – the
> supreme consummation of a large number of revolutionary
> British women – make no appeal to an Indian woman. Her
> strongest impulses are to fulfil her womanhood, to experience
> love, and to bear children. That is her vocation, her ambition,
> and joy.[48]

The *Freewoman* magazine which represented the tiny sex reforming tendency within feminism before the war, carried articles on
systems where polygamy was practised by male apologists in
1911 and 1912. Heape recommended polygamy in *Sex Antagonism*. It was gaining popularity as an answer to the problem of
uppity women. The spectre of unmarried women caused Gallichan great discomfort:

> Another cause of (reason for ?) polygyny especially in Great

145

Britain is to be sought in the preponderance of women in the population. The surplus of marriageable women who remain single is often overstated. None the less there is an immense army of compulsorily celibate women. Certain city areas are inhabited chiefly by unmarried women.[49]

Antifeminism before the First World War took the form of an attack upon spinsters and militant feminism combined with the creation of an ideal of motherhood which masqueraded as a 'new' feminism and was beginning to have its converts among women. Sexological ideas gave ammunition to antifeminists, and sexologists like Havelock Ellis were in the forefront of the onslaught on that form of feminism which threatened them. This was a feminism in which women saw themselves as having interests separate from men and in which they proclaimed their right not to marry or engage in sex with men. This was a feminism based upon social and economic changes which rescued some women from total dependence upon men and thus offered a real challenge to men's dominance. The sexological response was to replace economic dependence with a new 'scientifically discovered' biological dependence. Since this 'new' dependence existed purely in the realms of ideology it required a massive propaganda campaign to ensure its acceptance. The ideal of sexually fulfilling motherhood which rendered the spinster 'superfluous' and dangerous by her example had by the 1920s been absorbed into the 'new feminism' of Eleanor Rathbone and other women in the National Union for Equal Citizenship. The development of this 'new feminism' and the simultaneous decline of the feminist campaign to transform male sexuality are described in the following chapter.

CHAPTER 8

The Decline of Militant Feminism

The face of feminism in the 1920s was very different from that of the militant suffrage movement before the First World War. The politics of direct action and the campaign to change men's sexual behaviour were replaced by a form of equal rights feminism which offered no direct challenge to men's dominance and had by the late 1920s acquired many of the characteristics of the Havelock Ellis ideal of 'new feminism'.

The Women's Social and Political Union of Emmeline and Christabel Pankhurst had split at the beginning of the war when Christabel made her dramatic conversion to nationalism and militarism. At the opening of the war the *Suffragette* viewed the war as an example of men's aggression. The feminist perspective disappeared almost immediately and WSPU energies were directed to supporting the war effort. Pacifists left the WSPU to join with the majority of other suffragettes who worked for peace in organisations such as the Women's International League for Peace and Freedom. During the war the WSPU transformed itself into the Women's Party to fight for parliamentary legislation. The Party was short-lived.

The war was an event of such magnitude that feminists were forced into a response and could not simply ignore it. In a somewhat similar way the issue of nuclear war has galvanised many feminists today, who have felt compelled to divert much of their energies into campaigning for nuclear disarmament. The phenomenon of mass male aggression seems consistently to drive women, feminist or otherwise, into a defensive position where they must struggle to maintain such principles as the continued existence of human life on earth. Directly feminist concerns which are aimed at increasing women's status and opportunities vis-à-vis men are at such times forced into abeyance.

During the First World War many feminists continued to maintain their pre-war interests in women's suffrage and a single standard of sexual morality. But the diversion of energies seems to have had a much more devastating effect on feminism at that time than the nuclear issue is creating within the contemporary women's liberation movement.

In 1918 women over 30 got the vote. Historians who have given undue importance to the struggle for the vote in the last wave of feminism have tended to see the force of the movement as declining inevitably once women were partially admitted to the franchise. Such an explanation fails to give weight to the other crucial concerns of feminism, particularly the campaign around transforming male sexuality. We must look further than a partial solution to the suffrage struggle to understand why these other feminist causes declined. The National Union of Women's Suffrage Societies, the non-militant wing of the suffrage campaign, was transformed after 1918 into the National Union of Societies for Equal Citizenship with Eleanor Rathbone at its head and the *Woman's Leader* as its journal. The Women's Freedom League continued to campaign on the suffrage issue, and many others, until 1928, when women were admitted to the franchise on equal terms with men.

Those very same women whom we have seen in Chapters 2 to 5 before the First World War taking up strong and radical positions on the issue of sexuality seem by the early 1920s to have lost all the forcefulness of their feminism. Christabel Pankhurst is the most notable example of this transformation. By 1921 Christabel had found her new mission in announcing the second coming of Christ. She went to Canada and then to America, engaged in Christian religious revivalism. In this respect her career has similarities with the careers of other feminists who found one variety of religion or another, for example, Annie Besant and Francis Swiney who took up theosophy. Religions like theosophy and Christianity, which made a virtue of sexual abstinence, offered consolation to women who were anxious to escape compulsory heterosexuality and compulsory sexual intercourse, particularly when, after the war, sex reform was stripping away all the prestige which feminists had sought to create for spinsterhood. In an article in the *Weekly Dispatch* in 1921 entitled 'Why I Never Married', Christabel Pankhurst showed how her politics had changed. In 1913, as we have seen, Christabel's fury at men's sexual abuse of women was so strong that she asserted that women should renounce men on the grounds of their moral inferiority. In the 1921 article she goes to great lengths to prove that she does not, and never did, hate men, and states that 'one sex should honour and reverence the other'.[1] This is a rather different position from the political celibacy she advocated before the war. By 1927, Christabel, who was still passionately opposed to the sexual abuse of women, interpreted the cause of sexual violence as the 'devil' rather than men. Writing about the reason for the rape and mutilation of a 12-year-old girl she explained: 'little girls are still at the mercy of lust, of murderous perversion ... God's answer is that the world lieth in the "evil one" and that sin and iniquity will abound until the Return of the Lord Jesus Christ.'[2]

Even that strong spinster theorist, Cicely Hamilton, had by 1921 lost the force of her feminism. In a *Weekly Dispatch* article entitled 'Women who repel men' she blamed an assault on Newnham women's college by male undergraduates, in which the gates of the college were damaged, on the women's reluctance to compromise and be amenable to men. She advised the women to play down their independence. It could be that strong spinster-hood was a more difficult position to take immediately after the war because of the outburst of virulent indignation and hostility which had greeted the increasingly independent behaviour of some spinsters within the war period. There had been opposition to the spinsters before the war, but not anything to match that which greeted them afterwards, as we shall see.

Few of the stalwarts of the prewar period seem to have been active in the feminism, of the 1920s. What then, was the new shape of feminism at this time? David Doughan, of the Fawcett Library, who is well informed about a period of feminist history which is seriously under-researched, has described 1920s feminism.[3] He suggests that feminists were concerned to look as sober and respectable as they could, that big flashy campaigns were out, constitutionalism was in, and feminists used parliamentary lobbying to achieve legal equality through complex legislation in specific areas. There was still some public campaigning, for example on equal pay, but lobbying was dominant. The lobbying was done by specialist organisations such as the Equal Pay Campaign Committee, Women for Westminster, the Married Women's Association, the Association for Moral and Social Hygiene, the National Union of Women Teachers, the National Association of Women Civil Servants, the Open Door Council and the Housewives' League. These lobbied for single issues, or on behalf of specific interests, they were not general-purpose feminist organisations. Doughan suggests that this fragmentation and multiplication of women's organisations caused feminists to lose sight of the unity of their campaign and 'weakened their theoretical base'.

There were umbrella feminist organisations in the early 1920s which were active in much the same areas and with the same tactics, though they were quite separate from one another. These were the National Union of Societies for Equal Citizenship, the Women's Freedom League, the Six Point Group, the National Council for Women and the London and National Society for Women's Service (later the Fawcett Society). This was different from contemporary feminism, in which specialist groups see themselves as a part of a Women's Liberation Movement rather than each organisation having to fight each battle independently. There is still no really adequate explanation as to why feminism lost its vital spark and degenerated into this multiplicity of fragmented organisations. Doughan directs us, helpfully, to consider the opposition to feminism in the form of the new fascists, the Freudians, Lawrence and Hemingway, the cult of machismo combined with increasingly obvious machismo on the political left, the way in which free love was becoming seen as progressive, and the impact of consumerism and press hostility.

Olive Banks, in her book *Faces of Feminism*, offers a rather different explanation of the changing form of feminism.[4] She describes how 'welfare feminism' developed in Britain in the 1920s as it had done in the USA. 'Welfare feminism' was concerned with the relief of poverty, the endowment of motherhood, and the health of children and attracted the support of women from the growing labour movement. A socialist woman, Wilma Meikle, in her 1916 book *Towards a Sane Feminism*, indicated the lines along which this alliance was to develop. She berated the 'older' more 'ladylike' feminists for their lack of enthusiasm for marriage and for sex with men. She described them as: 'the women who crammed their shelves with pamphlets on venereal diseases, who suspected all their male acquaintances of harbouring a venereal taint ... who regarded the majority of men as conscious and wilful oppressors.'[5] She attacked their concentration on agitating for the vote and explained that feminism's main task should be to organise around working women. She argued that agitation for the vote should be a platform for other reforms and it is her listing of these which shows the alliance between welfare feminism and the Labour party, and the way in which a new kind of feminism was developing. Meikle proposed that feminists should work for the following reforms: 'socialism, school clinics, schools for mothers, and the endowment of motherhood.'[6]

It seems that, at this time, some socialist women saw themselves as feminists simply because they were women operating with a new and unaccustomed independence in the field of social work. They did not see feminism as requiring a struggle for equality with men or as being in any way threatening or challenging to men's behaviour or to the advantages that men had gained at women's expense. A challenging form of feminism in which women's interests could be seen as conflicting with those of men would have been hard to sustain for women involved in a mixed-sex labour movement in which all were supposed to be united and working for a common goal. A reaction to this constraint was to adopt welfare goals in the place of feminism and to represent them as one and the same.

In the mid-1920s pre-war militant feminism was not in evidence, but there were two distinct varieties of feminism whose proponents engaged in a debate. There were those like Lady Rhondda, who wanted feminism to be about equal rights, and others who wanted a 'new feminism' which would be concerned with women's special, meaning biological, needs. Eleanor Rathbone is the most notable example of those who promoted the 'new feminism'. Rathbone's career, as described in Mary Stocks's biography, shows that she was the perfect 'type' of welfare feminist.[7] Her first experience of social and political work was in the Victoria Women's Settlement in Everton, a working-class neighbourhood of Liverpool, in the 1890s. In settlement houses university-educated young women and men lived among the working classes and engaged in social missionary work. From 1904 Rathbone was honorary secretary of the Women's Settlement. At the same time she did much unpaid social work in Liverpool, writing in 1909 an article about the living conditions of a casual labourer. Rathbone's ideas were beginning to move towards the cause for which she is most remembered, the endowment of motherhood, by 1913, when she was on Liverpool Women's Industrial Council and writing about the condition of widows under the Poor Law. She proposed that widowed mothers of young children should receive state-aided pensions, on the grounds that their labour in looking after children was as valuable to the state as the paid work of any man. In making this argument she showed the trait which was to be characteristic of her attitude to feminism.[8] She explained that although equal pay might be a good idea, there were too many obstacles in the way, such as the idea that men received a 'family' wage. Rather than struggle for equal pay, she suggested that women should campaign for the endowment of motherhood, envisioned by Rathbone as a wage, rather than a small allowance. Thus she betrayed the cause of spinsterhood and the independent woman. She deserted a feminist option because it was too difficult and embraced the simpler alternative of emphasising woman's mission of motherhood. It is particularly surprising that Rathbone should opt to support the married woman and mother at the expense of the spinster considering that she was herself a lifelong spinster.

Mary Stocks described Rathbone, in no uncertain terms, as having no interest in men and being hostile to the idea of heterosexual sex. Mary Stocks found it necessary to emphasise this point and it is important still when the strength of women's determination to choose for women emotionally and against men is continually ignored or omitted from the history books. Stocks pointed out that 'colourful commentators' had invented male lovers for Florence Nightingale, Emily Brontë and Octavia Hill because their determined spinsterhood and bonds to women could not be understood. She said that there was not even the suspicion of evidence on which male lovers could be invented for Rathbone. Rathbone, Stocks explained, had little contact with men at Oxford: 'Nor does the minutest record of her subsequent career offer any suggestion of susceptibility to male attraction.'[9] Eleanor met the woman she was to love and live with for the rest of her life at Victoria Settlement in Liverpool. Stocks described their relationship thus: 'Elizabeth Macadam became in due course the friend and companion of Eleanor's existence until death did them part, and at no subsequent period was Eleanor lonely.'[10]

Mary Stocks was a member of Eleanor's circle of women friends who holidayed and worked politically together. It was brave of Stocks in 1949 to make such a deliberate and moving record of the relationship between Eleanor and Elizabeth. This was after all a time when hostility towards lesbianism was growing steadily stronger to the extent where Vera Brittain in 1940, as we have seen, felt forced to make a public renunciation of her relationship with Winifred Holtby in *Testament of Friendship*.[11]

Eleanor Rathbone committed herself to the cause of biological motherhood, and submerged all the interests of all women into the glorification of reproduction. In her exposition of the 'new feminism' in a 1925 speech to NUSEC, reprinted in the journal the *Woman's Leader* which she edited, she characterised the 'old feminism' as the pursuit of legal equality and equal pay. Rathbone was scathing about this sort of feminism and called for it to be abandoned on the grounds that it would be difficult to achieve and likely to enrage various bodies of men in the process.

This defeatism symbolises the failure of feminist energy in the 1920s when Rathbone could call for the abondonment of feminist aims simply because they were unpopular and difficult to achieve. The *Woman's Leader* became the mouthpiece for the ideas of Rathbone's 'new feminism' whose concerns were outlined in a policy statement later in 1925. The article attacked a definition of feminism offered by the novelist Rose Macauley which was that feminism represented 'attempts by women to possess privileges (political, professional, economic or other) which have previously been denied to them on account of their sex'.[12] The aims of 'new feminism' were to be as follows: 'that the whole structure and movement of society shall reflect in a proportionate degree their experiences, their needs, and their aspirations.' Rathbone called this a 'wider conception of feminism'. At first sight it might seem so. In fact Rathbone's idea of women's needs and aspirations was limited to what she saw as the dictates of their biology. She wanted women to 'fulfil the potentials of their own natures' in the way that Havelock Ellis and the other sexologists had declared to be appropriate, in motherhood. Rathbone's belief in this separate sphere for women led her to concentrate on bettering the conditions of motherhood and gaining more respect and reward for motherhood as an occupation:

> we demand that this particular occupation shall focus the same measure of social attention and respect as any large and nationally important occupation in which men are engaged. . . . We demand that the economic basis of motherhood shall be the kind of economic basis that men would regard as acceptable for any occupation in which they themselves were engaged.[13]

There was opposition to the 'new feminism' from feminists who were not prepared to renounce the idea of equality with men. Elizabeth Abbott in the *Woman's Leader* 1927 declared that the 'new feminism' was not feminism at all:

> The issue is not between 'old' and 'new' feminism. (There is no such thing as 'new' feminism, just as there is no such thing as 'new' freedom. There is freedom; and there is tyranny.) The issue is between feminism – equalitarianism – and that which is *not* feminism.[14]

Abbott explained that the status of motherhood could not be raised until the status of women generally was changed. Motherhood would be valued when women were valued and to be valued women must have the same rights and opportunities as men. Trying to raise the status of motherhood whilst abondoning the fight for equality, she asserted, was doomed to failure.

In embracing the cause of motherhood the new feminists offered no challenge to the traditional sex-role system. No suggestion was made that men might share childcare or domestic work. There was no suggestion that the state should provide so that men might stay at home and look after children whilst women went out to work. But it was in the reiteration of the idea that women had 'laws of their own nature', the basis of separate spheres ideology, that the new feminists were most at variance with those pre-war feminists who had fought so hard for the right of women to work outside the home and earn a living wage, so that they would have a choice not to be wholly dependent upon men. In abandoning the fight for equality and embracing the endowment of motherhood, Rathbone betrayed the interests of spinsters, lesbians, and any women who wished to escape from unsatisfactory relationships with men.

In 1927 the equal rights supporters on the council of NUSEC resigned. In 1928 after the final stage of franchise extension to women, the 200 local suffrage societies in NUSEC split into two wings. One was the National Council for Equal Citizenship which was to press for further equal rights legislation and the other was the Union of Townswomen's Guilds which was modelled on the Women's Institutes and intended to play an educational role. The Townswomen's Guilds grew and thrived whilst the political wing of the organisation declined so that by 1932 there were 51 delegates to the NUSEC conference from the politcal societies and 183 from the guilds. The decline of the politcal societies accelerated from this time.[15] The Townswomen's Guilds were mainly concerned with home-making and crafts. They pursued interests such as anti-litter campaigns, improvement of shopping facilities and consumer protection. The only evidence of earlier feminist concerns was a continuing interest in moral standards.[16]

Amongst all the explanations that have been offered by historians for the decline of feminisim in the 1920s, one has generally been overlooked. This is the impact of sexology and of a changing sexual ideology. The change in sexual morality in the 1920s is seen by many historians today as wholly positive and it is not surprising therefore that it has not been seen as part of a reaction against feminism and women's independence. The American historian William O'Neil reports with glee that feminist campaigns around sexuality were subverted by the new 'enlightened' sexual ideology of the 1920s:

> By closing their eyes to the sexual elements regulating the life of women, feminists prevented themselves from developing a satisfactory analysis of the female dilemma. And, as we shall see, when the great changes in female sexual behaviour became visible in the 1920s, feminists were unable to react to it in such a way as to command the respect of emancipated young women. It was their sexual views more than anything else that dated the older feminists, after World War I, and made it difficult for them to understand or speak to a generation moved by quite different ambitions.[17]

In very important ways the impact of sexology was to undermine feminism and women's independence. The propaganda campaign against the spinster undermined the possibility of spinsterhood being seen as a positive choice for women. The promotion of the ideology of motherhood and marriage together with the stigmatising of lesbianism helped to reinforce women's dependence upon men. The new sexual ideology of the sexologists, that sexual intercourse was vital, that celibacy was dangerous for women, that male sexuality was uncontrollable and that heterosexual sex must take the form of men's aggression and women's submission, was antithetical to the feminist theory of sexuality which lay behind earlier feminist campaigns. Women's anger at men's sexual abuse was a potent and fundamental motivation behind militant feminism up until the war. It is not surprising then that as the feminist theory was denounced under the growing impact of 'science' and sex reform societies, women's rage was sapped and their challenge blunted. Most 1920s feminists showed no more overt enthusiasm for heterosexual sex than their predecessors, but their confidence in their own judgment was now undermined and it was harder to express their criticisms. Some 'new feminists' became fervent missionaries for the wonders of and the necessity for sexual intercourse.

Stella Browne was promoting the joys of sexual intercourse, at the same time as she attacked older feminists, in her article for the British Society for the Study of Sex Psychology in 1915:

> This [variability] is the cause of much cant and bitterness
> between women, for there is a considerable and pretty steady
> percentage of cold natures, who may yet be very efficient and
> able and very attractive to men. These cold women generally
> have a perfect mania for *prohibition* as a solution for all ills.
> But surely, we do not want the new world to be built up only
> by women who have long ago forgotten what sex means, or
> who have never experienced strong sexual emotions, and
> regard them as a sign of grossness or decadence.
>   I think no one who knows the 'personnel' of many social
> reform movements, can doubt that this is very real danger.[18]

The BSSSP was formed in 1914 to campaign for better public education on the scientific facts of sex. Jeffrey Weeks points out in his history of the homosexual reform movement *Coming Out* that the initiative behind the Society and much of its membership derived from a secret male homosexual reform organisation called the Order of Chaeronea.[19] Edward Carpenter was the chairman of the BSSSP, Havelock Ellis was closely involved, and Stella Browne is the only woman to appear in the published papers. It was the concerns of male homosexuals rather than the interests of any group of women that dominated this society, 'Its membership and support was wide among progressive intellectuals.'[20] Members and supporters included George Bernard Shaw, Radclyffe Hall, Una Troubridge, Dora and Bertrand Russell, and Alexandra Kollontai, the Russian feminist. These intellectuals spread sex reforming ideas through their published works. Wilma Meikle in 1916 described the impact of Bernard Shaw and H.G. Wells on the ideals of the new feminists concerning sex:

> Mr Shaw and Mr Wells remained, however involuntarily, the
> apostles of the new feminism. Young women at the
> universities pored over their works and at last came out into
> the world earnestly convinced that there was something

certainly wonderful and possibly glorious about this mystery called sex and that it was their business to discover it.[21]

Marie Stopes did not see herself as a feminist campaigner but her ideas were similar to those of the sex reform tendency and derived from her study of sexological literature in the British Library, and resembled the ideas of the sex reforming new feminists. She elevated sexual intercourse to the status of a blissful religions ritual which fitted into a kind of pagan universe reminiscent of D.H. Lawrence:

> Welling up in her [woman] are the wonderful tides, scented and enriched by the myriad experiences of the human race from its ancient days of leisure and flower-wreathed love-making, urging her to transports and self-expressions, were the man but ready to take the first step in the initiative or to recognise and welcome it in her. Seldom dare any woman still more seldom dare a wife, risk the blow at her heart which would be given were she to offer charming love-play to which the man did not respond. To the initiate she will be able to reveal that the tide is up by a hundred subtle signs, upon which he will seize with delight.[22]

Stopes, in her sex advice books, along with Lawrence in his novels, helped to create a religion of sexual intercourse by providing the sensual and emotional scenery that was absent from the more arid sexual descriptions of the sexologists. In Stopes's work the woman is almost entirely passive and is allowed no sexual opportunities beyond sexual intercourse. But Stopes had in her writings a vital ingredient which the male sexologists could not emulate. She wrote about sex from a woman's point of view, showing a clear and urgent understanding of the pain and distress caused to women by men who satisfied their sexual needs on women in a blatantly insensitive manner:

> It can therefore be readily imagined that when the man tries to enter a woman whom he has *not* wooed to the point of stimulating her natural physical reactions of preparation, he is endeavouring to force his entry through a dry-walled opening too small for it. He may thus cause the woman actual pain, apart from the mental revolt and loathing she is likely to feel for a man who so regardlessly uses her.[23]

Marie Stopes's promotion of the use of birth control through

157

clinics, letters and articles similarly stemmed from her sympathy with women's needs. Stopes is generally remembered as the woman who, more than any other, helped to 'liberate' woman's sexuality. This is only so if we understand as the full extent of woman's sexuality a passive response to being pursued and wooed by men with the objective of sexual intercourse. She recognised clearly the horrifying realities of unregulated hetero-sexual life for women and sought to alleviate them rather than breaking the mould. It was sexual first aid.

Dora Russell is often quoted as an example of the kind of 1920s feminist who proclaimed woman's right to sexual pleasure and helped to stamp out the 'puritanism' of the older generation of feminists. David Mitchell describes her book *Hypatia* (1925) as 'the most mettlesome feminist manifesto of the time'.[24] Dale Spender writes in *Women of Ideas* '*Hypatia* is today still a good read; Dora Russell's analysis shares much with contemporary feminism.'[25] The last part of Spender's comment may well, I fear, be true. *Feminist Theorists*, edited by Dale Spender (1983) is dedicated to 'Dora Russell, one of the best feminist theorists'.[26] Russell continues the tradition of the male sexologists of attack-ing the 'early' feminists for their prudery and for their spinster-hood. She saw herself as a new feminist. Whilst stressing the importance of motherhood she went further than new feminists like Rathbone, by stressing the preeminence of sexual intercourse. Russell decided that good sexual intercourse was the aim of feminism. It would reconcile the sexes to each other and provide the key to solving all women's problems:

> To me the important task of modern feminism is to accept and proclaim sex; to bury the lie that has too long corrupted our society – the lie that the body is a hindrance to the mind, and sex a necessary evil to be endured for the perpetuation of our race. To understand sex – to bring it to dignity and beauty and knowledge born of science, in place of brute instinct and squalor – that is the bridge that will span the breach between Jason and Medea.[27]

She was not concerned with women's right not to engage in sex with men. She seemed to have believed that the sexes had distinct and different roles to perform as did the different economic classes:

> The second aim [of the women's movement] was to prove they

could jolly well do without them. In exactly the same way the worker, rising in the social scale, seeks to prove himself a *Bourgeois*. Both efforts are mistaken! Each class and sex has a special contribution to make.[28]

There's not much room here for spinsters. Russell's sex and class determinism makes her feminism look as dubious as her socialism. Russell worked with Norman Haire, an eminent male homosexual sexologist who opened the Walworth Marriage Advice Centre in 1921. They organised the 1929 congress of the World League for Sex Reform which was held in London. Dora Russell was influential in propagating sex reforming ideas within that wing of the feminist movement which was allied to the labour movement. She is important today because she is held up by historians as an example of a progressive right thinking feminist of the time. Both Dora Russell and Stella Browne, who also carried the sex reform torch into the feminist arena, were closely involved with the labour movement, and might have suffered from constraint and the need for men's approval when writing about sex. They both emphasised the joys of sexual intercourse with little criticism of it. The campaign around sexuality which Browne and Russell promoted, within the feminist movement and on the left, was very different from earlier feminist campaigns on the issue. They did not seek to transform men or agitate against the sexual abuse of women and girls. They accepted the importance of sexual intercourse and sought to remove some of the disadvantages for women of this sexual practice. Both women were involved in campaigning for birth control. There can be no doubt that the possession of birth control information and appliances was important in improving the quality of women's lives, and became more vital the less option women had regarding their sexual practice. But by itself it was first aid and did not challenge the sexual status quo, in which women were expected to be dependent on men and to do sexual intercourse whether they liked it or not. They did not seek to question the form of heterosexuality but only to relieve its symptoms.

As we saw in Chapter 4, earlier feminists had opposed birth control on the grounds that it contributed to reducing the woman to an object on whom the male could act out his sexual desires and because they saw the avoidance of sexual intercourse as a more effective and palatable form of contraception than what they described as 'artificial' methods. The transformation of sexual

ideology in the 1920s which depended on affirming sexual intercourse as the main, if not only sexual practice for both sexes,
required the development of a birth control campaign. Dr Hannah Stone explained, in her paper on birth control to the 1929 Sex
Reform Congress: 'There can be little doubt that the so-called
"sexual revolution" which is apparently now taking place in all
civilised countries is dependent to a large degree upon the spread
of contraceptive knowledge.'[29] The papers of the congress offer
us a glimpse into the ideas and practice of the women birth control
campaigners. Stone called her paper 'Birth Control as a Factor in
the Sex Life of Woman'. She, and Elise Ottesen-Jensen in her
paper entitled 'Birth Control Work among the Poor in Sweden',
represent birth control as being crucial to women's sexual pleasure. Women could not relax and enjoy sex, meaning sexual
intercourse, they contended, if they were worried about becoming
pregnant. The case studies they describe indicate, on the contrary,
that birth control was mainly crucial to the man's pleasure and a
factor in the sex life of men.

In her first case study, Stone described how a wife was forced by
her husband and his psychiatrist to resume sexual intercourse,
which she had abandoned for fear of pregnancy:

> The husband became nervous, irritable, and quarrelsome, and
> at the end of a year he frankly stated that he could stand the
> strain no longer. The wife, anxious to avoid a marital
> disruption, urged that they resume a more normal sex life, and
> acquired from a friend some information which she thought
> would safeguard her from conception. (She became pregnant
> again and there was another two years of continence.) The
> husband had gradually become incompetent in his work, lost
> his position, and later suffered a complete breakdown and had
> to be sent to a sanatorium. The psychiatrist who was treating
> the husband was of the opinion that the difficulties were due
> primarily to the abnormal sex life.[30]

It was clearly the husband who suffered strain from lack of sexual
intercourse. The wife merely suffered his annoyance. The
psychiatrist did not seek to treat the husband for the very alarming degree of dependence for his very safety and wellbeing upon
one kind of sexual practice. Instead the wife was treated. The
second case study shows even more clearly that it was the
husband's sexual interests that were to be served through the
woman's use of birth control. The wife declined to take part in

sexual intercourse after having two abortions due to failure of the husband's contraceptives. She is described as 'obtaining sexual gratification at times through mere external contact or auto-erotic practice', i.e. practices other than penetration of the vagina by the penis.[31] The husband told his wife that he had begun to ejaculate frequently, even at the sight of an attractive woman passing by. The birth control campaigners did not see it as their task to ask why the men were suffering such acute physiological difficulties simply as a result of being deprived of one variety of sexual practice. The necessity of sexual intercourse was assumed, and the women were expected to adjust their bodies and minds to this necessity. Ottesen-Jensen gave an example of a woman who was forced, by her husband's emotional blackmail, to engage in sexual intercourse even though her vagina was, as she described it, 'like an open wound'.[32] The woman was given birth control and hygiene advice, so that she might divert her husband's psychological violence by engaging in sexual intercourse. Ottesen Jensen offers no criticism of the husband's behaviour.

Historians have consistently made the error of seeing birth control as a causal factor in the development of women's sexual freedom, despite the fact that birth control is associated with only one form of heterosexual practice, and that a 'sexual freedom' which was only a freedom to do more sexual intercourse, with no alternative, was no real freedom at all. Feminist historians in particular have seen this supposed 'sexual freedom' as resulting from the way in which birth control allowed a separation between 'sex' and 'reproduction'. Sheila Rowbotham pursues this line of analysis in *Hidden From History* (1973):

> the separation of sexual pleasure from procreation, contained a vital political freedom for women in making differentiation between the 'erotic and the reproductive functions'
> practicable. Only when women were freed from 'that terror of undesired pregnancy' could they begin to enjoy sex freely.[33]

Here Rowbotham is commenting on Stella Browne's work as a birth control campaigner. She makes the mistake of equating sex with sexual intercourse; sexual activity between women after all had never contained the threat of conception, and nor indeed did many sexual practices between women and men. Birth control campaigners who promoted birth control as crucial to the liberation of women's sexuality did not separate sex from reproduction, but on the contrary they reduced sex simply to one specifically reproductive practice.

In the 1920s feminists had not entirely abandoned campaigning around those issues in the field of sexuality which had exercised pre-war feminists, although the impetus was much blunted. In the area of prostitution the feminists campaigned to achieve an equitable law regarding women and men gained a pyrrhic victory. Feminists working within organisations like the Association for Moral and Social Hygiene wanted to make it illegal for either men or women wilfully to cause annoyance to any person in the street. They wanted it to be necessary for the person annoyed to appear in court so that no one might be prosecuted simply on the word of a policeman. These provisions were introduced into Parliament in a Bill entitled 'The Public Places Order Bill' in 1925. The Bill failed, but feminists do seem to have been having some effect through the pressure of their opinion on police and magistrates. An article in the *Woman's Leader* in 1925 explained that the figures for arrests of prostitutes in London had fallen from 2,504 in 1921 to 538 in 1923.[34] The article suggested that this change came about because 'magistrates stiffened by the opinion of the public and the press are reluctant to convict a woman on the sole word of a policeman, and the police either cannot or do not produce an independent witness.'

The 1928 McMillan Report on Prostitution recommended precisely the kind of law on annoyance in the streets that the feminists wanted. This should have been a crowning success but the recommendations were never implemented. In 1959 the solicitation laws against women were made even more severe and in 1960 the Association for Moral and Social Hygiene admitted defeat after nearly a century of struggle for the civil rights of prostitutes. They concluded: 'The law makes the prostitute the scapegoat for the sins of society . . . in these matters the man enjoys a favoured position due to a false position and our comfortable acceptance of a double moral standard.'[35] The feminist campaigners had recognised very clearly that the basic idea on which prostitution was justfied and considered to be necessary, was that of the man's uncontrollable sex drive. They sought to point out that men were not injured by occasional continence. With the idea that continence was harmful the sexologists undermined the gathering strength of the feminist assault on the abuse of women in prostitution.

One campaign in which feminists were successful was that to persuade railway companies in the 1920s to provide single-sex accommodation for women and girls so that they might escape men's sexual harassment. The need for such carriages was a constant theme in feminist journals of the period. The *Vote* of 1925 promoted a campaign of letter-writing to railway companies. The Women's Freedom League used the following wording in their prototype letter:

> We submit that cases of assault or annoyance to women by men on trains are all too frequent, and as women now form a large part of the travelling public, we think that their interests should be taken into consideration by the railway companies, and that they should be protected from the risk of insult, annoyance, or assault while travelling in the companies' railway carriages.[36]

We saw in Chapter 3 what happened to the feminist campaign against sexual abuse of girls in the 1920s, when its force was undermined by the intrusion of psychological explanations. Other aspects of the earlier feminist campaign around sexuality seem to have been entirely absent in the 1920s. The immense propaganda effort which had been directed towards demanding a transformation of male sexual behaviour faded away. Marital rape was no longer a strong focus of concern, and the single standard of sexual morality was no longer a burning issue, although it was on the list of aims of the National Union of Societies for Equal Citizenship as well as that of the Women's Freedom League. Eleanor Rathbone explained her lack of enthusiasm for pursuing these goals in the same way that she abandoned other feminist goals. This was to say that the equal moral standard was too difficult to achieve and could not be simply put through by the means of reform which she favoured, act of Parliament:

> An Equal Moral Standard is something intangible. It cannot be brought about by one or a dozen parliamentary Bills, only by a change of heart, of mental outlook, on the part of society and its members. . . . These questions are much more difficult and delicate and controversial than those embodied in the Bills which are approaching their completion. General public opinion is more backward; expert public opinion is more divided; the existence of a strong ad hoc Society entirely devoted to these questions and affiliated to our Union restricts the part which a wholly women's organisation like ours can profitably play.[37]

Earlier feminists had not restricted their campaign to the demand for legislative change, but had understood the necessity for a massive campaign of public education to change attitudes and transform male behaviour. The 'society' Rathbone mentions which was dedicated to acting around sexual morality was the Association for Moral and Social Hygiene. The fact that the AMSH, under the leadership of the spinster and feminist Alison Neilans, maintained its dedication to feminist principles around sexuality was no excuse for their abandonment by other feminists. Rathbone's abandonment of such a campaign could have been encouraged by the change in sexual ideology since she mentioned that 'expert' opinion was divided. She was quite right about that. By the 1920s there existed a large body of professional and progressive opinion which was promoting ideas about sexual morality which were in total contradiction to that of a single moral standard.

The main weapon which the sexologists used in the 1920s to pressure women into adjusting themselves to men's sexual behaviour and to undermine the feminist critique of male sexuality, was the concept of women's frigidity. Feminists, spinsters, lesbians, any women who showed reluctance to adjust, were attacked as frigid man-haters. In the following chapter we will see why the idea of the 'frigide' developed and the purposes to which it was put.

CHAPTER 9

The Invention of the Frigid Woman

The 1920s have been seen both by some contemporary commentators and by historians as a decade which witnessed dramatic changes in sexual morality. Some historians have seen the 1920s as the first 'sexual revolution' of the twentieth century and the 1960s as the second.[1] What did the 1920s sexual revolution consist of? The American feminist historian Linda Gordon explains that the 1920s sexual revolution in America was specifically heterosexual. It was 'not a general loosening of sexual taboos but only of those on marital heterosexual activity.'[2] Gordon makes it clear that this change intensified taboos on homosexuality. At the same time it altered the rules of heterosexual behaviour. For some 'free love' meaning sexual intercourse outside marriage became a possibility. In America, according to Gordon, such 'free love' was carried out in communities of bohemians and intellectuals in the immediate post-war period. This was not a wonderful liberation for women since woman's 'survival and success largely depended upon pleasing men' and women had to 'meet new male demands'.[3] Dora Russell, in her autobiography *The Tamarisk Tree* (1975), describes experiments happening in Britain at the time which reflected the Greenwich Village experience.[4] This kind of sexual practice probably did not affect a very large proportion of the population. Commentators on working-class sexual behaviour during and after the First World War bemoaned a phenomenon they described as 'amateur prostitution'. 'Amateur' prostitution seems to have meant many young women engaging in sexual intercourse before or outside marriage or in some cases the latter practice combined with the acceptance of minor favours or presents from men.

Charlotte Haldane used the term in its latter sense when

deploring the post-war change in morals in her book *Motherhood and its Enemies* (1927). Haldane was a novelist and married to a well-known Cambridge biologist. She had been a suffragette in her youth and explained 'Lest anyone accuse me of bias, let me here confess that at 18 I myself joined the Women's Social and Political Union, and sold its weekly paper . . . on Hampstead Heath.'[5] She attributed the change in morals to the effects of the war and specifically to the phenomenon of war babies. The historian Arthur Marwick uses an extract from the diary of Mary Agnes Hamilton to demonstrate the war's effect on morality:

> Life was less than cheap: it was thrown away. The religious teaching that the body was the temple of the Holy Ghost could mean little or nothing to those who saw it mutilated and destroyed in millions by Christian nations engaged in war. All moral standards were held for a short time and irretrievably lost. . . . The great destroyer of the old ideal of female chastity, as accepted by women themselves, was here. How and why refuse appeals, backed up by the hot beating of your own heart, or what at the moment you thought to be your heart, which were put with passion and even pathos by a hero here today, and gone tomorrow.[6]

War babies became a *cause célèbre* not so much because there was a small rise in the illegitimacy rate as because the government felt compelled, under wartime conditions, to reward these 'fallen' women with financial help, since they had fallen pregnant by the soldier heroes of the day and were bearing the soldier heroes of tomorrow. The war babies may not have evidenced a change in women's sexual behaviour so much as the difficulty during the war of women marrying whilst pregnant because of military postings.

It seems unlikely that the phenomenon of 'free love' was the most significant change in sexual ideology and behaviour in the 1920s. The greatest change was in the eroticising of the married woman. The 1920s saw a massive campaign by sexologists and sex advice writers to conscript women into marriage and ensure that once within it they would engage cheerfully and frequently in sexual intercourse. Marriage was seen to be primarily about sexual intercourse which was to be the pivot and focus of the relationship.

Ideal Marriage, by the Dutch sexologist Van de Velde, was published in 1926. This book achieved such success that it was republished consistently until well into the second 'sexual revolution' of the twentieth century. The 37th impression was published in 1961. *Ideal Marriage* was translated by the socialist feminist Stella Browne. Thomas Van de Velde explained in his introduction why he considered marriage to be so important. This was because it was sacred to the believing Christian, indispensable to the social order, absolutely necessary in the interests of the children, it offered to woman security in which she could love and provided for men 'the best background for useful and efficient work'.[7] He asserted that there were four cornerstones to marriage of which by far the most important was 'a vigorous and harmonious sex life'. He wrote that this had to be:

> solidly and skilfully built, for it has bear a main portion of the weight of the whole structure. But in many cases it is badly balanced and of poor materials; so can we wonder that the whole edifice collapses, soon? Sex is the foundation of marriage. Yet most married people do not know the ABC of sex.[8]

This picture of marriage is very different from that of the ideal Victorian marriage. Sexual intercourse was now to play a vastly inflated role. This reflects changes that had been taking place in the relations between the sexes. Some of those pressures which had forced women into marriage and ensured their complete dependence upon men had been alleviated. The most punishing legal disabilities of marriage for women had been relieved by the 1920s. The Married Women's Property Acts made women less dependent. The 1923 Divorce Act equalised the grounds for divorce so that women could get a divorce on the grounds of their husbands' adultery without having to prove other bad behaviour like incest or bestiality as well. These changes fought for by feminists, caused great anxiety to many of the male sex reformers, even those of apparently progressive outlook. One of the latter was the socialist and self-professed pro-feminist Alec Craig. In his book *Sex and Revolution* (1934) he applauded the changes in sexual morality and declared that he was a 'modernist' following the programme of Bertrand Russell for sex reform. The modernists were apparently for birth control, the emancipation of women and sex education and they thought that sexual intercourse should be justified simply on the basis of mutual attraction. Craig bemoaned the changes in divorce law in particular because he saw them as anti-men: 'The English law, it will be observed, is heavily weighted in favour of the woman, this is due to changes that have been made with increasing effectiveness during comparatively recent times.'[9] The result was, in his opinion, that woman had been given freedom without responsibility, and the equilibrium of English family life was unstable.

The development of new work opportunities meant that women were less financially dependent upon men and marriage, and feminist spinsters had been proclaiming the joys of independence and hostility to marriage. Women's new work role in industry during the war created enormous anxiety amongst antifeminsts of all persuasions. Charlotte Haldane saw as the most significant 'enemy' of motherhood, the development through the experience of war work of what she called the 'warworking woman', the 'more or less unsexed or undersexed female type' or 'intersex woman':[10]

> the 'warworking' type of 'woman' – aping the cropped hair, the great booted feet, the grim jaw, the uniform, and if possible the medals, of the military man. If this type had been transitory its usefulness might be accorded, but it is not doubtful, as I propose to show, that in a long run we shall have to regret its social and political influence, much as we may applaud its wartime works.[11]

Haldane's words are an example of the backlash against independent women, spinsters and lesbians which was a significant aspect of the campaign to promote marriage and motherhood throughout the 1920s. The image of the warworking woman also appeared in fiction. Radclyffe Hall's solution to the problem of the woman who became used to independence and fulfilment through war work in the war years, when she discovered that she was to be allowed no place in the ranks of 'normal' women after the war, was to have her discover that she was really, deep down, a man. In Hall's short story *Miss Ogilvy Finds Herself* (1926) the warworking woman's post-war plight is examined with pathos and Miss Ogilvy discovers that she has the soul of a prehistoric man. Hall did not choose the feminist explanation of attributing the heroine's troubles to the limitations placed upon women's lives under male domination. She chose a mystical/biological explanation which fitted in with sexological stereotypes of lesbians.[12]

An important motivation behind the writings of the sex reformers in the 1920s was the desire to shore up marriage. This was to be done by introducing a new binding ingredient in the form of woman's sexual response to sexual intercourse, to compensate for the lost legal and economic restraints. Another likely motivation for this change in men's sexual taste in wives is the decline in the use of prostitutes in the first two decades of the twentieth century. Contemporary sources generally agree that such a decline took place. Some attribute it to the growth of 'amateur' prostitution.[13] It could also be that there was a change in public opinion regarding the use of prostitutes. The sex reformers were in fairly general agreement that the purchase of sexual pleasure was not desirable. The massive campaigning efforts of feminists against the use of women in prostitution, coupled with anxiety over venereal disease, may well have caused such a change of attitude. If men were not to use prostitutes then they would require from their wives the same response of simulated passion which they had previously been able to buy. Wives could be indifferent no longer and must fulfil the prostitute's role.

There was a problem with the implementation of this new role for sexual intercourse. The work of the sexologists testifies to the existence of strong resistance by women. A 'scientific' explanation had to be invented to account for this resistance. It was assumed that the 'normal' woman would enthusiastically embrace sexual intercourse. The deviant woman who failed to respond with enthusiasm was classified as 'frigid'. Prior to the 1920s the concept of the 'frigide' had not been necessary because normal women had not been expected to have such a response to sexual intercourse. The fear of being labelled 'frigid' was to be used as a weapon, by the sexologists and their popularisers, to force women to adapt themselves to the demands made by the new role for sexual intercourse. The attack on the resisting women within marriage was combined with a massive renewed onslaught of propaganda against spinsters, feminists, 'man-haters', lesbians; all those categories of women who were seen as rejecting not only sexual intercourse but marriage itself.

The experts disagreed over the percentage of women who were frigid, and over whether all frigidity was curable or whether some was biologically ordained. Wilhelm Stekel was a Freudian analyst who seems to have specialised in the problem of women's frigidity. His two-volume work, entitled *Frigidity in Woman in Relation to Her Lovelife* was published in New York in 1926. It was one of many studies of 'sexual impotence' or 'deficient sexual sensibility' (the terms for describing the problem were not yet fixed because it was so new), which were published in the 1920s. He estimated that 40-50 per cent of women were frigid and considered that the problem particularly afflicted women of the 'higher cultural levels'. He asserted that there was no such thing as an 'asexual' being and that frigidity was the result of repression. Weith Knudsen was a professor of jurisprudence and economics at the Technical College at Trondheim, Norway. He was an antifeminist whose work *Feminism — The Woman Question from Ancient Times to the Present Day* was translated into English in 1928. Gallichan quoted sympathetically from his work which clearly had an audience among the British sex reformers. Weith Knudsen quoted estimates from various sources which placed the percentage of women who were frigid at between 40 and 60 per cent. He divided women into five classes according to their sexual responsiveness and estimated that 20 per cent of women were cold, 25 per cent indifferent, 30 per cent compliant, 15 per cent warm and 10 per cent passionate. He claimed that the first 20 per cent of 'cold' women were incurable and that part of the next 25 per cent could be assisted but that 40 per cent of women overall were incurable.[14]

The reasons offered for women's fridgity were many and various and included both physiological and psychological factors. Stekel suggested homosexuality as one cause of frigidity and considered this to be curable with analysis which would help the patient 'improve her attitude to men'. However, the description he gives of the 'homosexual' woman conforms closely with the caricature image of an independent woman of the time:

> She wishes to dominate and is afraid to submit. Orgasm means to give in, to be the weaker one, to acknowledge the man as master. This type is keeping back the orgasm because of pride. She plays the 'she-man', trying to imitate the habits, qualities, dress and sporting qualities and even the shortcomings of men, smoking, drinking, fighting and the like. She hates motherhood, she despises nursing, is afraid of giving birth, of labour pains, and she tries to suppress her monthly period.[15]

A sexual interest in women was not necessary to be classified a homosexual under this definition. The sexual habits of the problem homosexual or intersexual woman might take the form merely of masturbation.

Gallichan also posed homosexuality as a cause of frigidity and having stated that 'unquestionably a considerable number of so-called "frigid" women are homosexual', demonstrated the gravity of the problem by stating his conviction that 'sexual inversion is more prevalent among women than among men'.[16] Some writers saw 'intersexuality' as the result of frigidity rather than as the cause. Haldane used this argument to encourage participation in sexual intercourse. She explained that the development of the 'secondary sex characters of the opposite sex' might appear through 'non-fulfilment of the normal sex functions'.[17] The bogeys of lesbianism or growing beards were part of the armoury of threats used to drive women into compulsory sexual intercourse. Often in the same book and according to the whims of the authors, inter-sexuality could be seen as cause or result of frigidity. Similarly feminism and manhating were cited as both cause and result of the same phenomenon.

Another favoured explanation for frigidity was 'arrested development'. The arrested development was said to be either psychological or physical. The former led to 'psychosexual infantilism' and the latter, according to Van de Velde led to 'genital infantilism' which took the form of a misplaced clitoris. Weith Knudsen attributed only 10 per cent of the amount of frigidity to feminism, and the rest to cerebral defects, defective secretion of the sexual glands and nervous disorders. Gallichan also mentions various biological causes such as ovarian inefficiency, amenorrhoea, prolapse of the womb, vaginitis and constipation. Gallichan cited masturbation as one of the causes of frigidity in woman. He stated that 'The habit, now generally referred to as an auto-erotic act, tends to blunt the finer sensibility for coitus in wedlock, and the practice is often preferred to the normal gratification.'[18] Often, he stated, mental masturbation or erotic daydreaming was as harmful as the physical variety. He cited another expert who claimed that many married women 'develop the habit of masturbation as their relief from coitus which they dislike.'[19] Masturbation is thus seen as both a result of women's dislike of sexual intercourse and as a reason for that dislike. It was not to be tolerated in either case, since women were to engage in sexual intercourse whether that was the activity which gave them most satisfaction or not.

It should be clear at this point that frigidity was not understood to mean lack of sexual response. Lesbianism and masturbation were likely to include some sexual response and were cited as cause and result of frigidity. Frigidity was quite simply woman's failure to respond with enthusiasm to one particular sexual practice, sexual intercourse.

Two other much favoured explanations for women's frigidity were ignorance due to lack of sex education and the trauma of the first night. The defloration was written about by most sex advice writers of the period as a fearful ordeal to be got over as swiftly as possible, like a visit to the dentist. Behind the anxiety about defloration lay the idea that women could not be expected to have a satisfactory sexual response at the outset of married life. Not only were women expected to be slower to arouse on each occasion on which sexual activity took place, but they were expected to take months or even years to learn how to respond sexually to their husbands. Van de Velde quotes two experts in *Ideal Marriage* who considered: 'inadequate sensibility in coitus at the beginning of sexual life, must be accounted physiologically normal in women: they have to learn how to feel both voluptuous pleasure and actual orgasm. The frequency of temporary anaesthesia, these specialists estimate as absolute, 100 per cent.'[20] Isabel Hutton wrote, in a marital advice book *The Hygiene of Marriage* (1923), 'It is quite normal, however, for a woman not to experience in any way the feelings of sexual excitement, even towards the man she loves, till some time after the marriage has been consummated.'[21] Sexual pleasure in intercourse was to be learnt by women, often with considerable difficulty, but was presumably pleasurable from the beginning for men since they entered into the activity with pleasure in mind and could not be expected to undergo lengthy distress and pain. This did not cause the experts to wonder, as we might now, whether this might indicate that sexual intercourse was not a form of sexual activity into which women fell most naturally, or a form of activity, in fact, most suited to male needs and contraindicated for women. The concept of frigidity could not be applied to men. Men could be classified as 'impotent' if they wanted to engage in sexual intercourse but couldn't manage it. Men who were indifferent to, or wished to avoid sexual intercourse were and are seen as exercising free will and freedom of choice rather than necessarily suffering from a medical or psychological complaint. The concept of frigidity removed that freedom of choice for women where sexual intercourse was concerned.

The sexologists listed an impressive array of dangers which would befall women, children, men, marriage, and 'society' from woman's failure to enjoy or engage in sexual intercourse. The sexologists assumed that there was a sexual instinct or drive and that if this instinct did not find its appropriate outlet in sexual intercourse, then women would suffer from 'repression', and thwarted instincts, which would cause them to be 'bitter', 'man-hating', 'destructive', 'fanatical', 'kill-joys', a 'threat to civilisation'. Ludovici, in his antifeminist classic *Lysistrata* (1924), employed this idea. Ludovici's book was a powerful fascist tract, in which he called for the return of the superman and the destruction of democracy in order to save the race from deterioration. The main problem, which necessitated these drastic measures, was women's withdrawl from sexual intercourse. Ludovici made it clear that he was terrified of feminism. The connection between fear of feminism and the rise of fascist ideology in the immediate post-war period would repay further study. It has been suggested that D.H. Lawrence's flirtation with fascist thought at this period, combined with the developing strength of his misogyny, might have stemmed from this source.[22]

Ludovici was concerned about 'surplus women', the 2 million women in excess of men in the population in Britain. He feared that, because these 'surplus women' had no access to sexual satisfaction with men, the women's 'thwarted instincts' would find some destructive outlet since 'A thwarted instinct does not meekly subside. It seeks compensation and damages for its rebuff.'[23] The danger was exacerbated by the fact that these women were spreading the doctrine that 'human beings can well get on and be happy without sexual expression' even to married women. Ludovici gave an alarming picture of the steadily increasing threat posed by these women. The main danger was that they were, in his opinion, hostile to men:

> As the number of these women increases every year, and, in their systematic depreciation of the value of life, they are joined and supported by thousands of disillusioned married women who also scoff at marriage and motherhood as the only satisfactory calling for women, swell with imposing rapidity.[25]

The dangerous effects of 'thwarting' the 'instincts' according to Ludovici was that women would compensate with the 'lust of exercising power' and alongside that a 'bitter hatred of men'. This led to the 'note of hostility to the male' in woman movements since woman movements were 'largely led either by spinsters or else by unhappy married women'.[25]

Ludovici painted a description of the future he envisaged if the 'disgruntled females' were successful. He feared that male dominance would be overthrown, the exercise of male sexuality severely curtailed and eventually the numbers of men in the population severely reduced:

> congress of male and female will have begun to seem much more guilty and disgusting even than it is today, and as the male will still be looked upon (as he is now) as the principal culprit in the matter, the age of consent will probably be extended to 35 or 40, if not to the menopause. Seduction and rape will be punished brutally, probably by means of emasculation; and men of vigorous sexuality will be eliminated in order to make way for a generation of low-sexed, meek and sequatious lackeys.[26]

His predictions about restrictions on male sexual behaviour are clearly based upon the demands of feminist campaigners of the day though much exaggerated. Women would go even further than the above, he claimed, and take to extracorporeal gestation and cease to cohabit with men, and at length, 'The superfluousness of men above a certain essential minimum (about 5 to every 1,000 women) will have become recognised officially and unofficially as a social fact.'[27] There would then be an annual slaughter of males or at least vigorous males and if sex choice were developed, only $\frac{1}{2}$ per cent of males would be reared yearly. Ludovici's concern with the 'problem' of women's refusal to participate in heterosexuality stemmed from a fear of feminism and its implications for men, particularly in the area of control of male sexual behaviour.

In the antifeminist classic, *Motherhood and its Enemies* (1927), Charlotte Haldane, favoured a more strictly biological theory of the connection between lack of sexual activity and dangerousness in women. She focussed her concern on virgins:

> We are revising all our opinions on the value of virginity — economic, social, political or religious. Scientific students cannot avoid scientific conclusions such as the demonstrable evidence that in certain animals, including man, the non-fulfilment of the normal sex functions due to atrophy or castration may cause the emergence in later life of the secondary sexual characters of the opposite sex.
>
> We do not yet have the means to investigate the psychological effects of permanent virginity in great detail, but enough is known to make us aware that in entrusting responsibility towards individuals and the State to elderly virgins we may be acting unwisely.[28]

The cruelty of this statement is remarkable considering the conscientious and self-sacrificing social service rendered by virginal spinsters at this time in voluntary social work, teaching and all kinds of work within the community. The definition of spinsters was changing at this time. Whilst previously the word spinster had simply meant unmarried woman, it was coming to mean, specifically, women who had not done sexual intercourse with men. Thus 'spinsters' like Stella Browne and Rebecca West were able to use 'spinster' as a dirty word to attack women who were not experienced with men. [29] Spinsters who did do sexual intercourse, though not married, were able to feel highly superior. This new meaning is much closer the present-day meaning of the word. Now, when women are expected to engage in sex with men whether married or not, the word 'spinster' is generally reserved for those who do not. Haldane identified the problem of the virgin as being that she might, in later life, develop masculine characteristics, and the further her habits and interests 'deviate towards the male, the greater must be the danger of her influence'.[30] She described those who had 'deviated' as the 'intermediate sex' which is the term used by the homosexual rights reformer Edward Carpenter to describe homosexuals in his pioneering work.[31] It is unlikely that Haldane did not know the meaning of the term she chose to use. She seems to have been very alarmed about unmarried women becoming lesbians. The 'intermediate' women were only, in her opinion, suited to:

> subordinate positions which do not call for great emotional development, or great experience of life, and for a wide and generous point of view in the executant. . . . But in dealing with education or in nursing, or medicine, intermediate women may do an enormous amount of harm.[32]

The influence of the virgin intermediates had 'grown alarmingly' in the past few years she said:

> Their fanaticism and crankiness have caused them to take up freak science, freak religions, and freak philanthropy. They are the chief supporters of movements such as anti-vivisection, which does its best to retard the advance of experimental science in this country; of dogs' homes and cats' homes; of missionary societies and 'Kill-joy' propaganda.[33]

Spinsters were dangerous, she argued, because they had interests which were not identical with those of men: 'Only the normal

175

wife and mother will consider her interests identical with those of her husband and children.'[34] She considered that spinsters were likely to become antagonistic to the mother and, more worrying-ly, they were guilty of having created hostility between the sexes by going outside the role of wife and mother: 'They have uncon-sciously or deliberately fomented "sex-antagonism" by compet-ing with men economically and refusing to conform, or to allow women in general to conform to the masculine ideals of sex relationships.'[35] Spinsters, it seemed, were upsetting the com-promises and adjustments which heterosexual married women had made to fit in with men's wishes and demands. Men's anger at the threat to their dominance was blamed on spinsters. They were scapegoated and sacrificed as women like Haldane rushed to reassure and comfort their men and keep their relationships with them peaceful.

Weith Knudsen saw frigidity in women as a 'threat to civilisa-tion'. It is clear that by the word 'civilisation' he meant male dominance. He sought to explain why 'psycho-erotic deficiency' was 'worth making such a fuss about' and how it was connected with feminism:

> it is not possible thus to dismiss the lurking social-biological danger that this sexual anaesthesia, so prevalent among civilised women, will intensify the misunderstanding between the sexes and contribute to make them even greater strangers to each other than Nature has already made them. Thus this (relative or absolute) feminine erotic sensibility actually reinforces the threats to our civilisation, which in a higher degree than in any former culture is based on the assumption of mutual understanding and co-operation between the sexes.[36]

Weith Knudsen's conclusion is that allowing what he calls 'eroti-cally impotent' women to have any political power would be dangerous to other women and men. No political power could be given to women since it was impossible to separate off 'erotically impotent' women from those who were potent. If women were allowed any political voice he considered, then decisions would:

> depend pre-eminently on the hyper-feministic, anaesthetic minority among the women. For it would not be unreasonable to assume that hyper-feminism has as its most numerous, most ardent and most fanatical adherents among the erotically

anaesthetic, neurasthenic women. Many of its monstrous assertions and proposals are simply only to be explained by an inborn and incurable blindness to all erotic phenomena.[37]

Weith Knudsen was convinced that peace in the 'open war between the sexes' could only be reached through the 'natural subordination (of women) which cannot be, and in the case of the white man, so long as history has known him and long before that, never has been synonymous with oppression; on the contrary'.[38] Weith Knudsen's alarm at women's frigidity stemmed from its connection with feminism and his fear of the results of feminism was profound. He described it as an agitation 'against Man, and the society created by him' and claims that everyone must be aware of the 'reality of Feminist disasters'. Anyone who was not was *consciously using* the Feminist movement as a wedge for the destruction of the white man's world'.[39]

Walter Gallichan also saw the results of female frigidity in apocalyptic terms. In his 1929 book *The Poison of Prudery* he wrote:

> The erotically impotent women have an enormous influence upon the young, the conventions and regulations of society, and even upon sex legislation. These degenerate women are a menace to civilisation. They provoke sex misunderstanding and antagonism; they wreck conjugal happiness, and pose as superior moral beings when they are really victims of disease.[40]

Gallichan produced many other diverse reasons why frigidity in women was dangerous, none quite so extreme as the above and mostly concerned with the frigidity of married women. In *Sexual Antipathy and Coldness in Women* (1927), he produced a formidable array of dangers including, as suggested in the title, the problem of manhating. A serious danger according to Gallichan was the effect of a mother's frigidity upon her children. 'The children of sexually cold mothers generally show signs of emotional and neurotic disturbance at an early age.'[41] Much of the disturbance, he claimed, came from the domestic disharmony and disappointment of the parents which stemmed from the wife's frigidity.

Wilhelm Stekel contributed an article entitled 'Frigidity in Mothers' to a 1930 collection called *The New Generation* which contained articles from many well known names in the sex reforming camp and was introduced by Bertrand Russell. Stekel's article detailed the dire effects of frigidity in mothers upon their children. According to Stekel frigidity meant 'repressed sexuality'. He states categorically that 'frigid women are not fit to be mothers. They should first get rid of their frigidity.'[42]

Van de Velde, in volume 2 of his trilogy on the relations between the sexes, *Sex Hostility in Marriage* (1931), explained precisely how the frigid woman became a manhater. He attributed the contempt for men displayed by 'unsatisfied women' to the reversal of feelings of attraction. Sexual antagonism, he explained, was 'nothing less than a fear of attraction' which developed from a knowledge of the power that 'sexual impulse' would have over them. Some women developed contempt for their husbands and men in general because they knew that sexual satisfaction was denied them through their husbands' selfishness or ignorance. The process of reversal is described thus:

> The mental processes referred to, sublimation, reversal and repression, often appear simultaneously, resulting in the familiar type of 'man-hater', which needs no further description. The contempt with which such women regard men is reversal of the respect they would have been ready to have paid him; and also of the desire to be subjected, which is frequently encountered, and is a characteristic quality of the feminine mind.[43]

Another reason for lamenting women's frigidity was that it inhibited the husband's pleasure and could make him feel uncomfortable when he was using her body in sexual intercourse. Weith Knudsen provides us with a graphic description of the tragic consequences for a man of having a frigid white woman for a wife instead of the Eastern woman whom he considered to be far more responsive:

> he who knows how terrible and degrading it can be, especially to a nobler masculine nature, to be reduced to mating with one of the numerous sexually anaesthetic white women, will understand the European returned from the tropics, who replies to the expert's enquiries that he prefers the Malayan, Polynesian or Japanese mistress, who screamed with joy if he only laid his hand on her, to the icy white woman, who regarded his erotic transports with contempt and did not even shrink from showing him that she only just bore with him

because it was supposed to be part of her wifely duties. And to make things worse, she wronged her husband in this by a feeling that precisely by doing so she showed herself a 'higher being' than he, though, of course, the truth is that she is a defective individual, a poor invalid, a presumptuous ignoramus in matters of love.[44]

Weith Knudsen's assumption that non-European, non-western women would be uncritically thrilled by any male sexual approach is a common feature of racist sexual stereotyping by white western authors. This form of sexual stereotyping was used to describe working-class European women as well. One of the favourite myths to be propagated by the sex reformers was that 'frigidity' was a problem of the middle-class woman and that the working-class woman was somehow more primitive, spontaneous and sensual. Stekel asserted that it was women of the 'higher cultural levels', by which he presumably meant middle-class, who were most likely to suffer from frigidity.[45] In fact sources such as the letters of the Cooperative Women's Guild, letters written to Marie Stopes after the publication of *Married Love*, and the reports on the work of marriage advice centres and birth control campaigners given at the 1929 Sex Reform Congress, all indicate that women's 'resistance' or 'frigidity' was a cross-class phenomenon at this time. Letters from members of the Women's Cooperative Guild, received in reply to questions about maternity in 1915, mostly describe the physical agonies and economic difficulties caused to the women through constant childbearing. They also include comments which would have earned some of the writers the appellation 'frigid' from the sex reformers. One woman wrote:

During the time of pregnancy, the male beast keeps entirely from the female: not so with the woman: she is at the prey of a man just the same as though she was not pregnant. Practically within a few days after the birth, and as soon as the birth is over, she is tortured again. If a woman does not feel well she must not say so, as a man has such a lot of ways of punishing a woman if she does not give in to him.[46]

Such sentiments are very similar to those of Francis Swiney. The letter writers had striking feminist analyses of the plight of wives in respect of their husbands' sexual demands. The following writer stressed that women in all classes shared a common situation in this respect:

No amount of State help can help the suffering of mothers until men are taught many things in regard to the right use of the organs of reproduction, and until he realises that the wife's body belongs to herself, and until the marriage relations take a higher sense of morality and bare justice. And what I imply not only exists in the lower strata of society, but is just as prevalent in the higher. So it's men who need to be educated most. . . . No animal will submit to this; why should the woman? Why simply because of the marriage laws, of the woman belonging to the man, to have and to own, etc.[47]

It may be that the male sexologists used the myth that non-western women and working-class women were ever willing and eager for sex with men to pressure women of their own class into sexual compliance. Josephine Butler and other women involved in the campaign against the Contagious Diseases Acts in the 1870s and 1880s particularly attacked the abuse and exploitation of working-class women by middle-class men. It could be that the sexual stereotyping of the sexologists helped to justify such exploitation and draw the sting of the feminist critique. The sexologists and their popularisers were skilled in the technique of playing off one group of women against another in order to achieve their propaganda objectives. So the desires of western and eastern women were counterposed, similarly the desires of working-class and middle-class women. In the same fashion the interests of the spinster and the married woman were represented as not only different but contradictory. This is the technique of divide and rule.

The non-participation of spinsters in sexual intercourse was held to be as dangerous to the interests of men and society as the 'frigidity' of the married woman. Alec Craig, the socialist and sexual 'modernist' was very worried that spinster schoolteachers might be dangerous to the young because they were not doing sexual intercourse; 'energy which is dammed up sexual urge, seeking another channel or outlet is rarely satisfactory in its results. Much might be said about the evils resulting from the almost exclusive employment of women in the teaching profession.'[48] Gallichan warned specifically against the employment of the 'frigide' as a teacher, because he thought she would make girls critical of men.[49]

The stereotype of the spinster which these writers were offering was so unattractive that spinsterhood would not have appeared a positive alternative to women. Haldane wrote: 'The sub-normal is a type chiefly prevalent among celibate women. They tend, for instance, to enjoy a less rich and varied diet than married women.'[50] Most writers about sex in the 1920s fought shy of mentioning the possibility that women might have sex with each other. They avoided using the words 'lesbian' and 'homosexual'. None the less it is clear from the descriptions they gave of the group of spinsters that worried them most, that they had lesbians in mind. Haldane's 'intersex' group has a list of supposedly masculine attributes precisely similar to Ellis's description of the female homosexual in Chapter 6.[51]

Women were required to enjoy sexual intercourse, not just take part in it. Sexual pleasure in intercourse was not expected to be positive or strengthening for women. The sexologists of the 1920s predicted with assurance that women could not gain pleasure in sexual intercourse unless they subjected themselves to the will of their husbands. This assumption had also underlain the work of other sexologists before the First World War, such as Ellis, Bloch, and Forel. The writers of the 1920s put much more emphasis upon the idea of the necessity of women's subjection in sexual intercourse, and expected it to fulfil a grandiose social and political function. Through the orchestration of women's sexual response, based upon submission, writers like Stekel and Van de Velde believed that all the problems which most alarmed them such as feminism, manhating and female resistance to male domination in general, could be overcome. A radical new significance was given to sexual intercourse. It became both a metaphor for the subjection of women and a method of effecting that subjection. The eagerness of the sexologists to help women with their 'frigidity' becomes easier to understand as we see how closely they associated women's sexual pleasure with their submission.

Many writers before Stekel had mentioned the connections between feminism, manhating and frigidity. The main theme of Stekel's work was his unequivocal proposition that female frigidity was a form of resistance to male domination, a weapon to be used against men in the battle of the sexes:

> We shall never understand the problem of the frigid woman unless we take into consideration the fact that the two sexes are engaged in a lasting conflict. . . . The social aspect of the problem, too, unveils itself before our eyes. We recognise

plainly that dyspareunia (frigidity in women) is a social problem; it is one of woman's weapons in the universal struggle of the sexes.[52]

Stekel considered that a woman must submit herself to her husband in order to experience sexual pleasure. He saw woman's refusal to experience pleasure as an unconscious or conscious refusal to submit or be 'conquered'. He believed that 'two bipolar forces struggle for mastery over human life: The will-to-power and the will-to-submission (or the self-subjection urge).'[53] It will be no surprise to discover that he expected the subjection urge to conquer the will-to-power in women but not in men. He argued that all lovers must yield in love but continued in the same breath to speak only of women being 'conquered':

A secret (unrecognised) notion of all persons who love is that to make another person 'feel' is to achieve a victory over that person. To give one's self to another, to permit one's self to be 'roused', means self-abandonment; it means 'yielding'! This act of submission is expressed symbolically even in woman's position during the sexual embrace. Alfred Adler very properly lays great stress upon the symbolisms of 'above' and 'below'. Indeed, certain women feel roused only if they are 'on top', i.e. by clinging to the fantasy that they are males and that they are the ones to 'rouse' their sexual partner, who is thus relegated to the passive or feminine role. To be aroused by a man means acknowledging one's self as conquered.[54]

Stekel did not see woman's 'will-to-submission' in sex as being isolated from the rest of her experience. As a psychoanalyst he was used to treating the whole personality and to treating the 'dyspareunia' as part of the woman's whole personality. He was indignant at the general 'obstinacy' of the women he treated, their refusal to submit and the fact that they wished to be personalities in their own right. Such a wish he associated with the 'will-to-power' which he saw as the desire of a woman to survive as a self-respecting, independent human being who still had some conception of herself as a person not subsumed into her husband. The following unsympathetic comment upon his patients illustrates his attitude:

We are still disposed to underestimate the infantile obstinacy of most women, their predisposition to 'resentment', their vengeful attitude, their inability to forget an insult and their play-acting propensitites which enables them to mask the inner motives of their emotional aloofness. There are women who refuse to be made happy; *they resent the thought that the man has saved them, that they owe him everything.*[55]

The way to cure 'dyspareunia', according to Stekel, was to uncover the motives for the obstinacy in the woman's whole personality and treat those. One of the symptoms of the obstinacy was woman's desire to see herself as a separate personality and only when the woman stopped fighting to maintain her separate personality would she, according to Stekel, be able to achieve sexual pleasure: 'I have emphasised repeatedly that the dyspareunia signifies an "inner negation". . . . Obstinacy cancels the will to submission and reopens the struggle for the maintenance of the feeling of personality.'[56] Stekel saw women's frigidity as a mass phenomenon and as a weapon used by women in the general war of the sexes. Curing individual frigidity but on a mass scale would aid the end of women's resistance to men in the battle of the sexes and ensure male dominance, not just on an individual but on a societal scale.

Van de Velde's *Sex Hostility in Marriage* makes it clear that the correct form of marriage ought to be male dominance and female submission, and that this power relationship was to be symbolised in sexual activity. Van de Velde refers frequently to Stekel and was much influenced by Stekel's ideas. His description of the desirable form of marriage was placed in capitals to give extra emphasis:

> As a result of characteristic sexual qualities (in particular as a result of her physiological vulnerability and plasticity) the woman is dependent on the man for protection and support. She demands this support – consciously or unconsciously. She not only accepts, but desires the dependence involved by this, because her highly developed intuitive feeling tells her the reasons for this dependence are based on natural (biological) causes.
>
> Dependence is always connected with submission, and the desire for the one involves the other. In addition to this, numerous powerful influences making for submission to the man are present in sexual connection, the sexual impulse is associated in the woman with a tendency to submit herself.[57]

The reader could be forgiven for thinking that it was Van de Velde rather than woman's 'intuitive' feelings that were telling her to submit. Van de Velde's main concern in all his work was the preservation of marriage and the elimination of that dangerous threat to marriage, 'hostility'. The hostility seems to have been caused by women's refusal to submit to their husbands. He writes that woman because of her 'emotional temperament':

> desires either power or subjection. She desires submission with her whole soul and being, but seeks to gain power. She, herself, sooner or later, (usually, however, from the very first) begins the struggle for power, and, if she wins the victory, she loses the very thing that she most needs, the protection and support of the man.[58]

Though it may seem hard to understand how to marry these contradictions, Van de Velde none the less found some logic in this and went on to say that there was only one possible outcome of the struggle. The woman can only win by losing, 'the woman who wins the game of the struggle for power, loses. Only if the man carries off the prize can both the husband and wife win. If the woman wins, then both lose.'[59] This very strange language which Van de Velde uses, in which words mean their opposites, at first sight a strange language for a scientist to use, is actually the language of sado-masochism. Men's pornographic literature of sado-masochism is full of women who choose to be conquered and win by losing, women for whom only slavery is freedom and for whom only being bound is being really 'free'.[60] Van de Velde was simply trying to extend the rules of the pornographic game into everyday sexual life, and discovering a disquieting amount of resistance in the women playmates. In sado-masochistic pornography women consent to their submission and are said to win by losing in order that the obvious cruelty inflicted upon them should not look too unfair and appear to be what the women really want.

Weith Knudsen was also greatly exercised by the problem of women's frigidity. He also saw woman's subjection to be necessary to her sexual pleasure, and was annoyed that feminism seemed to be interfering with women's natural inclination to submit:

> It is therefore only to be expected that a mental atmosphere like that of present-day Feminism, which in a number of women actually precludes the psychical submission,

abandonment and self-effacement under the man's will – *one* of the most important requirements for the woman's attaining maximum erotic gratification with all that follows therefrom – should of itself be calculated to increase the already large number of white women who are erotically impotent from other causes of a more physical nature.[61]

Many different solutions were offered for the problem of the woman who was not participating in sexual intercourse. For spinsters the favoured solution was concubinage or polygamy. Ludovici recommended it and was able to support his plan with a congratulatory letter in the introduction to *Lysistrata* from Norman Haire, liberal British sexologist, founder of the Walworth Marriage Advice Centre in 1921. Haire asserted that the normal woman could not be happy 'unmated' and agreed that concubinage was the right solution.[62] Solutions offered for the married woman included sending her to a psychoanalyst or gynaecologist, better sex education and more firmness and resolve from the husband on the wedding night. The most effective solution is likely to have been the sex advice literature itself, not because of the factual information if offered, but because of the fear and feelings of inadequacy which would be instilled into resisting women. To be 'normal', women had to do sexual intercourse willingly. They were also pressured by threats. Wives were told that they would lose their husbands to the divorce courts or to prostitutes if they failed to do sexual intercourse willingly.[63]

The picture which the historians have painted of the 1920s as a period of dawning sexual freedom does not look nearly so rosy on closer examination. The sexologist offered the 'freedom' only to marry and engage willingly in sexual intercourse. Spinsterhood, lesbianism, celibacy and heterosexual practices apart from sexual intercourse were condemned. The concept of the 'frigid woman' was invented to explain why women were resisting this change in men's sexual expectations and was used as a weapon to worry women into compliance. The sexologists did not suddenly take a humanitarian interest in maximising women's sexual response. Rather they took an interest in quelling feminism and women's critique of men's sexual behaviour by eliciting from women a sexual response the sexologists believed to be intrinsically linked with total surrender to men's power and dominance.

CHAPTER 10

The 'Prudes' and the 'Progressives'

The terms of the debate around sexuality had changed dramatically by the late 1920s. The combined impact of the work of the orthodox sexologists, who were inventing the 'frigid woman', and the work of the 'progressive' sex reformers, was to transform the whole way in which sex could be spoken about or thought about. The pre-First World War challenge to male sexual behaviour had become unthinkable. There were only two positions possible on sexuality: the pro-sex position and the anti-sex position. The pro-sex camp, which included the sexologists and the sex reformers, characterised the feminists as 'anti-sex', as prudes and puritans.

The sex reformers represented themselves as knights tilting at the enemy – the 'puritan' attitude. Puritanism was commonly seen to be the result of the 'ascetic ideals' of the Christian religion, which were seen as having survived for 2000 years for want of the brave challenge of sex reform. Max Hodan's *History of Modern Morals* was published in 1937, translated by Stella Browne. Hodan had been involved in the sex reform movement in Germany. His book gives us a good example of the pride which the sex reformers took in what they saw as the dangerous struggle with puritanical ideas. Hodan wrote that the history of sexology was a 'record of the resistance of the champions of obsolete ideas and customs, threatened in their security and supremacy by the pioneers of constructive progress'.[1]

The Congress of the World League for Sex Reform which took place in London in 1929 marks the high point of sex reform in Britain. By the early 1930s the sex reform movement, and particularly its radical and socialist elements such as Magnus Hirschfeld and Wilhelm Reich, were under attack in Europe. Hirschfeld's

186

Berlin Institute was raided and the books and research destroyed in 1933. In Britain, according to Dora Russell's biography, the impetus to sex reform died out in the 1930s also, under the impact of the depression, the threat of fascism and preparation for war. The ideas of the sex reformers were by no means wiped out and forgotten, however, though they may not have developed any further in the 1930s. The papers and participants at the 1929 congress show the strength, influence and respectability which the sex reform movment had gained and the extent to which sex reforming ideas had become the common parlance of many academic disciplines.

The Congress was organised by the British branch of the World League for Sex Reform. The main work was done by Dora Russell and Norman Haire. The Congress brought together many of those whose work and influence are considered in this book. The contributors included Dora Russell, Dr Helene Stoecker, Marie Stopes, Stella Browne, Laurence Housman, Norman Haire and Magnus Hirschfeld. Amongst the supporters and/or members of the congress were Havelock Ellis and August Forel (who were, along with Hirschfeld, presidents of the World League), Gallichan, Max Hodan, and Wilhelm Stekel. The contributors and supporters also included an impressive cross-section of the most well-known names in the arts, the academic world, particularly anthropology and the biological sciences, medicine and psychoanalysis, and in politics. Literary figures included Vera Brittain, Naomi Mitchison, Ethel Mannin, George Bernard Shaw, Arnold Bennet, E.M. Forster, D.H. Lawrence and Somerset Maugham. The Congress brought together many whom one might otherwise have thought to have little in common. This apparently disparate collection of men and women disagreed on many details of the sex reform programme such as birth control and sterilisation, and infanticide of the unfit. They were, however, in agreement over the main themes of the Congress. These were: an attack on 'puritanism', the problem of women's frigidity, the vital importance of sexual intercourse.

Some of the aims of the 'progressive' sex reformers, such as the promotion of sex education and birth control, would have been of some benefit to women. However it was not women's interests which actually lay at the root of these aims, and the advantage which would have accrued to women was limited by the hidden agenda of the sex reformers which was very clear at the Sex Reform Congress of 1929. There were no papers which dealt with male homosexuality – though many of the supporters of the congress were male homosexual rights campaigners – let alone any paper on lesbianism and only two papers included positive mention of spinsters, celibacy or any heterosexual practice apart from sexual intercourse. (Naomi Mitchison wrote one of these two papers. She questioned the primacy of sexual intercourse in a fascinating contribution.[2]) The hidden agenda was the conscription of all women into sexual intercourse with men. This motive is best illustrated by a paper given by R.B. Kerr entitled *The Sexual Rights of Spinsters*. Kerr, like other sex reformers, spoke of 'rights' when he actually meant 'obligations'. This subtle distortion of language enhanced the progressive image of his paper and served to conceal the hidden agenda. Kerr explained that since the mid-nineteenth century in all civilised countries there had been a phenomenal growth in the number of spinsters, so that in England and Wales, out of the marriageable women over the age of 15, the number annually married declined by 18 per cent. He estimated that in 1929 40 per cent of women over the age of 30 had never been married. He lauded the great achievements of these spinsters in the fields of animal welfare, the abolition of slavery and child labour, promoting peace and other good causes. He left out their contribution to feminism. He concluded that despite these great achievements, 'Nothing can compensate, in the life of the average woman, for the lack of full sexual experience.' He considered that something of 'immense importance' (sexual intercourse), was missing from these women's lives. He asserted the 'right' of such women to have lovers though there 'is no possibility of every woman having a man to herself'. There were plenty of women lovers available, of course, but he did not consider this. Every spinster ought to have a sexual relationship with a man: 'Nothing is more common than to see two sisters living together protected only by a dog. In very many cases they would prefer a man, and there are many men who would gladly avail themselves of such an opportunity. The only obstacle is Mrs Grundy [the archetype prude].'[3] It did not occur to him that these spinsters might have relationships of importance with each other. Nor does it seem to have occurred to him that ensuring every spinster related to a man might destroy all their wonderful work since it was precisely their independence of men which gave them their dynamism.

The Congress is important not only because it demonstrates the extent of the influence gained by sex reforming ideas in the European intellectual community but because it shows that the ideas of the 'pre-war' feminists had been almost completely swamped by the doctrine of sex reform. The World League declared itself to be fighting for the 'political, economic and sexual equality' of women. That variety of feminism which had dominated the debate around sexuality in the pre-war period, with its fierce attacks on male sexual behaviour and understanding of a fundamental connection between the 'oversexualisation' of women and women's oppression, was represented at the Congress by only one paper, by Joanna Elberskirchen. Elberskirchen argued that less, not more, sexual intercourse was necessary to the emancipation of women. She argued that the matriarchate was suppressed by the patriarchal state when sexual periodicity gave way to men's preoccupation with woman as an object of pleasure. 'Sex, the desire for pleasure, became the great power in the life of man, Man became the slave of pleasure. Woman became the victim, the slave to man's pleasure.'[4] The result of this was the 'sexual dictatorship of men over women' which led to the general dictatorship of men over women:

> Patriarchal marriage and civilisation were attained at the cost of the prostitution of all womankind, and women were brought up to be victims . . . [man] robs her of her natural rights, her right to determine her own life, her freedom of choice, her right to enjoyment, her right to work. . . . Her economic existence, indeed her whole existence, is now based fundamentally on her sexual function and on her sexual relation to the male.[5]

The whole tone of her contribution was at total variance with the others at the Congress. Though the equality of women was one of the planks of the World League platform of reform, the form of feminism espoused by the league was carefully circumscribed. Only that propounded by 'new' feminists or modernists like Dora Russell, Vera Brittain or Stella Browne, was acceptable. Elberskirchen's feminism was critical of men and attributed responsibility to men for the wrongs done to women. Rather than seeing sexual intercourse as a joyful opportunity, she saw it as the main means through which women had been oppressed. Elberskirchen, who had been a militant suffragist in Germany before the First World War, was the lone representative of a defeated tradition at the Sex Reform Congress.

The most significant achievement of the sex reformers was to contribute to changing the terms of the debate on sex with the effect that the pre-war feminist critique of male sexual behaviour was muzzled. A new dominant ideology emerged within which the feminist campaigns against the crippling effects of male sexual behaviour on women's lives in the form of sexual abuse of children, the use of women in prostitution and sexual coercion in marriage were discredited and undermined. The pre-war feminist message drew strength from a prevailing ideology which priortised self-control and placed a low value on the sexual side of married life. A new generation of feminists whose ideas on a whole range of feminist questions differed from their predecessors, began to promote the importance of motherhood, of relationships with men and the joy and necessity of sexual intercourse. The new feminists, in their eagerness to promote the joy of sex, avoided or ignored the unpleasant realities which earlier feminists had been fighting. Their ideas and activities were far less radical than those of the earlier campaigners in the challenge they offered to male dominance. The feminists who had launched the critique of male sexual behaviour had not only refused co-operation with the sexual demands of men but promoted the value of women's independence of men and marriage and the importance of women's clubs, societies and companionship. The dimensions of the threat posed by such a feminist development is revealed by the scale of the defensive reaction it caused. Later feminists urged enthusiastic co-operation in heterosexual relationships in return for the promise of some sexual gratification during sexual intercourse. The earlier feminist critique of male sexual behaviour was supported by anger at men and a distancing from them. Later feminists, lulled into participation, were unable to stand back and launch such a critique. In order to be a part of a movement, sex reform, which was seen in the intellectual community as wholly progressive and backed up by the 'truths' of science, women had to adapt themselves to a new kind of feminism, acceptable to their socialist brothers. Alec Craig described this change in feminism with approval: 'The sex antagonism which was often at least tacitly assumed by the old pre-war feminism was laid aside. In post-war feminism woman-interests and man-interests merge into human interests.'[6] To achieve this new feminism, Craig 'hoped that the women's societies which still survive from the pre-war world will soon disappear as segregated congregations of females.' After the First World War, despite an increased 'surplus' of women over men, the popularity of marriage and the rate of marriage increased steadily.

The silencing of the feminist critique was not inevitable or accidental. As we have seen, both male and female, 'progressive' sex reformers and orthodox sexologists, made savage attacks on the pre-war feminists and their attitudes. An important weapon in those attacks was the concept of the 'prude' which was refined during the 1920s with the aid of psychoanalytic 'insights' about repression. The concept of 'repression' explained the development of the 'prude'. It was asserted that 'repression' of the supposedly innate and powerful sexual urge would cause that urge to find its outlet in a lurid interest in things sexual disguised as disgust and condemnation. Gallichan's book *The Poison of Prudery* published in 1929 shows how the model of the 'prude', a woman of course, had been refined. A Weith Knudsen quotation shows clearly the nature of the problem to which the book was devoted: 'It is the unfeeling and impotent women who dominate the whole discussion with their folly, their reproaches, and their abuse of Man.'[7] Another quotation, from a Professor McCurdy, further shapes the 'prude' concept: 'Prudery is a feeble bluff, which the woman who is, or was, subject to sex fantasies makes in an effort to persuade herself and others that her mind is pure.'[8] Not only could the indignant feminist now be dismissed as merely having repressed her sexual urge, she could now be accused of having secret desires for precisely those forms of male behaviour which she criticised. Gallichan described the making of the 'prude' thus: 'Hence prudery arises as reinforcement of resistance against the forbidden thoughts, and the resistance may be so heightened that it becomes a pathological symptom.'[9] Alec Craig characterised the pre-war feminists as prudes and puritans:

> The feminist movement was not without undesirable results. In the first place, the women who gained most in political, economic and social influence were generally celibates. Their influence on the national life tended towards puritanism, drabness and a safety first attitude to sociological problems.[10]

There was now an effective weapon with which to dismiss women who persisted in criticising male sexual behaviour.

To the sexologists and sex reformers pre-war feminism had presented a frightening spectacle of female solidarity, of women who seemed prepared to live independently of men and to launch a vigorous critique of male behaviour. The fears expressed about 'intersexuality', about women who refused to be feminine, dress in feminine attire and behave with deference to men, show great alarm at the development of determinedly independent and critical women. There had been a general weakening of the pressures which had, in the nineteenth century, kept women, and particularly women of the middle classes, dependent on men and trapped within marriage, in the form of educational, legal and economic restraints. The dependence of women upon men in heterosexual relationships which provided the foundation stone of male dominance, appeared to the sex reformers to be under serious threat. The apparently surprising alliances which developed to fight for sex reform, of socialists, liberals, conservatives and even proto-fascists, can be explained by recognising that there was a common fear of and determination to end, the threats to male dominance felt by representatives of all shades of political opinion.

In this period of flux in the relations between the sexes it was necessary, if male dominance was to survive, to strengthen those structures which underpinned it. The execration of the spinster, the glorification of motherhood and the idea that sexual intercourse was a vital necessity of everday life, were all used to strengthen the basic heterosexual relationship. Sexual intercourse was seen to be essential for the welding together of the married couple in a way in which it never had been in the nineteenth century. By the many writers who assumed that female submission was an inevitable concomitant or result of sexual intercourse, that activity was promoted to shore up male power in marriage. Concubinage was promoted as a way of conscripting independent women into this activity and into relationships with men.

One serious threat which the sex reform movement was able to defeat, was that posed to male pleasure by the criticism of male sexual behaviour. The much vaunted change in sexual mores was not a change in the expected behaviour of men, but a change in the expectations made of women through a massive campaign to conscript women into enthusiastic participation in sexual intercourse with men. The pre-war feminist critique which had been building up momentum throughout the last quarter of the nineteenth century, threatened to deprive men of the use of prostitutes without providing them with a substitute in the form of wifely enthusiasm. The decline in prostitution required compensation. The 1920s witnessed a concerted onslaught on the problem of the 'resisting' woman, to persuade, blackmail or therapise her into the performance of an activity, namely sexual intercourse, for which it was recognised that she would require months or perhaps years of training. Rather than being about the opening up to men and women of the possibility of sexual choice, the 1920s sexual revolution was about narrowing women's options to the role of complements to men in the act of sexual intercourse. The 1920s paved the way for the continuing progress of the 'sexual revolution' from the late 1950s onwards. The process does not seem to have been inevitable at any point, and certainly was not the result of women spearheading a crusade for sexual freedom, but a story of man's war against woman's resistance to the use of her body as the basis for the maintenance of the structures of male dominance.

AFTERWORD

Most historians have been remarkably uncritical in their treatment of this episode (1880–1930) in the history of sex. They have tended to duplicate the version of events offered by 1920s and 1930s propagandists of the 'sexual revolution'. Alec Craig's interpretation in *Sex and Revolution* (1934) presents the standard analysis beyond which historians have not much advanced. Craig saw the 'revolution' of the 1920s as entirely positive, especially for women. He explained the change in sexual mores mainly in terms of economic development, rather than in terms of the changing relations between the sexes. He also attacked pre-war feminists for their puritanical attitude to sex. It is this latter distortion which should be of most serious concern to those who are interested in developing a balanced history of sexuality or of feminism. Pre-First World War feminists had constructed a theory of sexuality and embarked upon campaigns around sexuality which were a hugely important aspect of the women's movement. Instead of being credited with having a worked-out theory around sexuality, these feminists have been dismissed as having an old-maid, prudish attitude of mind. However if the campaign to transform male sexual behaviour and protect women and girls from abuse had not been so important a part of feminism then antifeminists in the 1920s would not have picked it out as a particular target for ridicule. No other aspect of pre-war feminism was seen as so challenging or so deserving of attack.

Today in Great Britain and the USA feminists are campaigning against men's sexual violence and challenging men's sexual behaviour in groups such as Women against Violence against Women. Again an analysis of sexuality is being developed which opposes the abuse and exploitation of women and girls, challenges the notion that men have an uncontrollable sex drive, and resists the enforcement of compulsory heterosexuality. These feminists today are being attacked as anti-sex, prudish, puritanical, reactionary and as potential allies of the moral majority. These detractors are supported by some socialist and socialist feminist historians who compare the women fighting male violence within feminism today, with the pre-First World War feminists who were fighting similar struggles, in an attempt to discredit the contemporary feminists by distorting the work and ideals of our foresisters. Two American historians, Linda Gordon and Ellen Dubois (1983), use this approach in an article in the British journal *Feminist Review*:

> We have tried to show that social purity politics, although an understandable reaction to women's nineteenth century experience, was a limited and limiting vision for women. Thus we called it conservative. Today, there seems to be a revival of social purity politics within feminism, and it is concern about this tendency that motivates us in recalling its history. Like its nineteenth century predecessor, the contemporary feminist attack on pornography and sexual 'perversion' shades at the edges into a right-wing and antifeminist version of social purity, the moral majority and pro-family movements of the new right.[1]

Gordon and Dubois do not include within their version of feminism a critique of men's use of women in prostitution and pornography. Consequently they have no grounds for understanding feminist anger at the institution of prostitution in the late nineteenth century and attribute it to an irrational 'fear of prostitution'. They have similar difficulty in understanding the feminist campaign against pornography today. They avoid the need to clearly express their politics by spreading confusion and distorting feminist campaigns now and in the past through the use of unsubstantiated allegations and smears. The confusion evidenced in the above article is an example of the difficulty most historians have had in differentiating between a critique of male sexual behaviour and being anti-sex.

The ideas of the sexual 'progressives' have had such an impact on the way sex is thought about, that historians are still trapped, for the most part, in the belief that there are only two positions possible on sex – pro and anti. In fact there is a third possibility. This is a revolutionary feminist position, which is currently establishing its strength and uniqueness in books such as *The Sexuality Papers* by Lal Coveney *et al.* and *Women against Violence against Women* edited by Sandra McNeill and Dusty Rhodes.[2] In the area of sexuality, more than in any other area of human social life, the inequality of power between men and women is most clearly expressed. Thus an analysis of sexuality which bases itself on economic class or which fails to accept as its starting point the power relationship between the sexes, is doomed to failure. When looked at closely, those two supposedly opposed positions on sexuality which are variously classified as pro- and anti-sex, sexual liberalism and sexual conservatism, or even left and right wing, can be seen to have a common thread which is much greater than their differences. This common thread is the idea of a powerful, well-nigh uncontrollable, imperative male sexual drive. According to the 'anti-sex' position, this is dangerous and requires all of a man's best energies in its control. According to the 'pro-sex' position it is good and necessary and women and girls of any age cannot be justified in resisting its demands. The possibility that this so-called 'drive' or 'urge' is a social construct and that male sexuality need not be uncontrollable, aggressive and exploitative, must be the basis of a feminist perspective on sexuality.

This feminist perspective must include the understanding that many women can and do live an alternative to male-orientated sexuality. Such a perspective must include acceptance of the need to build a world in which loving women is seen as a positive choice for women, where the spinster and the lesbian are not stigmatised, and in which sexual intercourse and heterosexuality receive no special emphasis as sexual possibilities. In such a world many more women would choose to be lesbian. For that very reason we are far from attaining such a world, and the idea that aggressive male sexuality should be the organising principle of the universe is promoted with such obsessive anxiety.

NOTES

Introduction

1   Judith Walkowitz, 'Prostitution and Victorian Society', *Women Class and the State*, Cambridge, Cambridge University Press, 1980.

2   Lawrence Stone, *The Family, Sex and Marriage in England 1500–1800*, London, Weidenfeld & Nicolson, 1977.

3   Two useful books on the social construction of sexuality are: J.H. Gagnon and William Simon, *Sexual Conduct*, London, Hutchinson, 1973, and, for a feminist approach, Stevi Jackson, *On the Social Construction of Female Sexuality*, London, WRRC Publications, 1978.

4   An example of this kind of writing is Jeffrey Weeks, *Sex, Politics and Society*, London, Longmans, 1981.

5   For the classic exposition of the social control argument see Susan Brownmiller, *Against Our Will: Men, Women and Rape*, London, Penguin, 1978. A recent British study which looks at the effects of male violence on women's lives is Jalna Hanmer and Sheila Saunders, *Well-Founded Fear: A Community Study of Violence to Women*, London, Hutchinson, 1984.

6   See Florence Rush, *The Best Kept Secret: The Sexual Abuse of Children*, New York, Prentice-Hall, 1980; Andrea Dworkin, *Pornography: Men possessing Women*, London, The Women's Press, 1981; Catherine Mackinnon, *Sexual Harassment of Working Women*, New Haven and London, Yale University Press, 1979. For British feminist theory on all aspects of male violence, see Sandra McNeill and Dusty Rhodes (eds), *Women against Violence against Women*, London, Onlywomen Press, 1984. Lal Coveney, Margaret

Jackson, Sheila Jeffreys, Leslie Kay, Pat Mahoney, *The Sexuality Papers*, Hutchinson, London, 1984. Onlywomen Press (eds), *Love Your Enemy? The Debate between Heterosexual Feminism and Political Lesbianism*, London, Onlywomen Press, 1981.

Chapter 1   Feminism and Social Purity

1   Robert Bristow, *Vice and Vigilance. Purity Movements in Britain since 1700*, London, Gill & Macmillan, 1977, p.2.
2   *Ibid.*, p.3.
3   *Ibid.*, p.3.
4   Josephine Butler, *Social Purity: An Address*, London, Social Purity Alliance, 1879.
5   *Ibid.*, p.5.
6   *Ibid.*, p.5.
7   Onlywomen Press (eds).
8   *Ibid.*, p.12.
9   Bristow, op. cit., p.97.
10   J. Ellice Hopkins, *A Plea for the Wider Action of the Church Of England in the Prevention of the Degradation of Women*, London, Hatchards, n.d.
11   *Ibid.*, p.5.
12   *Ibid.*, p.7.
13   *Ibid.*, p.8.
14   *Ibid.*, p.9. Emphasis original.
15   *Ibid.*, p.9. Emphasis origianl.
16   *Ibid.*, p.14.
17   The White Cross League, *Aims and Methods*, London, White Cross League, n.d., p.5.
18   *Ibid.*
19   *Ibid.*
20   J. Ellice Hopkins, *The Ride of Death*, White Cross League, London, n.d., p.5.
21   *Ibid.*
22   J. Ellice Hopkins, *Grave Moral Questions Addressed to the Men and Women of England*, London, Hatchards, 1882, p.53.
23   *Ibid.*, p.7.
24   Laura Ormiston Chant, *Chastity in Men and Women*, White Cross League, London, n.d.

25 *Ibid.*
26 National Vigilance Association for the Defence of Personal Rights, *Personal Rights*, November 1881, p.90.
27 *Ibid.*
28 Hopkins, *A Plea*, op. cit., p.13.
29 Judith Walkowitz, 'We are not beasts of the field: Prostitution and the campaign against the Contagious Diseases Acts 1869–1886', University of Rochester, New York, unpublished PhD thesis, 1974, p.323.
30 Moral Reform Union, *Annual Reports 1881–1897*, 3rd report, p.3.
31 *Ibid.*, 1st report, p.3.
32 Title page of each report.
33 Moral Reform Union, *Annual Reports 1881-1897*, 2nd report, p.3.
34 *Ibid.*, 3rd report, p.3.
35 *Ibid.*, 4th report, p.5.
36 *Ibid.*, 15th report, p.3.
37 *Ibid.*, 4th report, p.3.
38 *Ibid.*, 3rd report, p.6.
39 *Ibid.*, 4th report, p.13.
49 International Council for Women, Washington 1888, *Report*, p.289.
41 Moral Reform Union, 9th report, p.12.
42 Moral Reform Union, 4th report, p.3.
43 *Alliance of Honour Record*, London 1912.

Chapter 2 Continence and Psychic Love

1 Dale Spender, *Women of Ideas (And What Men Have Done To Them)*, London, Ark Paperbacks, Routledge & Kegan Paul, 1982, p.11.
2 Elizabeth Wolstenholme Elmy, Letters and Papers, British Library, May 1895, no.47450.
3 Sylvia Pankhurst, *The Suffrage Movement*, London, Virago, 1977, 1st published 1931, p.31.
4 Ellis Ethelmer (Elizabeth Wolstenholme Elmy), *The Human Flower*, Congleton, Women's Emancipation Union, 1892, p.43.
5 Ignota, 'Judicial Sex Bias', *Westminster Review*, 1898, p.284.

6   Ellis Ethelmer, *Phases of Love*, Congleton, Women's Emancipation Union, 1897, p.9.
7   Ellis Ethelmer, *Woman Free*, Congleton, Women's Emancipation Union, 1893, p.20.
8   *Shafts*, March 1897, p.87.
9   *Ibid.*, p.87.
10 Ethelmer, *Woman Free*, p.100.
11 Francis Swiney, *Women and Natural Law*, London, League of Isis, 1912, p.44.
12 Francis Swiney, *The Bar of Isis*, London, C.W. Daniel, 1912, 1st published 1907, p.38.
13 Francis Swiney, *The Sons of Belial and Other Essays on the Social Evil*, London, C.W. Daniel, n.d., p.29.
14 Swiney, *The Bar of Isis*, p.43.
15 Francis Swiney, *Man's Necessity*, Cheltenham, League of Isis, n.d., p.21.
16 Francis Swiney, *The League of Isis*, leaflet, Cheltenham, League of Isis, n.d.
17 Swiney, *Woman and Natural Law*, p.15.
18 Swiney, *The Bar of Isis*, p.38.
19 *Shafts*, January 1898, p.10.
20 Elizabeth Wolstenholme Elmy, Letters and Papers, letter to M. McIlquham, 13 December 1896.
21 Lucy Re-Bartlett, *The Coming Order*, London, Longmans, 1911, p.51.
22 Lucy Re-Bartlett, *Sex and Sanctity*, London. Longmans, 1912, p.59.
23 *Ibid.*, p.59.
24 *The Woman's Leader*, January 1925.
25 Harry Quilter (ed.), *Is Marriage a Failure?*, London, Sonnenschein, 1888.
26 *Westminster Review*, July 1899, p.100.
27 Westminster Review, July 1899, p.95.
28 Annie Besant, *The Law of Population*, London, Freethought Publishing, 1877, p.28.
29 Peter Fryer, *The Birth Controllers*, London, Secker & Warburg, 1965, p.155.
30 Annie Besant, *Theosophy and the Law of Population*, London, Freethought Publishing, 1901, p.6.
31 National Union of Women's Suffrage Societies, *Women's Suffrage or Party?*, London, n.d.
32 *The Suffragette*, 22 April 1913, p.782.

33 *Ibid.*
34 Christabel Pankhurst, *Plain Facts about a Great Evil (The Great Scourge and how to end it)*, London, Women's Social and Political Union, 1913, p.20.
35 Cicely Hamilton, *Marriage as a Trade*, London, Chapman & Hall, 1909, p.36.
36 The *Freewoman*, 13 November 1911, p.31.
37 Adrienne Rich, *Compulsory Heterosexuality and Lesbian Existence*, London, Onlywomen Press, 1981.
38 The *Adult*, September 1897, p.41.
39 *Ibid.*, June 1897, final page.
40 Swiney, *Sons of Belial*, p.38.
41 Christabel Pankhurst, *The Great Scourge*, p.15.
42 The Suffragette, 29 August 1913.
43 The *Freewoman*, 1 August 1912, p.219.
44 Ursula Roberts, *The Cause of Purity and Women's Suffrage*, London, Church League for Women's Suffrage, n.d.
45 Francis Swiney, *Man's Necessity*, p.29.
46 Annie Besant, *Theosophy and the Law of Population*, p.6.
47 Lady Sybil Smith, *Women and Evolution*, London, Women's Freedom League, n.d.
48 Pankhurst, op. cit. p.17.
49 The *Freewoman*, 18 April 1912.
50 The *Freewoman*, 9 May 1912, p.497.

Chapter 3   'The sort of thing that might happen to any man'

1   The *Vote*, 20 March 1925.
2   *Vigilance Record*, December 1895.
3   *Personal Rights Journal*, 15 September 1882.
4   *Ibid.*
5   *Assaults on Children*, Report of the Conference on Criminal Assaults on Children, London, 1914, p.25.
6   *Ibid.*
7   *Ibid.*, p.24.
8   The *Vote*, 20 March 1925.
9   Association for Moral and Social Hygiene, *Committee on Sexual Morality*, London, AMSH, 1919. Evidence of Mr W. Clarke Hall.
10 *Ibid.* Evidence of Miss Costin.
11 National Society for the Prevention of Cruelty to Children,

Occasional Paper XVII, containing evidence submitted to the Departmental Committee on Sex Offences, 1926.

12 *Assaults on Children*, op. cit.
13 The *Shield*, 1914–15.
14 *Votes for Women*, 1 January 1915.
15 *Ibid.*, 8 January 1915.
16 *Ibid.*
17 *Ibid.*, 19 February 1915.
18 The *Vote*, 29 January 1910.
19 National Vigilance Association, Committee Minutes, 3 January 1889.
20 The *Shield*, December 1937.
21 Association for Moral and Social Hygiene, Report on the 10 Towns Enquiry, 1916.
22 The *Vote*, 14 May 1915.
23 Moral Reform Union, Annual Report 1890, p.13.
24 *Ibid.*
25 M. Lowndes, *Child Assault in England*, London, Office of 'The Englishwoman' Ltd, n.d.
26 *Ibid.*
27 *The Woman's Leader*, 6 March 1925.
28 Sheila Jeffreys, 'The Sexual Abuse of Children in the Home', in S. Friedman and E. Sarah (eds), *On The Problem of Men*, London, The Women's Press, 1982, p.63.
29 Parliamentary Debates, Commons, 12 July 1923.
30 The *Shield*, December 1937.
31 *Votes for Women*, 8 January 1915.
32 *Assaults on Children*, p.4.
33 *Ibid.*, p.12.
34 *Ibid.*, p.15.
35 *Ibid.*, p.15.
36 Association for Moral and Social Hygiene, 1916, p.21.
37 *Report of the Departmental Committee on Sexual Offences against Young Persons*, HMSO, Cmd 2561, 1925.
38 National Society for the Prevention of Cruelty to Children, Occasional paper XVII, p.37.
39 *Ibid.*, p.38.
40 *Report of the Departmental Committee on Sexual Offences*, op. cit.
41 Evelynne Viner, 'Protective Work among Children', vol. II, 1918, p.48.
42 The *Vigilance Record*, 1908.

43 Association of Moral and Social Hygiene, 1916, p.26.
44 *Assaults on Children*, p.4.
45 National Society for the Prevention of Cruelty to Children, Miscellaneous Papers, 1910.
46 *Report of the Departmental Committee on Sexual Offences*, op. cit.
47 National Society for the Prevention of Cruelty to Children, Occasional Paper XVIII, p.30.
48 *Ibid.*
49 *Ibid.*
50 *Ibid.*, p.31.
51 Sheila Jeffreys, op.cit. p.65.
52 The *Shield*, 12 July 1923.
53 *Report of the Departmental Committee on Sexual Offences*, p./5.
54 The *Shield*, April 1932, pp. 12–24.
55 The *Woman's Leader*, 22 January 1926.

Chapter 4   'Henpecking'

1 National Vigilance Association Executive Committee Minutes, 27 May 1902.
2 *Ibid.*, 8 June 1886.
3 *Ibid.*, 13 November 1886
4 *Guardian*, 11 November 1938.
5 Parliamentary Debates, Commons, 9 July 1885.
6 National Vigilance Association Executive Committee Minutes, 28 January 1901.
7 *Ibid.*, 31 July 1889.
8 A.M. Ludovici, *Lysistrata or Woman's Future and Future Woman*, London, Kegan Paul, Trench Trubner, 1924.
9 For the attitudes of Victorian males to incest see: Anthony S. Wohl, 'Sex and the Single Room: Incest among the Victorian working classes', in Anthony S. Wohl (ed.), *The Victorian Family*, London, Croom Helm, 1978.
10 *Ibid.*, p.199.
11 *Report on Sexual Offences*, 15th report from the Criminal Law Revision Committee, HMSO, 1984.
12 NVA Executive Committee Minutes, 29 January 1901.
13 Millicent Fawcett, *On the Amendments required in the*

Criminal Law Amendment Act 1885, London, Women's Printing Society Ltd, n.d.

14 *Ibid.*
15 *Ibid.*
16 *Vigilance Record*, December 1895, p.65–6.
17 Criminal Law Amendment Committee, *The Age of Consent*, London, C.L.A. Committee, 1912.
18 *Ibid.*
19 *Vigilance Record*, April 1917.
20 *Ibid.*
21 *Ibid.*
22 Association for Moral and Social Hygiene, Annual Reports, 1922–30.
23 *Ibid.*
24 Parliamentary Debates, 5 July 1922.
25 *Ibid.*
26 Parliamentary Debates, 3 March 1921.
27 *Ibid.*
28 Sheila Jeffreys, op. cit., pp. 56–66.

Chapter 5   Spinsterhood and Celibacy

1 Rosemary Auchmuty, 'Victorian Spinsters', Australian National University, unpublished PhD thesis, 1975, p.9.
2 *Ibid.*, p.12.
3 *Ibid.*, p.19.
4 Patricia Hollis, *Women in Public*, London, Allen & Unwin, 1979, p.36.
5 W.R. Gregg, 'Why are Women Redundant?', *National Review*, April 1862, quoted in Hollis, op. cit., p.37.
6 Maria Grey and Emily Shirreff, *Thoughts on Self Culture*, quoted in Hollis, op. cit., p.12.
7 Auchmuty, op. cit., p.108.
8 Christabel Pankhurst, *Plain Facts about a Great Evil, (The Great Scourge and How to End It)*, London, Women's Social and Political Union, 1913, p.98.
9 Lucy Re-Bartlett, *Sex and Sanctity*, London, Longmans, 1912, p.25.
10 *Ibid.*, p.26.
11 *Ibid.*, p.44.

12 *Ibid.*, p.32.
13 Cicely Hamilton, *Marriage as a Trade*, London, Chapman & Hall, 1909, p.37.
14 *Ibid.*, p.251.
15 *Ibid.*, p.252.
16 *Ibid.*, p.278.
17 The *Freewoman*, 8 August 1912.
18 The *Freewoman*, 23 November 1911.
19 *Ibid.*
20 Joan Lidderdale and Mary Nicholson, *Harriet Shaw Weaver*, London, Faber & Faber, 1970, p.47.
21 *Ibid.*, p.46.
22 The *Freewoman*, 23 November 1911.
23 *Ibid.*
24 The *Freewoman*, 30 November 1911.
25 The *Freewoman*, 15 February 1912.
26 *Ibid.*
27 The *Freewoman*, 7 March 1912.
28 Christabel Pankhurst, op. cit., pp. 129–30.
29 *Ibid.*
30 The *Freewoman*, 15 February 1912.
31 *Ibid.*
32 *Ibid.*

Chapter 6   Women's Friendship and Lesbianism

1 Carroll Smith-Rosenberg, 'The Female World of Love and Ritual: Relations between women in nineteenth century America', in N.F. Cott and E.H. Pleck (eds), *A Heritage of Her Own*, New York, Touchstone Books, Simon & Schuster, 1979.
2 Lillian Faderman, *Surpassing the Love of Men. Romantic Friendship and Love between Women from the Renaissance to the Present*, London, Junction Books, 1981.
3 *Ibid.*, p.164.
4 Rosenberg, op. cit.
5 Rosemary Auchmuty, 'Victorian Spinsters', Australian National University, unpublished Phd thesis, 1975.
6 For an example of this kind of criticism of Faderman see Sonia Ruehl, 'Sexual Theory and Practice: Another Double

Standard', in Sue Cartledge and Joanna Ryan (eds), *Sex and Love. New Thoughts on Old Contradictions*, London, The Women's Press, 1983.

7 Faderman, op. cit. p.312.

8 Nancy Sahli, 'Smashing: Women's Relationships before the Fall', *Chrysalis*, no. 8, p.18.

9 Jeffrey Weeks, *Coming Out: Homosexual Politics in Britain from the Nineteenth Century to the Present*, London, Quartet Books, 1977.

10 Havelock Ellis, *Sexual Inversion, Studies in the Psychology of Sex, volume 2*, Philadelphia, F.A. Davis, 1927, 1st published 1897, p.250.

11 Edward Carpenter, *Love's Coming of Age*, London, Allen & Unwin, 1913, 1st published 1896, p.66.

12 Magnus Hirschfeld, Presidential Address, in Norman Haire (ed.), *The Sex Reform Congress*, London, Kegan Paul Trench Trubner, 1930.

13 Iwan Bloch, *Sexual Life in Our Time*, London, Heinemann, 1909.

14 Havelock Ellis, op. cit., p.262.

15 Iwan Bloch, op. cit.

16 *Ibid*.

17 Ellis, op. cit., p.257.

18 Richard von Krafft-Ebing, *Psychopathia Sexualis*, London, William Heinemann, 12th German edition, n.d., p.400.

19 Ellis, op. cit., p.200.

20 *Ibid.*, p.221.

21 Faderman, op. cit. and Sahli, op. cit.

22 Auchmuty, op. cit.

23 Radclyffe Hall, *The Well of Loneliness*, London, Virago, 1982, p.207, 1st published 1928.

24 Parliamentary Debates, Commons, 1921, vol. 145, 1799.

25 *Ibid.*, 1800.

26 *Ibid.*, 1805.

27 *Ibid.*, 1799.

28 *Ibid.*, 1804.

29 *Ibid.*, 1804.

30 *Ibid.*, 1800.

31 Sheila Rowbotham, *A New World for Women: Stella Browne, Socialist Feminist*, London, Pluto Press, 1977.

32 *Ibid.*, p.89.

33 *Ibid.*, p.102.

34 *Ibid.*, p.102.
35 *Ibid.*, p.102–3.
36 *Ibid.*, p.103.
37 *Ibid.*, p.101.
38 Stella Browne, 'Studies in Feminine Inversion', *Journal of Sexology and Psychoanalysis*, 1923, p.51.
39 *Ibid.*, p.55.
40 *Ibid.*, p.55.
41 *Ibid.*, p.58.
42 *Ibid.*, p.57.
43 *Ibid.*, p.58.
44 Ruth Hall, *Marie Stopes*, London, Virago, 1978, p.39.
45 Marie Stopes, *Enduring Passion*, London, Hogarth Press, 1953, 1st published 1928, p.29.
46 *Ibid.*, p.30.
47 *Ibid.*, p.30.
48 Winifred Holtby, *The Crowded Street*, London, Virago, 1981, 1st published 1924, p.41.
49 Sahli, op. cit.
50 Holtby, op. cit., p.41.
51 *Ibid.*, p.41.
52 Vera Brittain, *Testament of Friendship*, London, Virago, 1981, 1st published 1940.
53 *Ibid.*, p.169.
54 *Ibid.*, p.117.
55 Rosamund Lehman, *Dusty Answer*, London, Penguin, 1981, 1st published 1927, p.161.
56 *Ibid.*, p.171.
57 G. Sheila Donisthorpe, *Loveliest of Friends*, London, Old Royalty Book Publishers, 1931, p.254.

Chapter 6   Antifeminism and Sex Reform before the First World War

1 Magnus Hirschfeld, Introduction to Norman Haire (ed.), *The Sex Reform Congress*, London, Kegan Paul Trench Trubner, 1930.
2 Margaret Jackson, 'Sexual Liberation or Social Control? Some aspects of the relationship between feminism and the social construction of sexual knowledge in the early twen-

tieth century', *Women's Studies International Forum*, volume 6, January 1983.

3 Edward Brecher, *The Sex Researchers*, London, André Deutsch, 1970, chapter heading for Havelock Ellis chapter.

4 Phyllis Grosskurth, *Havelock Ellis: A Biography*, London, Quartet, 1981.

5 Sheila Rowbotham and Jeffrey Weeks, *Socialism and the New Life*, London, Pluto Press, 1977, p.142.

6 Lillian Faderman, *Surpassing the Love of Men: Romantic Friendships and Love Between Women from the Renaissance to the Present*, London, Junction Books, 1981.

7 Havelock Ellis, *Man and Woman. A Study of Secondary and Tertiary Sexual Characters*, London, Heinemann, 1934, 1st published 1894, p.iii.

8 *Ibid.*, p.447.

9 Havelock Ellis, *Studies in the Psychology of Sex, volume 3, Analysis of the Sexual Impulse, Love and Pain, the Sexual Impulse in Women*, Philadelphia, F.A. Davis 1913, 1st published 1903, p.68.

10 Havelock Ellis, *The Erotic Rights of Women*, London, British Society for the Study of Sex Psychology, 1917.

11 Havelock Ellis, quoted in Margaret Jackson, op. cit., p.14.

12 Havelock Ellis, *My Life*, London and Toronto, Heinemann, 1940.

13 Eric Trudgill, *Madonnas and Magdalens. The origins and development of Victorian sexual attitudes*, London, Heinemann, 1976, p.276.

14 Alex Comfort, *The Joy of Sex*, London, Quartet Books, 1974, p.123.

15 Ellis, *Studies* volume 3, p.89.

16 *Ibid.*, p.90.

17 *Ibid.*, p.92.

18 *Ibid.*, p.103.

19 *Ibid.*, p.226.

20 Anna Davin, 'Imperialism and Motherhood', *History Workshop*, issue 5, Spring 1978, p.15.

21 *Ibid.*, p.12.

22 Havelock Ellis, *The Task of Social Hygiene*, London, Constable, 1913, p.46.

23 *Ibid.*, p.63.

24 *Ibid.*, p.86.

25 *Ibid.*, p.103.

26 *Ibid.*, p.310.
27 Ellis, *Man and Woman*, p. vi.
28 *Ibid.*, p.vi.
29 Havelock Ellis, *Sex in Relation to Society, Studies in the Psychology of Sex*, volume 6, London, Heinemann, 1946, p.247.
30 *Ibid.*, p.247.
31 Iwan Bloch, *The Sexual Life of Our Time*, London, Heinemann, 1909, p.72.
32 *Ibid.*
33 *Ibid.*, p.84.
34 August Forel, *The Sexual Question*, New York, Medical Arts Agency, 1922, 1st published 1908, p.93.
35 *Ibid.*, p.504.
36 C. Gasquoigne-Hartley, *The Truth about Woman*, London, Eveleigh Nash, 1913, p.xi.
37 *Ibid.*, p.263.
38 *Ibid.*, p.364.
39 *Ibid.*, p.61.
40 Walter Heape, *Sex Antagonism*, London, Constable, 1913, p.4.
41 *Ibid.*, p.6.
42 *Ibid.*, p.207.
43 *Ibid.*, p.208.
44 *Ibid.*, p.208.
45 Walter Gallichan, *Modern Woman and How to Manage Her*, London, T. Werner Laurie, 1909, p.46.
46 *Ibid.*, p.49.
47 *Ibid.*, p.48.
48 Walter Gallichan, *Woman Under Polygamy*, London, Holden & Hardingham, 1914, p.73.
49 *Ibid.*, p.295.

Chapter 8   The Decline of Militant Feminism

1 Christabel Pankhurst, 'Why I Never Married', *Weekly Dispatch*, 13 April 1921.
2 David Mitchell, *Queen Christabel*, London, MacDonald & Jane's, 1977, p.297.
3 David Doughan, *Lobbying for Liberation: British Feminism*

1918–1968, London, City of London Polytechnic, 1980.

4 Olive Banks, *Faces of Feminism*, Oxford, Martin Robinson, 1981.

5 Wilma Meikle, *Towards a Sane Feminism*, London, Grant & Richards, 1916, p.84.

6 *Ibid.*, p.86.

7 Mary Stocks, *Eleanor Rathbone*, London, Victor Gollancz, 1949.

8 *Ibid.*, p.62.

9 *Ibid.*, p.48.

10 *Ibid.*, p.58.

11 Vera Brittain, *Testament of Friendship*, London, Virago Press, 1981, 1st published 1940.

12 Eleanor Rathbone, 'Is Birth Control a Feminist Reform?', *Woman's Leader*, 2 October 1925.

13 *Ibid.*

14 *Woman's Leader*, 11 February 1927.

15 Banks, op. cit.

16 *Ibid.*

17 William O'Neill, *Everyone was Brave*, New York, Quadrangle, 1976, 1st published 1971, p.32.

18 Stella Browne, 'Sexual Variety and Variability among Women and their Bearing upon Social Reconstruction' (1915), reprinted in Shelia Rowbotham, *A New World for Women: Stella Brown – Socialist Feminist*, London, Pluto Press, 1977, p.87.

19 Jeffrey Weeks, *Coming Out: Homosexual Politics in Britain, from the Nineteenth Century to the Present*, London, Quartet Books, 1977, p.122.

20 *Ibid.*, p.122.

21 Wilma Meikle, op. cit.

22 Quoted in Ruth Hall, *Marie Stopes*, London, Virago, 1978, p.130.

23 Marie Stopes, *Married Love*, London, Putnams, 1924, 1st published 1918, p.65.

24 Op. cit., p.294.

25 Dale Spender, *Women of Ideas (And What Men Have Done to Them)*, London, Routledge & Kegan Paul, 1982, p.669.

26 Dale Spender (ed.), *Feminist Theorists*, London, The Women's Press, 1983.

27 Dora Russell, *Hypatia or Woman and Knowledge*, London, Kegan Paul, Trench, Trubner, 1925, pp.24–5.

28 *Ibid.*, p.21.
29 Hannah Stone, 'Birth Control as a factor in the sex life of Woman, in Norman Haire (ed.), *The Sex Reform Congress*, London, Kegan Paul, Trench, Trubner, 1930, p.155.
30 *Ibid.*, p.156.
31 *Ibid.*, p.156.
32 Elise Ottesen-Jensen, 'Birth Control Work amongst the Poor in Sweden', in Haire, op. cit., p.175.
33 Shelia Rowbotham, *Hidden From History*, London, Pluto Press, 1973, p.158.
34 The *Vote*, 17 July 1925.
35 *An Injustice to be remedied*, Association for Moral and Social Hygiene, London, AMSH pamphlet, 1960.
36 The *Vote*, February 1925.
37 Eleanor Rathbone, 'The Old and the New Feminism', *Woman's Leader*, 13 March 1925.

Chapter 9   The Invention of the Frigid Woman

1 Lawrence Stone, *The Family, Sex and Marriage in England 1500–1800*, London, Weidenfeld & Nicolson, 1977, p.658.
2 Linda Gordon, *Woman's Body, Woman's Right*, London, Penguin, 1977, p.194.
3 *Ibid.*, p.194.
4 Dora Russell, *The Tamarisk Tree: My Quest for Liberty and Love*, London, Virago, 1977.
5 Charlotte Haldane, *Motherhood and its Enemies*, London, Chatto & Windus, 1927, p.107.
6 Arthur Marwick, *Women at War*, London, Fontana, 1977, p.111.
7 Thomas Van de Velde, *Ideal Marriage*, London, Heinemann, 1961, 1st published 1928, p.4.
8 *Ibid.*, p.5.
9 Alec Craig, *Sex and Revolution*, London, Allen & Unwin, 1934, p.44.
10 Haldane, op. cit., p.94.
11 *Ibid.*, p.94.
12 Radclyffe Hall, 'Miss Ogilvie Finds Herself' (1926), in Seymour Kleinberg (ed.), *The Other Persuasion*, New York, Vintage Books, 1977.

211

13 Haldane, op. cit., p.93.

14 K.A. Weith Knudsen, *The Woman's Question from Ancient Times to the Present Day*, London, Constable, 1928, p.97.

15 Wilhelm Stekel, 'Frigidity in Mothers', in V.F. Calverton and Samuel D. Schmalhausen (eds), *The New Generation*, London, Allen & Unwin, 1930, p.251.

16 Walter Gallichan, *Sexual Antipathy and Coldness in Women*, London, T. Werner Laurie, 1927, p.28.

17 Haldane, op. cit., p.154.

18 Gallichan, *Sexual Antipathy*, p.30.

19 Van de Velde, *Ideal Marriage*, p.227.

20 *Ibid.*, p.227.

21 Isabel Elmslie Hutton, *The Hygiene of Marriage*, London, Heinemann, 1923, p.51.

22 Hilary Simpson, *D.H. Lawrence and Feminism*, London, Croom Helm, 1982.

23 A.M. Ludovici, *Lysistrata or Woman's Future and Future Woman*, London, Kegan Paul Trench, Trubner, 1927, p.37.

24 *Ibid.*, p.5.

25 *Ibid.*, p.47.

26 *Ibid.*, p.89.

27 *Ibid.*, p.95.

28 Haldane, op. cit., p.154.

29 See the debate between Stella Browne and Kathryn Oliver in the *Freewoman*, February and March 1912.

30 Haldane, op. cit., p.155.

31 Edward Carpenter, *The Intermediate Sex*, London, Allen & Unwin, 1905.

32 Haldane, op. cit., p.155.

33 *Ibid.*, p.156.

34 *Ibid.*, p.168.

35 *Ibid.*, p.168.

36 Weith Knudsen, op. cit., p.119.

37 *Ibid.*, p.121.

38 *Ibid.*, p.287.

39 *Ibid.*, p.289.

40 Walter Gallichan, *The Poison of Prudery*, London, T. Werner Laurie, 1929, p.184.

41 Walter Gallichan, *Sexual Antipathy*, p.11.

42 Wilhelm Stekel, 'Frigidity in Mothers', p.254.

43 Thomas Van de Velde, *Sex Hostility in Marriage. Its Ori-*

gins, Prevention and Treatment, London, Heinemann, 1931, p.16.

44 Weith Knudsen, op. cit., p.111.

45 Wilhelm Stekel, *Frigidity in Women in Relation to her Love Life*, volume 2, New York, Livewright, 1936, 1st published 1926, p.96.

46 Margaret Llewellyn Davies (ed.), *Maternity. Letters from Working Women*, London, Virago, 1978, p.49.

47 *Ibid.*, p.278.

48 Alec Craig, op. cit., p.96.

49 Walter Gallichan, *Sexual Antipathy*, p.13.

50 Haldane, op. cit., p.137.

51 See Ellis's description of the female invert in chapter 7.

52 Wilhelm Stekel, *Frigidity*, op. cit., p.1.

53 *Ibid.*, p.2.

54 *Ibid.*, p.1.

55 *Ibid.*, p.12, emphasis added.

56 *Ibid.*, p.25.

57 *Ibid.*, p.61.

58 Van de Velde, *Sex Hostility*, pp.64–5.

59 *Ibid.*, p.64–5.

60 *Ibid.*, p.66.

61 Weith Knudsen, op. cit., p.116.

62 Ludovici, op. cit., p6.

63 Hutton, op. cit.

Chapter 10   The 'Prudes' and the 'Progressives'

1 Max Hodann, *History of Modern Morals*, London, Heinemann, 1937, p.x.

2 Naomi Mitchison, 'Some comments on the use of contraceptives by intelligent persons', in Norman Haire (ed.), *The Sex Reform Congress*, London, Kegan Paul, Trench, Trubner, 1930.

3 R.B. Kerr, 'The Sexual Rights of Spinsters', in Haire, op. cit.

4 Joanna Elberskirchen, 'The Altero-centric Dynamic of the Female and the Ego-centric Dynamic of the Male: Their Part in the Development of Life and Civilisation, and the Transformation of the relations between Men and Women', in Haire, op. cit., p.651.

5 Elberskirchen, op. cit., p.651.
6 Alec Craig, *Sex and Revolution*, London, Allen & Unwin, 1934, p.18.
7 Walter Gallichan, *The Poison of Prudery*, London, T. Werner Laurie, 1929, p.8.
8 *Ibid.*, p.10.
9 *Ibid.*, p.13.
10 Craig, op. cit., p.16.

Afterword

1 Linda Gordon and Ellen Dubois, 'Seeking Ecstasy on the Battlefield: Danger and pleasure in nineteenth century feminist thought', *Feminist Review*, 13, London, Spring 1983, p.50.
2 Lal Coveney, Margaret Jackson, Sheila Jeffreys, Leslie Kay, Pat Mahoney, *The Sexuality Papers*, Hutchinson, London 1984. Sandra McNeill and Dusty Rhodes (eds), *Women against Violence against Women*, Onlywomen Press, London, 1984.

BIBLIOGRAPHY

Books

Rosemary Auchmuty, 'Victorian Spinsters', Australian National Univiersity, unpublished PhD thesis, 1975.

Olive Banks, *Faces of Feminism*, Oxford, Martin Robinson, 1981.

Annie Besant, *The Law of Population*, London, Freethought Publishing, 1877.

Annie Besant, *Theosophy and the Law of Population*, London, Theosophical Publishing, 1901.

Iwan Bloch, *The Sexual Life of our Time*, London, Heinemann, 1909.

Edward Brecher, *The Sex Researchers*, London, André Deutsch, 1970.

Robert Bristow, *Vice and Vigilance. Purity movements in Britain since 1700*, London, Gill & Macmillan, Rowan & Littlefield, 1977.

Vera Brittain, *Testament of Friendship*, London, Virago Press, 1981, 1st published 1940.

Susan Brownmiller, *Against Our Will. Men, women and rape*, London, Penguin, 1975.

Josephine Butler, *Social Purity. An Address*, London, Social Purity Alliance, 1879.

V.F. Calverton and S.D. Schmalhausen (eds), *The New Generation*, London, Allen & Unwin, 1930.

Edward Carpenter, *The Intermediate Sex*, London, Allen & Unwin, 1908.

Sue Cartledge and Joanna Ryan (eds), *Sex and Love*, London, The Women's Press, 1983.

Laura Ormiston Chant, *Chastity in Men and Women*, London,

White Cross League, n.d.

Alex Comfort, *The Joy of Sex*, London, Quartet, 1974.

N.F. Cott and E.H. Pleck (eds), *A Heritage of Her Own*, New York, Touchstone Books, Simon & Schuster, 1979.

Lal Coveney *et al.*, *The Sexuality Papers*, London, Hutchinson, 1984.

Alex Craig, *Sex and Revolution*, London, Allen & Unwin, 1934.

M. Llewellyn Davies, *Maternity. Letters from Working Women*, London, Virago, 1978, 1st published 1915.

Arabella Dennehy, 'Women of the Future', *Westminster Review*, July 1899.

G.S. Donisthorpe, *The Loveliest of Friends*, London, Old Royalty Book Publishers, 1931.

David Doughan, *Lobbying for Liberation: British Feminism 1918–1968*, London, City of London Polytechnic, 1980.

Andrea Dworkin, *Pornography: Men Possessing Women*, The Women's Press, 1981.

Havelock Ellis, *Man and Woman. A study of secondary and tertiary sexual characteristics*, London, Heinemann, 1934, 1st published 1894.

Havelock Ellis, *Studies in the Psychology of Sex*, volume 2, *Sexual Inversion*, Philadephia, F.A. Davis, 1927, 1st published 1897.

Havelock Ellis, *Studies in the Psychology of Sex*, volume 3, *Analysis of the Sexual Impulse, Love and Pain, the Sexual Impulse in Women*, Philadelphia, F.A. Davis, 1913, 1st published 1903.

Havelock Ellis, *The Task of Social Hygiene*, London, Constable, 1913.

Havelock Ellis, *The Erotic Rights of Women*, London, British Society for the Study of Sex Psychology, 1917.

Havelock Ellis, *Studies in the Psychology of Sex*, volume 6, *Sex in Relation to Society*, London, 1946, 1st published 1937.

Havelock Ellis, *My Life*, London and Toronto, Heinemann, 1940.

Ellis Ethelmer (Elizabeth Wolstenholme Elmy), *The Human Flower*, Congleton, Women's Emancipation Union, 1892.

Ellis Ethelmer, *Woman Free*, Congleton, Women's Emancipation Union, 1893.

Ellis Ethelmer, *The Phases of Love*, Congleton, Women's Emancipation Union, 1897.

Lillian Faderman, *Surpassing the Love of Men. Romantic*

Friendship and Love Between Women from the Renaissance to the Present, London, Junction Books, 1981.

August Forel, *The Sexual Question*, New York, Medical Art Agency, 1922, 1st published 1908.

Sigmund Freud, 'Some psychical consequences of the anatomical distinction between the sexes', in *Freud, On Sexuality* volume 7, London, Pelican Freud Library, 1977.

Peter Fryer, *The Birth Controllers*, London, Secker & Warburg, 1965.

Walter Gallichan, *Modern Woman and How to Manage Her*, London, T. Werner Laurie, 1909.

Walter Gallichan, *Woman under Polygamy*, London, Holden & Hardingham, 1914.

Walter Gallichan, *Sexual Antipathy and Coldness in Women*, London, T. Werner Laurie, 1927.

Walter Gallichan, *The Poison of Prudery*, London, T. Werner Laurie, 1929.

J.H. Gagnon and W. Simon, *Sexual Conduct*, London, Hutchinson, 1973.

Linda Gordon, *Woman's Body. Woman's Right*, London, Penguin, 1977.

Linda Gordon and Ellen Dubois, 'Seeking Ecstasy on the Battlefield: Danger and Pleasure in nineteenth century feminist thought', *Feminist Review*, 13.

Phyllis Grosskurth, *Havelock Ellis: A Biography*, London, Quartet, 1981.

Norman Haire (ed.), *The Sex Reform Congress*, London, Kegan Paul, Trench, Trubner, 1930.

Charlotte Haldane, *Motherhood and its Enemies*, London, Chatto & Windus, 1927.

Radclyffe Hall, 'Miss Ogilvy Finds Herself' (1926) in *The Other Persuasion*, Seymour Kleinberg (ed.), New York, Vintage Books, 1977.

Radclyffe Hall, *The Well of Loneliness*, London, Virago, 1982, 1st published 1928.

Jalna Hammer and Sheila Saunders, *Well Founded Fear. A Community Study of Violence to Women*, London, Hutchinson, 1984.

Cicely Hamilton, *Marriage as a Trade*, London, Chapman & Hall, 1909.

C. Gasquoigne Hartley, *The Truth About Woman*, London, Eveleigh Nash, 1913.

Walter Heape, *Sex Antagonism*, London, Constable, 1913.

J. Ellice Hopkins, *A Plea for the wider action of the Church of England in the prevention of the degradation of women*, London, Hatchards, 1879.

J. Ellice Hopkins, *Grave Moral Questions addressed to the men and women of England*, London, Hatchards, 1882.

J. Ellice Hopkins, *The Ride of Death*, London, White Cross League, n.d.

Max Hodann, *A History of Modern Morals*, London, Heinemann, 1937.

Patricia Hollis, *Women in Public*, London, Allen & Unwin, 1979.

Isobel Hutton, *The Hygiene of Marriage*, London, Heinemann, 1923.

Stevi Jackson, *On the Social Construction of Female Sexuality*, London, WRRC publications, 1978.

Margaret Jackson, 'Sexual Liberation or Social Control', *Women's Studies International Forum*, volume 6, January 1982.

Sheila Jeffreys, 'The Sexual Abuse of Children in the Home', in Scarlet Friedman and Elizabeth Sarah (eds), *On the Problem of Men*, London, The Women's Press, 1982.

Richard von Krafft-Ebing, *Psychopathia Sexualis*, London, Heinemann, from 12th German edition, n.d.

Rosamund Lehmann, *Dusty Answer*, London, Penguin, 1981, 1st published 1927.

J. Lidderdale and M. Nicholson, *Harriet Shaw Weaver 1876–1961*, London, Faber & Faber, 1970.

A.M. Ludovici, *Lysistrata or Woman's Future and Future Woman*, London, Kegan Paul, Trench, Trubner, 1927.

Katherine Mackinnon, *Sexual Harassment of Working Women*, New Haven and London, Yale University Press, 1979.

Sandra McNeill and Dusty Rhodes (eds), *Women against Violence against Women*, London, Onlywomen Press, 1984.

Arthur Marwick, *Women at War*, London, Fontana, 1977.

Wilma Meikle, *Towards a Sane Feminism*, London, Grant & Richards, 1916.

David Mitchell, *Queen Christabel*, London, MacDonald & Jane's, 1977.

National Society for the Prevention of Cruelty to Children, Occasional Paper XVII, London, NSPCC, 1926.

William O'Neil, *Everyone Was Brave*, New York, Quadrangle,

1976, 1st published 1971.

Onlywomen Press, *Love Your Enemy? The Debate between Heterosexual Feminism and Political Lesbianism*, London, Onlywomen Press, 1981.

Christabel Pankhurst, *Plain Facts about a Great Evil (The Great Scourge and How to End It)*, London, Women's Social and Political Union, 1913.

Sylvia Pankhurst, The Suffrage Movement, London, Virago, 1977, 1st published 1931.

Lucy Re-Bartlett, *The Coming Order*, London, Longmans, 1911.

Lucy Re-Bartlett, *Sex and Sanctity*, London, Longmans, 1912.

Adrienne Rich, *Compulsory Heterosexuality and Lesbian Existence*, London, Onlywomen Press, 1981.

Ursula Roberts, *The Causes of Purity and Women's Suffrage*, London, Church League for Women's Suffrage, n.d.

Sheila Rowbotham, *Hidden from History*, London, Pluto Press, 1977.

Sheila Rowbotham and Jeffrey Weeks, *Socialism and the New Life*, London, Pluto Press, 1977.

Sheila Rowbotham, *A New World for Women*, London, Pluto Press, 1977.

Florence Rush, *The Best Kept Secret: The Sexual Abuse of Children*, New York, Prentice Hall, 1980.

Dora Russell, *Hypatia or Woman and Knowledge*, London, Kegan Paul, 1925.

Dora Russell, *The Tamarisk Tree: My Quest for Liberty and Love*, London, Putnam's, 1975.

Nancy Sahli, 'Smashing: Women's relationships before the fall', New York, *Chrysalis*, no.8.

Hilary Simpson, *D.H. Lawrence and Feminism*, London, Croom Helm, 1982.

Lady Sybil Smith, *Woman's Evolution*, London, Women's Freedom League, 1913.

Dale Spender, *Women of Ideas (and what men have done to them)*, London, Ark paperbacks, Routledge & Kegan Paul, 1982.

Dale Spender (ed.), *Feminist Theorists*, London, The Women's Press, 1983.

Wilhelm Stekel, *Frigidity in Woman in Relation to Her Love Life*, volume 2, New York, Livewright, 1926.

Lawrence Stone, *The Family, Sex and Marriage in England*

1500–1800, London, Weidenfeld & Nicolson, 1977.

Marie Stopes, *Married Love*, London, Putnam's, 1924, 1st published 1918.

Marie Stopes, *Enduring Passion*, London, Hogarth Press, 1928.

Francis Swiney, *The Bar of Isis*, London, C.W. Daniel, 1912, 1st published 1907.

Francis Swiney, *Women and Natural Law*, London, League of Isis, 1912.

Francis Swiney, *The Sons of Belial, and other essays on the social evil*, London, C.W. Daniel, n.d.

Francis Swiney, *Man's Necessity*, Cheltenham, League of Isis, n.d.

Eric Trudgill, *Madonnas and Magdalens: The origins and development of Victorian sexual attitudes*, London, Heinemann, 1976.

Thomas Van de Velde, *Ideal Marriage*, London, Heinemann, 1961, 37th impression, 1st published 1928.

Thomas Van de Velde, *Sex Hostility in Marriage*, London, Heinemann, 1931.

Judith Walkowitz, *Prostitution and Victorian Society, Women, Class and the State*, Cambridge, Cambridge University Press, 1980.

Judith Walkowitz, "We are not beasts of the field": Prostitution and the campaign against the Contagious Diseases Acts 1869–1886', New York, University of Rochester, unpublished PhD thesis, 1974.

Jeffrey Weeks, *Coming Out: Homosexual Politics in Britain from the Nineteenth Century to the Present*, London, Quartet, 1977.

Jeffrey Weeks, *Sex, Politics and Society*, London, Longmans 1981.

K.A. Weith Knudsen, *The Woman Question from Ancient Time to the Present Day*, London, Constable, 1928.

Anthony Wohl, *The Victorian Family*, London, Croom Helm, 1974.

Manuscript sources

The letters and papers of Elizabeth Wolstenholme Elmy, British Library.

National Vigilance Association Executive Committee Minutes, Fawcett Library.

Journals and newspapers

The *Adult*, journal of the Legitimation League.

The *Freewoman*, A Weekly Feminist Review.

Personal Rights, journal of the National Vigilance Association for the Defence of Personal Rights.

The *Suffragette*, Journal of the Women's Social and Political Union.

Shafts, an independent journal.

The *Shield*, journal of the Ladies National Association and later the Association for Moral and Social Hygiene.

The *Weekly Dispatch*.

The *Westminster Review*.

The *Woman's Leader*, journal of the National Union of Societies for Equal Citizenship.

The *Vigilance Record*, journal of the National Vigilance Association.

The *Vote*, journal of the Women's Freedom League.

Votes for Women, journal of the Women's Social and Political Union up to 1912. Thereafter an independent journal edited by Emmeline and Frederick Pethick-Lawrence until 1914 when it became the journal of the United Suffragists.

INDEX